# General Zieten

# General Zieten
## Frederick the Great's Renowned General of Prussian Cavalry

TWO VOLUMES IN ONE EDITION

The Life of General de Zieten

Madame de Blumenthal

*General Zieten*
*Frederick the Great's Renowned General of Prussian Cavalry*
*The Life of General de Zieten*
by Madame de Blumenthal

TWO VOLUMES IN ONE EDITION

Leonaur is an imprint of Oakpast Ltd
Copyright in this form © 2022 Oakpast Ltd

ISBN: 978-1-915234-62-9 (hardcover)
ISBN: 978-1-915234-63-6 (softcover)

**http://www.leonaur.com**

Publisher's Notes

The views expressed in this book are not necessarily those of the publisher.

# Contents

Preface 9
The Life of de Zieten 11

TO THEIR ROYAL HIGHNESSES THE DUKE AND DUCHESS OF YORK,
THE FOLLOWING MEMOIRS OF A HERO,
THEY BOTH OF THEM KNEW AND ADMIRED,
ARE INSCRIBED WITH THE HIGHEST RESPECT,
BY THEIR ROYAL HIGHNESS'S MOST OBLIGED
AND DEVOTED HUMBLE SERVANT,

THE AUTHOR.

# Preface

The Reign of Frederick the great makes an epoch in the history of the world his military talents were unrivalled, and he became the acknowledged master in the art of war to every nation in Europe.

The most glorious period of his reign, the Seven years' War, must be peculiarly interesting to Britons. He was then the ally of England, and we were the partners of his triumphs. The names of Granby and Wolfe were not more familiar to our ears than those of the Prussian generals, and every street in the metropolis and every village in the country, displayed the testimonies of our admiration of their heroic monarch.

The increasing importance of our army in the present circumstances of Europe, makes every lesson in the military science peculiarly valuable; but in presenting to the public the life of one of the greatest generals, whose reflected lustre augmented the glory of Frederick the Great, we not only exhibit a picture most interesting to professional men, but an example of the brightest virtues which can adorn humanity.

The life of this hero is remarkable for the vicissitudes of his fortune. He was involved in early youth in a variety of difficulties, without protection, and without advice. Zieten was indebted to himself alone, for the distinction which his eminent virtues and manly conduct deserved, and obtained. Envy and calumny repeatedly plunged him into disgrace, and drove him from the service of his country. Many years did the displeasure of Frederick the Great continue, but the truth could not always be concealed from his penetrating mind. At the time of the most imminent public danger, Zieten was reconciled to his sovereign, and to the end of his illustrious life, enjoyed in the highest degree, his confidence and friendship.

To do justice to the great actions of Zieten, it was necessary to take a view of the war. This part of the work contains many important particulars and interesting Anecdotes, never before published, and also his private correspondence with Frederick the Great.

To delineate the private and domestic life of Zieten was by far the most agreeable part of the author's work. She deemed it necessary to represent him in his childhood, youth, manhood, and age, as a subject, a husband, and a father; and thus, to demonstrate by facts the moral and religious principles of this excellent man.

It is superfluous to say that no biography can possess a higher degree of authenticity than that now offered to the public; the author, a person of the first distinction, not only possessing herself means of information much more extensive than usually falls to the lot of those who undertake to write the actions of illustrious persons, but many officers of high rank in the Prussian Army being still living, (1803), who were witnesses of the principal facts.

# The Life of de Zieten

John Joachim de Zieten was born on the 18th of May, 1699, at Wüstrau, a village belonging to his family, situated in the county of Ruppin, seven German miles from Berlin. His father, Joachim Matthias de Zieten, was a country gentleman who resided on his own estate, unemployed either in a civil or military capacity. He married Elizabeth Catherine de Jurgas of the house of Ganzer, by whom he had four daughters and two sons; of the latter one died in his infancy.

M. de Zieten's fortune did not exceed five hundred *rix*-dollars a year, which arose from the produce of his Wüstrau estate. (The village of Wüstrau was at this time possessed by three different proprietors. M. de Zieten's portion amounted to about a sixth part). On this moderate income did this gentleman and his family, whose wants were few, live, as people lived in good old times, towards the close of the seventeenth century. The tricks and chicaneries of his wealthy neighbours which often bore hard upon him, alone could make him feel the want of fortune, and under the pressure of these injurious proceedings he commonly displayed a command of temper not a little rare among the old Germans.

Young de Zieten, in his father's house, was utterly unprovided with the means of instruction or culture. Left to himself at a time of life in which, at the present day, young men of condition are engaged in their studies and various exercises, his natural dispositions alone developed themselves and gave him that character of originality which the hand of art in polishing would have much defaced.

He employed the leisure of his early days in forming plans for the future. The void that prevailed in the life of his father, the small fortune which one day was to fall to his share, the narrow and gloomy limits of the mansion-house, to which he found himself confined, instead of afflicting and dismaying him, tended only to inflame his courage and foster his ambition. When yet a mere child his imagination was busied in embellishing the inheritance of his ancestors, and when grown old he has often acknowledged, that the plans he afterwards executed were in part the dreams of his youth.

He betrayed from his early childhood a decided partiality for everything that related to the military life. Whenever a soldier passed through Wüstrau on a furlough, a circumstance that rarely happened, young Zieten followed him closely, could never sufficiently admire him, and was eagerly solicitous of the honour of imitating and resembling him. The Prussian soldiers, it is well known, wear their hair tied in a queue. Every Saturday young Zieten requested his father's leave to go to Ruppin, a German mile from Wüstrau, where a soldier of the garrison "with whom he had formed an acquaintance dressed his hair *à la prussienne*, and made him a large queue well stiffened and powdered, which served to ornament him for the ensuing week. He was at this time nine years of age.

Nature had endowed him with a quick perception of right and wrong, and with the strongest propensity to resist oppression. These dispositions manifested themselves from his very childhood and rendered him a correct and judicious observer of everything that passed within the sphere of his notice. The unbecoming procedure of his neighbours irritated his mind, his father's mortifications became his own, and in the bitterness of his soul he has been often heard to swear he would one day put an end to them.

When he was thirteen years old, his parents provided him with a kind of tutor, a man whose irregularity of conduct ill fitted him for the task. Young Zieten soon perceived this and withdrew his esteem and confidence. The preceptor one day preparing to inflict a bodily correction upon his pupil, the youth repulsed him with disdain, impeached him to his father, and having supported his accusations with proper proof, the pedagogue was immediately dismissed.

At the age of fourteen he left Wüstrau to enter into the service, of Frederick William I. king of Prussia. His father procured him the post of standard bearer in the regiment of Schwendy (now Zenge) which after having been engaged in the siege of Stralsund, was garrisoned at Spandau, Frankfort on the Oder, Cottbus, Treuenbrietzen and Belitz.

His relations were unable to furnish him either with letters of recommendation or money. He was low of stature and of a puny unhealthy appearance. Without patron, friend or fortune, he felt himself in his new career in a strange city, as if he had just dropped from the clouds. His father, indeed, had some slight knowledge of General de Schwendy; they were neighbours and their estates bordered upon each other, but they had scarce any intercourse together. M. de Zieten strongly recommended to his son to take the first opportunity of paying his court to the general and of soliciting his patronage. He promised himself great advantage from this step, and we shall see in what manner it ended.

The young man appears before his general, executes his father's commission and finishes with the usual phrase, that he was come to pay his devoirs to him, "Well, pay them then," said Schwendy with the most insulting coolness; and without adding a civil word either for the youth or his parents, he opened the window and looking out of it, turned his back upon his visitor, whom he left standing near the door. Zieten did not long remain in this awkward situation; deeply hurt at the rude reception he had met with, he flung out of the chamber without taking the least pains to dissemble his resentment. He was never able to forget this scene, and even in his old age could never speak of it without the keenest indignation.

Although unpatronised in his new career, and having entered it under the most unpromising auspices, his zeal for his profession remained uncooled, and his genius lost nothing of its original energy. On the contrary, it seemed as if oppression fortified his breast, and that the neglect in which he was vegetating nourished his ambition and imparted new elasticity and vigour to his mind. Thus, situated he was not, however, the less alive to insult, nor less prone to avenge his wrongs. The first person he chastised was a veteran sergeant who had behaved improperly to him. He wounded him desperately in the face and escaped unhurt himself. Soon after this, he crippled one of his comrades. This early courage, though it bordered upon ferocity, acquired young Zieten that esteem for which his diminutive stature and undignified appearance seemed at first to have disqualified him, and procured him a kind of relief.

After having passed some years in learning the detail of the military service, frequently mounting guard in the capacity of a common sentinel, and in acquitting himself of every duty his station imposed upon him, he was appointed ensign on the 7th of July, 1720. In a short time, the regiment to which he belonged was given to count de Schwerin, afterwards field marshal general of Prussia. The count, who was a native of the dutchy of Mecklenburg, had entered early into the army in the service of his own country, and after having retired for awhile to his paternal estate, he again launched into the military life under the banners of the king of Prussia.

He had many imitators among the young and wealthy part of his own countrymen, who were eager to serve in his regiment, into which he admitted them to the prejudice of the senior officers, and of Zieten in particular, whom he disliked on account of his low stature and the shrillness of his voice, which he said was not formed to give the word of command. Zieten after finding himself, in four successive instances, superseded to make way for others, demanded his dismission with reluctance, and immediately obtained it.

This first essay of the military life was ill calculated to soften the asperity of his manners. Of this I shall give the reader a single example. The Germans, it is well known, have always had the reputation of great drinkers. This vice which prevailed in the Prussian Army was particularly in vogue in the regiment of Schwerin, and the following custom was always religiously observed. The officer of the day took care to provide the guardhouse with a hogshead of beer, which he and his comrades never failed to empty. Each in his turn was obliged to swallow at one draft a full quart-mug: He who could not perform this feat was derided, and none were allowed on any pretext whatever to be exempted from this Bacchanalian exercise.

This proved no small embarrassment to young Zieten whose puny stomach was unable to contain such floods of beer, and who of course was extremely averse to the ceremony. He was at a loss how to act in order to avoid a thousand disagreeable contingencies and being every moment under the necessity of fighting a duel. At last he was able to prevail on his comrades to allow him instead of emptying the monstrous jug, to drink a small glass of brandy, which was less disagreeable to him as well as less detrimental to his constitution.

To this excess in drinking, to these gross customs which bore the stamp of the age and which fashion had rendered honourable, were joined excesses of another kind more conformable to nature, to which young Zieten, whose passions now began to unfold themselves with ardour, found himself more inclined, and which he had begun to teach himself to think he might indulge with impunity. How fortunate was it for him that he was checked in the beginning of a career which threatened such mischief to his moral character! In his peaceful retirement he had full leisure for reflection, to foster those meditations of which he himself was the subject, and to prepare in silence for his real destination.

Ardent, ambitious and naturally inclined to excess, he might have been plunged into inextricable difficulties, had he met with that reception at his first entrance into life which is commonly given to young men favoured by fortune. He would probably have lost sight of, or never attained the splendid part he was one day to act. His lot involved him in a series of perplexities, recalled his attention to himself, and taught him that he could only gratify the ambition with which he was inspired and advance his fortunes, by depending on himself alone and founding all his plans and all his hopes on the basis of real desert. To listen to such dictates and to follow such counsels both genius and resolution were required. Zieten was not deficient in either the one or the other, and thus it was that the first germs of that moral force, that vigour of character which were afterwards so much admired, developed themselves in his young mind.

After having quitted the army, he had no other resource than that of retiring to his own estate, where his father had died in the year 1719. His first care was to examine into the true state of his affairs, to put them in order, to make provision for his mother and sisters, and to unravel the complicated lawsuits in which his father had been so long involved with his neighbours, and which not only had brought him to the brink of ruin, but likewise contributed to shorten his days.

In spite of all these occupations which were well calculated to engross his whole attention, he never lost sight of that sphere of greater activity in which he hoped one day to be engaged. His inclination for a military life was far from being abated; he meditated upon the subject with unremitted ardour, yet two years elapsed before he was enabled to realise his wishes. At the expiration of this time, after having paid a visit to his old comrades of the regiment he had quitted, he was induced by curiosity to visit Berlin to be present at a gala which was given by the French ambassador.

One morning when he was on the parade opposite the royal palace, Frederick William I. observed him; and his regimentals, which he had not left off wearing, having caught the attention of the king, he inquired who he was. Zieten on satisfying His Majesty's curiosity, mentioned likewise the reasons that had induced him to quit the army; but not having expressed any desire to resume the profession, nothing farther at this time took place.

Some months after this, being obliged to attend the progress of a lawsuit at Berlin, he learnt with great satisfaction, that de Wuthenow's dragoons, who were quartered in Prussia, were shortly to be augmented from five squadrons to ten. This information revived all his hopes. He anticipated the long wished for moment of changing the sedentary and inanimate life he now led, for scenes of greater activity and pursuits more adapted to his genius. He was determined, however, not to avail himself of the recommendation or interposition of any one: His fortune, he was resolved, should be his own work;—such was his unconquerable aversion to everything that looked like patronage and dependency.

Thus determined, he frequently appeared on the parade, and though he was aware that his diminutive size would be far from recommending him in the eyes of Frederick William, he was not the less eager to appear before that prince and to attract his notice. To further his design, he had again taken care to dress in regimentals, and the king soon remarked him. His Majesty not only asked his name, but having received the same answer as was formerly given, he made him an offer of a new commission. It may be easily imagined with what readiness Zieten accepted the gracious proposal; he ventured, however, to stipulate conditions which might indemnify him in point of rank for the time he had lost in his retreat and the partiality shewn to the Mecklenburg officers who, as it has been already observed, had been put over his head. Having received His Majesty's assurances that he should rank agreeably to his wishes, he entered into Wuthenow's dragoons as fourth lieutenant.

It was in the year 1726 that Zieten, now twenty-seven years of age, thus launched for the second time into that element for which nature seemed to have formed him. Full of hope and ardour, and painting in the most vivid colours the picture of his future life, he was far from dreaming that vexations of a more disagreeable nature awaited him in the cavalry, than those he had experienced in the infantry. He repaired to his new quarters, but before he arrived there, he had a disaster to encounter which nearly cost him his life.

When he was on the point of setting out for his garrison, (Tilsit, a town in the Prussian Lithuania), in the month of February, a staff officer of his own regiment, who had come to Berlin to procure of supply of horses, having been informed that Zieten was appointed lieutenant, consigned a quantity of them to his care. The officer set out a day before him and passed the Vistula with no small difficulty, as the ice was beginning to break up. When Zieten arrived the next day on the bank of the river, the ice was already afloat and he was obliged to take a circuitous way of more than twenty German miles to cross the river over the bridge of Naugarten.

This tottering structure had been often impaired by the inundation of the Vistula, and at this moment seemed on the point of giving way. What could he do? It was necessary to avail himself of the present instant, and Zieten accordingly began to march the horses over the bridge, and remained behind himself to preserve order. During these proceedings the Polish toll-man shut the gate on the opposite side and refused to suffer the horses, which were now crowded on the bridge, to pass till the toll was duly paid. This incident rendered the personal interference of Zieten absolutely necessary, and he was obliged to make his way over the narrow and crazy bridge, justling along by the horses which now began to grow unruly and much startled at the dashing of the waters.

Scarcely had he, by dint of threats and promises, prevailed on the man to throw open the gate, scarcely had the horses in the rear lightened the bridge, which their weight had hitherto tended not a little to keep entire, when one arch after another began to yield to the violence of the current, and the last horse having touched the bank, the last arch gave way and the whole bridge disappeared in a few minutes.

Thus did Zieten owe his safety to the merest accident. Had he remained in the rear, and had not the well-timed perverseness of the toll-man forced him to quit that dangerous post, he would most probably have been swallowed up with the bridge, and found a grave in the Vistula. But having escaped this danger, he seemed to derive new intrepidity from it, and became the better fitted to encounter the perils that still awaited him.

Being happily arrived at his garrison, he gave himself up with unremitting ardour to his vocation, and the more so as the cavalry was a new school to him; and being incapable of doing anything by halves, he resolved to accomplish himself in a profession, in which it was one day his lot to act so brilliant a part. However, after having been present at the first review of his regiment, he was obliged at the beginning of winter to solicit for leave of absence in order to terminate a tedious lawsuit which had for so many years employed and embittered the life of his father.

The difficulties he had to combat engaged him not only to solicit a prolongation of his furlough but likewise to make direct application to the king for the purpose of hastening a definitive sentence. The sentence was accordingly obtained and this unhappy suit which had lasted forty years, was at length determined in favour of the family of Zieten. After having settled this weighty business, and, at the same time, redressed many abuses and reformed many irregularities of less moment; after having obtained justice against his neighbours and restored peace and competency to his aged mother, he left Wüstrau in the month of February, 1727, and returned to his garrison.

This journey proved as perilous as the former. Zieten had just enlisted two very promising Saxon deserters, and was under the necessity of escorting them himself to the regiment. He set off with them from Berlin in a sledge on a clear frosty day, but they were hardy arrived at Schwedt, when it suddenly began to thaw, and Zieten was obliged to change his sledge for a waggon. He arrived with much difficulty at Dantzick, but was unable to proceed any further on account of the melting of the snow which had damaged the roads. In vain he endeavoured to truck his waggon for a carriage of more solid construction, or to inquire for some travelling companions in order to be accommodated with double the number of post-horses. He offered likewise considerable sums to all the carriers of the place to induce them, to take him further on; not one of them, however, would hear him, as they were all fearful of inundations and the breaking up of the ice.

Of all measures to be chosen, that of remaining at Dantzick and waiting for the thaw seemed the least conformable to his impatience. He quickly came to a determination, and went on in his waggon with the two recruits over the Frisch-haff, an arm of the sea lying between Dantzick and Königsberg. (In imitation of the Great Elector, Frederick William, who when he was driving the Swedes out of Prussia transported his army, with his artillery, over the Frisch-Haff, in sledges). The Haff was still frozen, but the ice in many places was so thin that the carriage wheels frequently cut it through and made the water spurt out. He was likewise unprovided with a guide, nor did he meet any person who was able to point out the way.

He himself therefore walked before the horses with an axe in his hand to try the thickness of the ice, and in this manner, being scarcely aware of the progress he was making, he advanced, though in a straggling way; and after prodigious labour, which lasted from nine o'clock in the morning till the approach of night, he arrived at an inn called the Haff-krug, where he was agreeably surprised at being informed, he had travelled more than seven German miles in the course of the day.

On the morrow he continued his route with his two deserters, whom he was under the necessity of watching very narrowly. The second part of the Haff was more difficult to pass than the first; but after having proceeded with the same caution, and undergone the same fatigues as before, Zieten arrived in the evening without any accident at Braunsberg where he passed the night. His landlord gave him many, useful hints relative to the rest of his journey, and advised him to be particularly cautious in his passage over the Pregel in a certain spot, where that river spreads itself into a kind of lake, and which is scarcely ever firmly frozen. Zieten thanked, him for his information and began early in the morning to avail himself of it. He came within sight of Königsberg and thought he had already passed the dangerous part of the river.

He was, however, soon convinced of his error. He had for some time followed, with equal pleasure and confidence, the track of a sledge containing two persons who seemed to be taking the same route. On a sudden the deserters gave a loud cry. Zieten asked the cause of this, but before they could make any answer his own eyes explained it. The sledge that preceded him sunk through the ice and disappeared in a moment. These unfortunate persons, as he afterwards learnt, were two young men belonging to a countinghouse in Königsberg, who in this manner paid with their lives for an innocent party of pleasure which they had just been making to the other side of the river. Zieten learnt at their expense that he was nearer than he had imagined to the treacherous spot, and taking in due time another way, he arrived safely with his two recruits at Königsberg.

At the inn where he lodged, he met with a merchant from Breslau, who informed him that he had crossed the Haff the day before and that his sledge had sunk in, that his horses were drowned, and that he himself escaped with extreme difficulty. He added that two clergymen of Braunsberg, who had followed him at a small distance, and who had lighted their pipes, from his but a few minutes before his disaster, not having come to his assistance though he had called to them nor overtook him afterwards, it was more than probable they had been swallowed up.

This recital feelingly convinced Zieten what risks he himself had run, and increased the satisfaction he felt at his own escape. To the gratitude which was due to his landlord of Braunsberg, he joined that which he owed divine providence, which had thus preserved him and irresistibly gained his fullest confidence. In his old age he could never speak of this perilous journey without feeling his confidence revive. He felt himself proud too of the courage he had manifested on the occasion; a courage which in his afterlife never failed him, whenever in the exercise of his hazardous profession he stood in need of it, and which rendered him always bold, often adventurous, but never rash.

Twelve months elapsed without involving him in the least embarrassment or disquietude. His zeal for the service increased with his military attainments, which being acquired in the double school of theory and practice were every day improving. His hours of relaxation were commonly taken up by the sports of the field, which had always been one of his most favourite diversions, and in two instances had nearly cost him his life. One day as he was tracing a hare over the snow, his horse foundered in a hollow way and he himself pitched upon his head. The horse rolled over him and he lay in a state of insensibility till a humane peasant coming to his assistance, drew him out of the snow and remained with him till he recovered his senses.

Another time, when he was pursuing the game on foot, he inadvertently rushed into a wood in which a great number of cattle which had died of a contagious distemper were lying in the highest state of putrefaction. The mephitic exhalations arising from these carcasses had such an effect upon him, that he began to feel his strength fail him. With the greatest difficulty he staggered to the high road, where being quite unable to proceed any farther, he fell into at swoon, but was soon enabled by timely assistance to recover himself. Had he fainted in the wood His death had been inevitable.

The genius of Zieten, his frank and noble deportment, did not long remain unobserved by his brother officers, nor fail to gain the esteem and friendship of all of them, except one who hated him and took every opportunity of doing him an ill turn. This person was the second captain of the colonel squadron, to which Zieten belonged. Being probably conscious that he was eclipsed by the merit of his lieutenant, he had long wished to get rid of him and had tormented him in every possible manner during a period of two years. Zieten bore all this with a degree of moderation which could hardly be expected from the natural warmth of his temper and the deep impression which every act of injustice made upon him even when he himself was not the object of it.

At length it became impossible to continue to act this painful part, notwithstanding all the empire he had acquired over himself since the broils in which he had been engaged during his service in the infantry, and he could no longer tolerate these insults. The mutual fire of the animosity of the two champions, which lay smothered under its ashes, waited only for an occasion to burst into a flame, and this occasion was now near at hand.

The squadron one Sunday morning had assembled as usual to appear at church in form, and only waited the arrival of the captain. The latter who was paying his court to a lady of the place forgot the parade and his duty. The moments stole away, and it was difficult to know how to act. The officers murmured, and the more so as the cause of the captain's delay was no mystery to them. At length they lost all patience and after having waited much later than the usual hour, Zieten, at the solicitation of his friends and in his capacity of lieutenant, ordered the troops to march.

The captain having been apprised of this, instantly joined them, and not satisfied with making the lieutenant a severe reprimand on the plea of breach of service, seemed happy to have this opportunity of giving full scope to his rancour towards him. During the whole march to the church, he continued muttering terms of abuse. Zieten being under arms refrained from making any direct reply; he, however, could not help lifting up his shoulders and shelving every mark of disgust and contempt for an officer, whose duty it was to examine into his conduct and punish it if reprehensible, but not to have recourse to ungentlemanlike expressions and indecent menaces. The captain perceived this, and his rage was redoubled.

"No more of these blackguard gesticulations if you please, lieutenant," cried he; and as if he foresaw the immediate consequence of this, he instantly alighted, and rushed into the church to which: he was close, and which he had never been accustomed to enter. Upon this Zieten lost all command of himself; he went into an inn opposite the church to wait for his enemy and to make sure of him as he passed by. As soon as he saw him come out of his retreat, he accosted him and demanded satisfaction for the word blackguard as well for the many other offensive expressions he had uttered.

The captain was averse to any explanation, and declining the challenge in the best manner he could, endeavoured to turn off the whole business as a jest. This affected indifference irritated Zieten beyond measure. He pressed him closer and insisted upon fighting him on the spot. His antagonist immediately took refuge in the general's quarters and made formal complaint against his lieutenant. The general ordered Zieten to be put under arrest, who now began to find he was entangled in a very disagreeable affair.

The captain, who had the ear of the general, abused his confidence as may be naturally supposed in order to place the whole transaction in the most advantageous view, and to screen himself from every suspicion of cowardice. The lady too with whom he was captivated was extremely useful to him in this business. The influence, she had over the mind of her own husband as well as of the general, enabled her to assert the innocence of her lover, and when the affair was canvassed everything was exhibited in a false light and discussed in favour of the captain and to the prejudice of Zieten.

A report was made to the king, and the monarch, to whom the conduct of Zieten had been represented in the blackest colours, ordered a court-martial to be held at Berlin, which instantly acquitted the captain and condemned Zieten to one year's imprisonment in the fortress of Friedrichsbourg near Königsberg. He was sent thither pursuant to his sentence towards the end of the year 1728.

The vexation he felt during his imprisonment was embittered by an incident which shewed to what degree the king believed him to be guilty. A dispute with the house of Hanover had made it necessary to give orders to certain regiments to hold themselves in readiness to march. That in which Zieten served being of this number, the prisoner was enlarged six weeks before the expiration of his time for the purpose of preparing his camp equipage; but he immediately received a counter order on the part of the king to return to the fortress and remain there the full time for which he had been sentenced. He was therefore obliged to take this disagreeable journey for the second time, impressed with the fullest conviction that the monarch's displeasure was not at all abated.

The severity with which he had been treated was a matter of great triumph for his enemy, who now flattered himself it would be an easy task, on his return to the regiment, to browbeat and oppress him. He had not, however, anticipated the hatred and contempt with which he himself was considered by the worthy part of his brother-officers. They had discovered the base expedients he had recourse to, and in spite of the support on which he plumed himself, they created him so many vexations that his situation in 'the regiment became extremely critical. His conduct towards Zieten was judged to be mean, his courage equivocal and his motives dishonourable. All he had now to do was to strike some blow in order to extricate himself from these embarrassments;—to such measure he had recourse, but in his own way and perfectly consistent with the principles by which he was governed.

For this purpose, he applied to an old *ci-devant* Austrian captain of the name of Soldan, who strolled from one garrison to another, and lived upon the quarrels of honour which he himself stirred up among the officers, and afterwards fomented in the capacity of second, and which he knew how to appease adroitly when the business came to be decided on the field of battle. The Prussian captain concerted with him on the means of regaining the esteem of the regiment without exposing his person to danger. Soldan in consequence of this took care to be at Friedrichsbourg a short time before Zieten left the place, and summoned him on the part of the captain to fight a duel before he joined his regiment, as the honour of both of them was equally at stake.

Zieten impatient as he had formerly been to attack his adversary, had too well learnt to know and despise him, not to dismiss his emissary with the following short reply: "I have no desire to lodge here a second time."

The captain was, however, no way remiss in his preparations against the time in which Zieten was expected and had everything in readiness for a regular duel. He sent his valuables out of the country, took a troop of *chasseurs*, grooms and lackeys into his immediate service, furnished them with firearms, and thus escorted, he sallied forth to meet Zieten, who had not the least intimation of what had taken place.

This extraordinary equipment made no small noise. Some foresaw that the catastrophe would turn out ridiculous; others trembled for the life of Zieten, who immediately on his enlargement repaired to an inn in Königsberg in order to pass the night previously to his setting off to his garrison the next morning. The landlord received him with an embarrassed countenance, and requested him to choose for the present evening another lodging; informing him at the same time that his antagonist had engaged several rooms in the house for himself and a numerous company, and that it would be very dangerous to receive both parties under his roof.

Zieten smiled at his alarms and protested he would not change his inn, as he was neither afraid of the captain nor of any man living. Upon this he took quiet possession of his chamber, and so far was he from meeting with any disturbance, that the captain, who arrived at Königsberg about an hour after him, did not think proper to alight at the inn, but went to lodge at another house. The road from the above city to the garrison threatening much danger to Zieten, his friends earnestly him to take a byway thither:

> Your enemy is treacherous and well escorted; you have nothing but courage to oppose to this, and you are alone.

These considerations, however, had so little effect upon, him that notwithstanding he was aware his antagonist had not made all these preparations in vain, but would probably attempt something desperate, he took no other precaution than that of providing himself with a brace of pistols and equipping a youth of fourteen years of age, who accompanied him, with an old sabre; asking him at the same time whether he had bravery enough to make use of it in case they were attacked by the whole troop; "for," added he, "should one or two only make up to us, you need not take the trouble of assisting me."

The boy promised to combat stoutly, and our two champions sallied forth at break of day.

Zieten learnt at the gate of the city, that the captain and his escort had passed through half an hour before and had taken the road he was going. He expected to find him in every village he passed, but his expectations were fruitless. Whatever place he came to, he was sure to learn that the other had proceeded forwards without having made any stay. On his arrival at each inn, it was in vain that he laid his pistols on the table before him; his antagonist had never thought fit to give him an opportunity of using them. Seized with a panic, he made the best of his way with his troop to the garrison, where, however incredible it may appear, he received Zieten in the most amicable manner when they met by accident at the colonel's quarters.

The laurels he had gathered in his late expedition were not splendid enough to allow him to make his boast of them. On the contrary, he pretended to be delighted at the return of the man whom he just before imagined he should have intimidated and subdued. How much ought he rather to have blushed at the sight of one so superior to him in courage and nobleness of mind!

His late proceedings, however, did not long remain a secret, and he began to find himself treated with still more neglect and contempt than before. His company was shunned, his brother-officers were ashamed to speak to him, and notwithstanding the countenance of the king and of his general and colonel, they gave him to understand they could no longer serve in the same regiment with him. To these measures Zieten alone, though the injured party, was an honourable exception. He gave him no disturbance whatever; and performed his military service under his command with the most rigid exactness. The more the other officers admired this conduct and respected the motives of it, the more they made the captain feel the effects of their hatred. Happy would he have been to recover his farmer credit;—it was now too late, he had lost the moment in which he might have done it in a proper manner.

He could now only have recourse to base and contemptible expedients: He even went so far as to determine to rid himself by assassination of a man whose presence now furnished him with a continual subject of self-reproach. He often laid wait for him in the street during night, and one evening in particular he certainly would have killed him had not Zieten turned about in time, and by the manliness of his looks and demeanour overawed his assassin, and palsied, his arm which was already lifted up to strike the blow.

May the young and boisterous who are engaged in the military life learn from Zieten, on the present occasion, how to model their own conduct! Let a man without education or culture be their pattern, when they are told, that the manner in which he corrected the assassin was by burying the act in silent oblivion!

This generous silence, however, was unable to still the public voice which nevertheless continued to run violently against him, and rendered him the object of universal indignation. His protectress even blushed to take his part. She had unavailingly exhausted every means of saving his reputation, or at least of casting a veil over his dishonour; and she would no longer share his disgrace, and even seemed determined to reject his amorous assiduities. Enraged at this reverse of fortune he made choice of the lady's birthday to try a last and desperate expedient.

Inflamed with love and wine, and tremblingly anticipating the fate that awaited him, if he did not wash away in the blood of his enemy the dishonour with which his reputation was soiled, he called forth the wrecks of his courage, attacked Zieten in the open street in the day time as he was coming out of a house, and involved him in a singular combat, which produced effects that gave birth to one of the most remarkable vicissitudes of his life.

Every advantage: was on the side of the assailants Zieten had scarcely time to draw his sword and stand upon his defence. A new disaster likewise befell him; his sword shivered in pieces while he was parrying a stroke which threatened to cleave his skull. The captain, as the reader may easily believe, would have been base enough to take advantage of this accident in order to terminate the quarrel, and Zieten would inevitably have been, lost, if he had not had the presence of mind to throw the hilt of his sword in his antagonist's face, who immediately staggered and fell, upon the pavement.

Zieten in the meanwhile laid hold of a new kind of weapon which was fortunately near at hand. This weapon was a large lever belonging to some brewing utensils which was reared against a pump. The young warrior, like another Hercules, brandishes his club; his adversary, who was now upon his legs again, waves aloft his sabre; the unequal conflict is renewed and address contends with superior force. A third person arrived; it was an officer and Zieten begged the use of his sword. The officer refuses his request, and rushing between the combatants protects the weaker of the two. The officer on guard appears, and having separated them, put them both under arrest.

This was what the captain desired. Fortune had been very favourable to him, and he imagined he had done wonders in having combated with a disarmed foe. He trusted he had given such proofs of courage as were sufficient to re-establish his reputation in the regiment, and he flattered himself besides that this second affray would completely blacken the lieutenant in the eyes of the king and hasten his final ruin.

This public achievement reinstated the captain in the good graces of the lady, who soon gained over the general and the next in command. In the inquiries which were made into this business the same steps were taken as in the former case; the facts were overcharged and the truth wholly disfigured. The report was sent to Berlin and the king was again imposed upon by false and partial representations.

Zieten was aware of the fate that awaited him. He saw himself in the power of his enemies and that what he had done in the defence of his own life was considered as a crime and was sufficient to ruin him. He could not disguise his just indignation, and being confined in the same guardhouse with his adversary during the whole process, due care was taken to prevent their being left alone together. Whenever the sentinels were relieved, a subaltern officer was stationed in the room to keep them in order.

Zieten, however, was not the more unhappy of the two. He derived, no small, consolation from the kind solicitude of his comrades who regularly visited him and exerted every means in their power to divert him and to render his confinement tolerable. The officer on guard dined with him, while the captain who sat in a corner of the room was never honoured with the least attention. A single officer, indeed, acted a different part; he declared himself the confident and partisan of the captain and the lady, and in concert with her and her complaisant husband, at the expense of every honourable feeling, he espoused the cause of their common friend, and his labours were crowned with success.

Six weeks elapsed, and the sentence of the court-martial arrived from Berlin and surprised everyone who heard it. The captain was condemned to suffer three month's imprisonment for drawing the first, and Zieten was broke for having thrown the hilt of his sword in the captain's face. This incident, which in fact was nothing more than a justifiable defence against an apparent attempt to assassinate him, became a pretext for loading the innocent, with the chastisement of the guilty. The severe and unjust sentence ought not, however, to be attributed to the king, as His Majesty had been taken by surprise and acted under the strongest prejudices in disfavour of Zieten. The prince, in fact, imagined he was doing an act of justice and rendering a service to the regiment in thus ridding it of an officer who had been represented to him as a hot-headed and dangerous man; and in this point of view, it was that he confirmed the sentence in every particular.

Thus was the military career of Zieten terminated for a second time in a humiliating manner, and to all appearance irretrievably, while his dastardly adversary enjoyed the completest triumph. This triumph, however, was not of long duration; the tardy vengeance of fate at length overtook him, and we shall see him make his appearance again in the sequel in a very different point of view.

Zieten acquired new consideration and esteem by the manly dignity with which he supported his adverse fortune. He gave way to no murmurs, nor complaints, nor did he meditate any act of vengeance against the authors of his disgrace. He yielded to his fate and retired in a peaceable manner to Wüstrau, where though to all appearance free and master of his actions, he could not help considering himself a captive, leading a life unenlivened by honour, profession and prospect: The vigour of his mind was cramped and his faculties were palsied. Had he possessed less delicacy and more levity of disposition, had he felt the glow of patriotism in a cooler degree or consulted either his resentment or his interest, he would have made a tender of his service to some foreign power. The idea, indeed, often came into his mind, yet he did what few would have done in his place—he opposed his duty to the keenness of his feelings, and happily preserved himself for his country.

What might not in fact be expected from a man in whom the inclination and the power to act agreeably to such motives were united, and who subjecting the emotions of his wounded heart to the sacred laws of honour and those of his country, was determined to recognise no other? The efforts he made upon himself, the many conflicts he endured doubtless contributed to render him that great character he invariably approved himself to be during the rest of his life.

Supported by the consciousness of his own innocence and convinced of the injustice of fortune, Zieten passed several months at Wüstrau in uninterrupted seclusion. This way of life at length grew intolerable, and he resolved to return to Berlin. Conscious that he was unable singly to push his fortune there, and that the king was too much exasperated against him to receive him again into his service without the mediation of powerful friends, he overcame on the present occasion the aversion he had to all adventitious recommendation. His pride bent under the yoke of necessity and his ardour to serve his country at length subdued his repugnance to act the part of a suppliant. He accordingly paid his court to some of the generals who lived on familiar terms with the king, and particularly to marshal de Buddenbrock and General de Flanz, who having soon discovered his merit and considering him as the victim of envy and intrigue, promised him their good offices as soon as it would be at all prudent to exert them in his behalf, for at the present moment the very mention of his name would be sufficient to put His Majesty into an ill humour.

The happy moment at last arrived. The king having paid a visit to his daughter, the Margravine of Bayreuth, observed at that court a small corps of hussars, which particularly attracted his notice. This troop which was chiefly employed in escorting the *margravian* family in the excursions they made, had been sent in their best accoutrements to meet the king on his arrival on the frontiers. At the sight of a corps so splendidly equipped and so completely mounted, Frederick William was seized with the most violent inclination to have a similar one in his own service, to which he was desirous to assign a more military destination, and which he wished to form under his own immediate inspection.

He had in the year 1722, created two companies of hussars in Prussia, and in the year 1730 his most favourite employment was the organisation of a third at Berlin, composed of the finest men of the Bayreuth company which the *margrave* had now given him, together with some volunteers of the same country, the flower of the hussars of the two Prussian companies, and some young recruits enlisted in Hungary. Such was the origin of the regiment of Zieten, which afterwards became so celebrated on account of their own bravery as well as that of their chief.

The king had named the captain and cornet of the new company; the lieutenant was not yet appointed. His Majesty commissioned General de Buddenbrock to look out for a man properly qualified for this kind of service. The general who knew and esteemed Zieten cast his eye upon him and proposed him to the king. He had foreseen the monarch's anger, and bore the first fury of it with patience. The king declared he would not hear Zieten any more spoken of; the general replied that he was a very worthy man and that he himself would be answerable for his conduct. At length General de Flanz added his solicitations in favour of the lieutenant, and the king struck with the good opinion his two favourites seemed to entertain of Zieten, yielded to their entreaties and expressed his desire to see him.

A courier was immediately sent to Wüstrau with these good tidings. He received orders to repair to Königs-Wusterhausen, and there wait His Majesty's pleasure, who was upon a hunting party in that place. He found the captain and cornet already arrived, and who were to be presented with him to the king. His Majesty, who had been put into a very good humour by the diversion the chase had afforded him, received the two other officers in the most gracious manner; but with regard to Zieten, he upbraided him in the presence of his comrades with every fault that had been laid to his charge and of which he was fully persuaded he had been guilty.

Zieten conscious of his own innocence observed nevertheless the most respectful silence. This was not the moment to enter upon his justification; he felt it, and the two generals, his patrons, were of the same opinion. A word might have impeded his fortune, and perhaps irretrievably. The king at length pleased with the submissive demeanour of Zieten began to soften the asperity of his language. A calm succeeded the storm, and Zieten was appointed lieutenant of the hussars, "on condition, however, that he should behave himself in an orderly manner, and that his superior officer would keep a watchful eye over him." (The king's own expression.)

This was no slight trial for the natural pride of Zieten's disposition; no small humiliation to him at his re-entrance into the military life. Yet the love he bore his country, and which had hitherto prevented his offering his services to any foreign power, again came to his aid and imposed silence upon him. During the rest of his life, he was unable to recollect this interview without emotion; and even at the most advanced stage of it, he could never speak on the subject without betraying the deep impression it still made upon him.

Zieten was thirty-one years of age when he entered the hussars, and it was not long before he began to find himself involved in new disasters. Captain de Benekendorf, his superior officer, had not forgot the scene of Wusterhausen, nor the orders he had received from the king to superintend the conduct of his lieutenant. He exercised the task in a manner incompatible with the honour and feelings of Zieten, whose moderation and patience were often put to the severest test. By frequent struggles with himself, however, he at last prevailed, and learnt in this new school, that those persons whom fortune destines to the rank of favourites have many mortifications to undergo preparatory to the enjoyments which are one day to fall to their share.

He perceived likewise that the king, now no longer the slave to his prejudices, began to shew him frequent marks of kindness and even to honour him with his confidence. This was no small encouragement to Zieten while it excited in Benekendorf both discontent and envy. The king's kindness seemed to increase daily, he treated him with distinction, loved to converse with him, and often charged him with his commissions, particularly with such as related to the dutchy of Mecklenburg. These circumstances gave umbrage to the captain, who now began to take every opportunity in his power to make him feel the effects of his ill humour.

One day the king speaking with Zieten had desired him to procure a skilful farrier from some other country. The captain who was informed of this the same evening while he was at supper with a party of his friends, sent to Zieten though very late in the night, and in a rude manner asked him what the king had said to him that morning, and why he had made no report of it. Zieten who on such occasions never carried his resentment farther than by eluding the indiscreet curiosity of his superior officer, replied coldly that the conversation had run upon indifferent affairs, and of which he did not at all conceive it his duty to make report.

The captain irritated at this answer and intoxicated with liquor had recourse to rudeness and invective. He advanced towards Zieten with his fist clenched and his eyes sparkling with rage. Zieten on his part could scarcely contain himself, his hand began to close mechanically and he was on the point of giving full scope to his anger, when he recollected in time the paternal exhortations of the king, which had been just before reiterated, together with His Majesty's declaration that his proneness to fall into variance was the only point on which he could now entertain the least distrust with regard to his conduct.

This recollection snatched him from the impending danger; he made a violent effort upon himself, and quitted the room in all the agony of stifled resentment.

Fortunately, neither this nor any of the quarrels that took place between the captain and his lieutenant reached the royal ear; the military service was well executed and the company was in the most perfect order. After the first year of its formation His Majesty created two new companies, and twelve months later he increased them to three squadrons, which he composed of the flower of the youth and of the choicest men of every other regiment. To this corps which he was pleased to notice in a very particular manner, he gave the name of body hussars and incorporated them in the army under that denomination and with the rank to which they were entitled. These changes, as we have seen, succeeded each other in the space of two or three years. At the expiration of the first year Zieten had the good fortune to be appointed captain (his commission bears date the 1st of March, 1731), and to command the second company annexed to the corps of Benekendorf.

This rapid advancement affords a new proof of the estimation in which the king now held him. It was not, however, solely to his conduct and the punctuality with which he acquitted himself of every duty that he owed this mark of royal favour; it arose chiefly from the deep impression the military merits of Zieten had made upon the king. His Majesty could perceive in him all those talents which seemed necessary to bring to perfection this militia which he himself had created and which was a new phenomenon in the Prussian Army. Hence was the king induced sometime after to intrust him with an expedition which he considered as a kind of touchstone for the corps, and which would display at once both their use and their peculiar advantage.

The king was not satisfied with having been in some sort the founder of the hussars, and employed during the latter part of his reign in organising them; he was desirous, at the same time that he intended to increase their number, to raise them from the infant condition in which they yet lay, and to give them opportunities of emulating his grenadiers. For this purpose, it was necessary to initiate them in the business of real service, and an occasion was soon at hand. France which had disputed the crown of Poland with Austria and Russia, had recently violated the neutrality of the empire and taken possession of the fortress of Kehl.

Frederick William not content with merely furnishing his quota, put himself at the head of ten thousand men whom he led to the banks of the Rhine. A fit of the gout or perhaps the inactivity of Prince Eugene who commanded the combined army, and who already began to feel the effects of age, soon induced His Majesty to return to Berlin. During this excursion he became acquainted with a famous Austrian partisan of the name of Baronay, and imagined he had found in this officer a man in whose school he might safely intrust his hussars. After having procured the consent of Prince Eugene to this measure he ordered sixty body-hussars (No. 2) with an equal number of those of Prussia (No. 1) to join the Austrian Army (in spring 1736), and gave the command of them to Captain de Zieten whom he recommended in very strong terms to General de Baronay.

Zieten marched with his six-score horse as soon as the season would permit, and having taken Potsdam in his way, the king gave him his last instructions there, and at the same time exhorted him to preserve the strictest order and discipline among the troops intrusted to his command. Zieten promised obedience to His Majesty's injunctions, but before he had arrived at his destination, he felt by sad experience that a man is not always master of his actions nor of their consequences, and that even without any fault on his own part, he may often risk the loss of reputation and burden his responsibility.

His march lay through the dutchy of Weimar. At Buttstädt, a small town belonging to that principality, where he was to take up his quarters for the night, he found the duke, who at the head of a small camp, was waiting to meet him, and who honoured him with the most distinguished reception. The officers were invited to the camp and regaled at the *ducal* table. The hussars were treated with the most cordial hospitality by the inhabitants of Buttstädt, and their horses were fed at the expense of; the duke. Plenty of provisions were displayed in the camp and in the town, and strong liquors, according to the custom of the times, were poured out in abundance. The hussars got drunk to the health of their hosts, and their commander made but slight resistance to, the quick circulation of the glass at the prince's table, and drank to an improper degree.

Many ladies from the capital, among whom was the duke's mistress, came to visit the camp and to grace with their presence a ball which was given to crown the festivity of the day. This fair and amiable lady made a deep impression on Zieten's heart. Inflamed with intemperance and lost in a tumult of sensations, he forgot he had a rival entitled to his respect and whose jealousy kept pace with the increasing captivation of his guest. The scene might have grown serious had not

Zieten, who was not much accustomed to drinking, sunk under the pressure of inebriation. He was taken from table, and the duke much delighted at this incident ordered him to be carried, in the state of insensibility in which he lay, to Buttstädt and locked up in his chamber.

The next morning Zieten with some difficulty broke loose from his confinement to assemble the troops and make ready for their departure. At length when he began to march at about noon, he was surprised to receive a visit from the duke. The prince had entirely laid aside his jealous apprehensions, and was the first to laugh at the scene that had taken place the preceding day. He expressed at the same time his desire to see the hussars make an evolution, and requested Zieten to gratify him with the spectacle. The captain, who thought it incumbent on him to return the kindness he had received at the hands of the duke, instantly began to make the necessary dispositions and divided his men into several platoons, but his complaisance had liked to have been attended with fatal consequences.

The hussars were not yet become perfectly sober, and besides this a violent animosity prevailed in the detachment which was composed of Berliners and Prussians against the others, so that, the sham combat became a real battle, and at the word given for firing, the two parties loaded their pistols with balls. Zieten was alarmed beyond description when he perceived his troops were thus hastening to destroy each other before they arrived in the presence of the enemy, and though he took instant measures to quell the affray, yet there were many wounded on both sides. The duke, who was much concerned at this incident, furnished them with carriages for their transport. Fortunately, not any of them died, and in a short time they were all cured of the wounds they had received. Zieten was fearful lest the affair should reach the kings ear and involve him in new troubles; His Majesty, however, happily remained in total ignorance of the transaction.

These late events proved a salutary lesson to Zieten and taught him to know both his troops and himself. From this time, he assiduously endeavoured to suppress that spirit of rivalry which prevailed among them, and even during the rest of his march he began to find that his labour had not been ill bestowed. He likewise introduced severer modes of discipline and by such exertions was afterwards enabled to prevent their falling into new excesses. As for himself he resolved never to give way again to intemperance, and his future life shews that his resolution was not taken in vain.

On the 12th of May he arrived with the detachment at the Austrian camp and was quartered in the neighbourhood of Mentz. His zeal and activity in the performance of his duty, and the regularity of his conduct soon gained him the approbation of the principal officers and particularly that of M. de Baronay. That able general was not slow in discovering his merit, and he became in a short time so attached to him that he was fond of calling him his disciple and declared himself proud of being his instructor. He took care to have him continually at his side, made him a party in all his expeditions, and taught him the art of war in the field of battle.

After having assisted in several skirmishes and being familiarised to desultory service, Zieten thought he might now venture to make trial of the strength and courage of his little squadron. He imparted his wish to the general who was delighted at his impatience to distinguish himself; he intrusted him with three hundred Austrian hussars to join the Prussians, and charged him with an enterprise of considerable importance. The object was to turn the enemy by passing through a defile, to flank them, to alarm their quarters, and to retreat before they could be able to collect their forces.

Zieten, to whom the general had left the task of making the necessary dispositions, conducted the enterprise with equal ability and prudence. He broke into the enemy's advanced quarters without being perceived, threw them into disorder, and made several prisoners. In the meantime, the adjacent posts taking the alarm, united and marched against him. This was the moment for retreat, and the Austrians, who had been accustomed to this kind of war, fell back in due time. Zieten's hussars, however, conceiving a degree of infamy to be connected with the word, spurned at the mention of it and kept their ground. Their obstinacy had well-nigh proved fatal to them; for while their commander was exhausting himself in exhorting them to consider their own safety, the enemy approached on all sides and had nearly cut off their retreat.

It was now necessary to make way through them in order to regain the defile, which was the only road they could take to their own camp, and Zieten conducted them without any loss to the spot. The moment they arrived there General de Baronay unexpectedly made his appearance among them. He had foreseen the danger of the undertaking and had lain in ambuscade at the head of twelve hundred horse in a neighbouring wood to be ready to support Zieten in case of need. He had seen the attack and retreat, and lay concealed till the moment in which he found it necessary to disencumber his pupil of the troops that were pursuing him, when falling in his turn upon the enemy he put them to flight, and after having taken several prisoners, he returned in triumph to the camp.

The proof which Zieten had just given of his talents gained him the applause of the general and a report in his favour to the king, who immediately advanced him to the rank of major, (January the 29th, 1736.) In the warrant which was transmitted to him it was stated:

> That His Majesty raised him to that rank in consideration of his good qualities, the military experience he had acquired, and the vigilance and courage he had manifested.

This was not, indeed, the only occasion in which Zieten distinguished himself during the course of his military excursion, but it is the only one of which we have been able to learn any particulars. The king having withdrawn his troops on the conclusion of the peace, Zieten quitted the imperial army with the reputation of a good officer, and favoured with every mark of friendship and esteem which General de Baronay could bestow upon him. At their separation neither of them could have entertained the least idea that in a few years they were to meet again as enemies.

This campaign proved of the greatest moment to Zieten; it procured him glory, experience and advancement. His garrison could not have afforded such advantages, and it was on the banks of the Rhine that his happier fate had destined him to serve his apprenticeship to the art of war. On his return to Berlin the king gave him the kindest reception, and expressed his satisfaction in the most flattering terms.

New disasters, however, were yet in store for him, and he began to experience them a short time after the late brilliant scenes in which he had been engaged. He was again entangled in military broils and had often occasion to regret the fortunate period of the year 1735.

During his late absence the king had been pleased to give M. de Benekendorf his dismission and to appoint Lieutenant-Colonel de Wurm in his stead, an officer who had hitherto served in the infantry. His line person probably recommended him to His Majesty's favour, for in other respects he was totally devoid of merit. At his entrance into the university, he had distinguished himself as a blustering youth, had killed four or five of his fellow-students in duels during the time he resided there, and owed his reputation for courage principally to the superiority of his bodily strength.

Elated with self-love and pride he never condescended to acquire any knowledge. When he first entered the army, his ignorance was remarkable, and when he removed into the cavalry it appeared in still more glaring colours, as he was possessed with the silly vanity of believing himself an adept in every military accomplishment. Such was the principal officer whom Zieten found on his return, and whom his own superior merit soon made his enemy. M. de Wurm, who doubtless was no stranger to the story of his former adventures, was persuaded it would be easy to create him new mischiefs. He took every opportunity to provoke him to anger, and endeavoured to draw him into situations which might force him to demand satisfaction and thereby forfeit the good graces of the king.

Zieten, however, who had learnt at his own cost to moderate his temper, still evaded the snares that were insidiously laid for him, and during a period of four years continued to act this painful part with unremitting patience. Curbing his frank and noble disposition and submitting to the yoke of subordination, he was always able to avoid coming to an open rupture with his persecutor. At one time redoubling his attention to his own conduct and laying a restraint upon his words and actions he gave no kind of hold to his enemy; At another, by the calmness and gravity of his deportment he was always able to keep him in due respect.

Though under these circumstances Zieten could not be happy, yet his heart, accessible to sentiments of the most tender nature, suggested to him that he might be happy in other respects, and prompted him to think of marriage. His choice fell on Leopoldine Judith de Jurgas, of the house of Ganzer and of the family of his own mother. The choice met with universal approbation. Mad. de Zieten was alike distinguished for her beauty, good sense, her virtues, and her amiable and dignified demeanour. Although the fortune of this lady was small, and his plans of aggrandising and embellishing his estate had not been laid aside, he solely consulted personal attachment in the choice he had made, undebased by the slightest consideration of interest.

The charms of domestic life continued for a while to temper the vexations with which the colonel strove to embitter it, yet, what was easy enough to foresee, at last took place. The unremitting malevolence of that officer at length tired out his major's patience, and they had recourse to the most violent measures. The distribution of a supply of horses was the immediate cause of their quarrel. The colonel had chosen the best for his own squadron although it was customary to draw lots for the more equal accommodation of the troops. The moment he was apprised of this innovation, Zieten conceived it to be his duty to expostulate with the colonel on the business.

He took care to wait on him before the parade began, and stating the inconveniency that would attend this new manner of selection, earnestly intreated him to suffer things to remain on their old footing. The despotic officer felt himself offended at this advice, fell into a passion, and grew rude. Zieten, who when the interests of the service were at stake was utterly incapable of giving way, answered him in the like tone. The dispute became serious, they fastened the door and drew upon each other. Their rancour which had been so long stifled and concentrated broke out with mutual violence, and they fought with equal fury. The colonel, however, had soon reason to be astonished at finding in Zieten an adversary who seemed to be a match for him, and over whom he was not likely to gain the least advantage.

Notwithstanding the low stature and apparent weakness of the major, he stoutly sustained the assault of his colossal foe. They were both wounded; the colonel in the head, and Zieten in the right hand (his middle finger remained ever after contracted.) M. de Wurm now suddenly broke off the combat with a view of carrying it on in another manner. He laid hold of his pistols and presented one of them to Zieten, who more wise and moderate than he, replied:

> We have both of us lost blood considerably, let us in the first place have our wounds dressed, and dispatch the business of the parade which waits for us. When we are cured, I shall expect to hear from you, and I shall leave to yourself the choice of weapons.

These words which were uttered in a cool and resolute manner had their proper effect. The colonel grew calm and a surgeon was immediately sent for. The guard was duly mounted, and the horses distributed by lot. The grudge, however, still rankled in the colonel's heart and only wanted a favourable occasion to break into explosion. An occasion soon happened, as we shall see in the sequel, and which made him pay dearly for his eagerness to take advantage of it.

The king being at this period extremely ill, it is probable he never heard of the affair; but had it reached his ear, his opinion had, been too much altered respecting Zieten, whom he loved and esteemed, and considered as a very accomplished officer, to have allowed him to judge with his former severity. His Majesty, moreover, had lately shewn the great confidence he had in him by having sent him to Vienna on a secret business. The exact time and object of this mission cannot be ascertained, and all that ever transpired on the part of Zieten was, that he was treated with much distinction at the imperial court. (The reigning emperor was Charles VI.)

The king died in the year 1740. In him Zieten lost a prince whom he loved as the author of his fortune, and whom he respected as the founder of the Prussian Army, who from a rigorous fudge had become a zealous patron, and whose severities had been transformed into benefactions and favours. Whenever he spoke of this monarch, it was always with impressions of admiration and gratitude, and with the flattering consciousness of having overcome his prejudices by mere dint of merit.

On the accession of Frederick II. all the splendid prospects of Zieten seemed on the point of vanishing away or at least of becoming extremely precarious. On ascending the throne this prince set about realising the plans which his genius had conceived in the silence of retreat. His system of government was already arranged and the instruments which were to assist him in carrying it on were already chosen. Zieten, who had always kept aloof and considered every kind of eagerness which bore any resemblance to flattery as beneath himself and incompatible with real desert, had not attracted the notice of that monarch. He was lost in the crowd; but while Frederick on his part was far from foreseeing that their names should one day be blended together in the annals of history and their glory reflect mutual splendour on each other, Zieten waited patiently for the moment in which his sovereign should mark him out and place him in his true sphere of action. The event has fulfilled his expectations and justified the confidence he had both in his own worth and the penetration of the monarch.

The beginning of the reign of Frederick II. was the epoch of the German war. On the decease of Charles VI. the last of the male line of the house of Austria, several powers made pretentions to a great part of his dominions. The commotion soon became universal and a general war appeared to be inevitable. The king of Prussia took advantage of the present juncture of affairs to make good the former rights his family had to a considerable portion of Silesia. The way of negotiation he considered as too tedious a measure, and while he published his manifestoes his troops took possession of the dutchy towards the end of the year 1740. The three squadrons of body-hussars under the command of Colonel de Wurm accompanied the army, and the Prussian hussars still remained in their quarters.

Such was the first appearance of Zieten on this theatre of war, in which the Prussian Army was destined to signalise itself both offensively and defensively, and under the banners of Frederick to merit the admiration of the universe, to raise its chief to the rank of the most powerful monarchs, and sustain his throne in the midst of the assaults of the combined force of Europe.

On this theatre it was Zieten's fate to gather a part of his laurels and to lay the foundation of his future glory.

This war, so important as to its consequences, was simple in its principle, while the world was far from foreseeing the events with which it was pregnant. The king marched into the heart of Silesia without noise and almost without resistance, took possession of its fairest provinces and completed the first half of the enterprise before the report of his having undertaken it had gained full credit at Vienna.

This happy opening of the first campaign afforded the highest encouragement to an army which its chief had destined to perilous warfare, inured to fatigue, and prepared to dispute one day under his command every inch of the territory they had conquered together.

If the occupation of Silesia afforded the hussars but slender occasions of distinguishing themselves it arose merely from their being as yet considered as in a state of infancy. Zieten was at their head, but the reputation he had acquired on the banks of the Rhine had been so far forgotten that during the course of the first campaign and as late as the middle of the second, he had never appeared on the scene with any degree of *éclat*; The provinces, the towns, the fortresses were conquered and occupied without the assistance of the hussars. They were peaceably cantoned in the villages and passed a considerable time before they came in sight of an enemy.

The application and utility of the light troops had been hitherto but little known and understood in the Prussian service, and hence the real cause of the inaction to which the hussars were condemned. M. de Wurm, moreover, who commanded them was but ill calculated to draw the attention of the army in general and acquire his troops the esteem to which they were entitled, and Zieten, circumstanced as he was with regard to that officer, was obliged to be satisfied with seeing, observing, and studying in silence, within venturing to hazard any attempts which might awaken his illiberal jealousy.

The apprenticeship which Frederick himself made in the business of war in this first campaign was connected with too many objects of higher importance to allow him to enter into every detail at once. He was rather inclined not to employ his hussars at all than expose them to be ill employed, and in this respect he approved himself to be more wise and humane than one of his oldest generals, who at this period thought proper to employ a party of them in such a manner as to render it doubtful whether he considered them as men or as a mere herd of cattle led to the slaughterhouse.

This general was posted near Frankenstein in Silesia with a division of the army and the hussars. Having received intelligence that a body of Austrian cavalry was advancing upon him, he was desirous to reconnoitre them in person, and taking twenty-four horse from Colonel de Wurm he set off for that purpose, when seeing the regiment of Lichtenstein drawn out, he halted and commanded Lieutenant de Müllwitz, who led on the hussars, to make a charge. The lieutenant despairing of success on account of the inequality of numbers ventured to make some representations to him; when being harshly asked by the general if he wanted courage, he ceased his expostulations, and turning to the hussars cried out, "Come, fellow-soldiers, follow me."

The little troop rushed forwards and fell upon the enemy, who on seeing them approach received them with loud fits of laughter, and asked them if they were out of their senses. But when they saw: this handful of men make ready to charge, they found it necessary to bring out a whole squadron to receive them. At the first shock the lieutenant and one hussar were killed, and the others overwhelmed or dispersed in an instant.

The reader may judge what impression this unhappy experiment of the efficacy hastily ascribed to these kind of troops made upon the whole body. Every officer felt himself offended in the person of the lieutenant, every hussar in that of his slain comrade; and Zieten, who felt this affront deeper than anyone, secretly regretted that, with the hussars at their head, the Prussian Army at that period could not produce a general like M. de Baronay. Though he had no resource but in patience, he did not, however, lose his time, but still endeavoured to turn it to account in observing the movements and exploits of the rest of the army.

At the close of the campaign the king saw himself master of Silesia, and considering it as an old province he took up his winter quarters there. The hussars were cantoned along the frontiers of Hungary.

The king, who during the winter had leisure to consider the great advantages that might be derived from the agency of these light troops, formed a body of regulations for them, and communicated it to their principal officers. Although these regulations were yet very defective and, as it were, the mere elements of the service, they, however, afforded Zieten the first splendid occasion he had of approving himself the worthy pupil of General de Baronay and of turning his own exploits to due advantage.

At the opening of the second campaign (April, 1741), he received orders to break up his winter quarters and join the king's army which was embodying at Michelau upon the Neisse, The troops under the command of Wurm had been reinforced by three squadrons of Prussian hussars (Brunikowsky's, No. 2), and though these two corps were not immediately blended into one regiment and put under the command of the same principal officer, their uniform was nearly alike, and they acted at one time in concert, at another separately, according to circumstances. The one was called the Life-guard or Berlin hussars, and the other the Prussian. The latter were commanded by Major de Soldan, the officer who had formerly carried a challenge to Zieten on the part of his captain. It is very probable that the king by not making either of these corps subordinate to the other was desirous of calling forth their emulation as well as that of their officers, in order to discover which should the more distinguish itself and prove of the greater service to the army.

On the 8th of April the king began his march and passed the Neisse at Michelau. The hussars, who had now for the first time the honour of composing the van, surprised a party of the enemy's hussars who far from expecting the attack as a deep snow had fallen during the night, had not even time to mount their horses and form themselves into order of battle. They lost forty men, and these were the first prisoners the Prussian hussars had ever taken. The rest saved themselves by flight, and the bad roads secured them from the pursuit of the conquerors. The king having proceeded at far as Mollwitz gave battle to Marshal de Neuperg on the 10th of April and gained a complete victory over him.

In this action the hussars had no part; they were placed on the left wing of the second line to guard the baggage and had received orders to remain inactive at their post while the second line was engaged in supporting the first. Zieten a mere spectator of the battle was taken up in admiring the bravery of the Prussian infantry triumphing over every obstacle, or in keeping in awe the parties of the enemy which might endanger the safety of the baggage; and being well aware that occasions of contemplating the shock of armies without bearing an active part would not often happen, he employed these important moments in observing the errors that were committed and in storing up the lessons they furnished him.

After the victory of Mollwitz and the reduction of Brieg, the king remained encamped at Strehlen from the 4th of May to the end of August. Having been convinced on the day of the 10th of April of the indispensable necessity of good cavalry he had already begun to exercise his own in patrols and rencounters, and had drawn two new regiments from Prussia which had been formed after that of Brunikowsky. To these he added the three Berlin squadrons, and employed them conjointly with the heavy horse in the execution of frequent manoeuvres.

This new arrangement proved of great utility to the service, and at length gave Zieten an opportunity of quitting a state of inaction so painful to an officer of his turn of mind, subjected by hazard to the control of an ignorant and jealous commander who was both unable and unwilling to lead the hussars into any enterprise of moment and give them an opportunity of distinguishing themselves. M. de Wurm, in fact, was so bad an officer and so imperfect was the discipline that prevailed in his own squadron, that at the Battle of Mollwitz his hussars had plundered the baggage they had under their guard without his being able to check their disorderly conduct.

But what chiefly tended to the loss of his reputation was want of courage in war (though the reader has seen he was troublesomely bold in peace) and his continual assiduity to avoid coming to action;—a conduct that repressed the ardour of his officers and kept his troops in a state of involuntary inaction.

It is not easy to imagine to what degree he lost all command of himself whenever he was employed in the execution of any military operation. One day when the king had charged him with an expedition, he began his march and led his troops during the whole night without having made a single disposition or informed the principal officers of the squadrons of the route they had to take, so that they continued to wander at random and in the dark without knowing whither they were going.

Suddenly a noise was heard behind the squadron of Zieten, who was bringing up the rear. Imagining it naturally to be the approach of the enemy he halted, faced about, and prepared for battle, when the discovery of a singular mistake of the colonel, who had marched his troops into a circle which occasioned the van to fall close upon the rear, surprised and shamed the whole corps. Instead of endeavouring to repair this false step by attempting some splendid action, be led back to the camp his brave hussars, who had eagerly expected an opportunity of distinguishing themselves in this expedition, yet only acquired from it new proofs of the incapacity of their commander.

No one was more irritated at this than Zieten, for no one was more capable of judging of it; yet still master of his temper, though more alive to affronts which he shared in common with the service than to such as were personal, his principles had triumphed over his resentment as long as the colonel acted merely a dastardly part; but finding, in an instance we are going to relate, that he added treachery to cowardice, and that himself and his squadron were on the point of becoming the victims of his perfidious machinations, he lost all patience and fell into in new broils with him more violent than the former.

At the beginning of June M. de Wurm was ordered by the king to observe the position of the enemy. On his way he met a patrol of some hundred hussars whom he attacked and dispersed. Having pursued them to the entrance of a defile, and perceiving that they halted and faced about, he halted likewise and permitted their flankers to harass him considerably. Zieten equally enraged at the sudden inactivity of his commander and at the audacity of the Austrians, was no longer able to contain himself. He pushed forward and cried out: "Colonel, will you not put these fellows to flight?"

"Why don't you do it yourself, since you are so bold? are you not' at the head of your squadron?"

"With all my heart," said Zieten, "provided you'll support me."

At the same moment he gave the word to march, and falling on the enemy he drove them into the defile and pursued them far beyond it, fully persuaded that the colonel had kept the position in which he had left him. He took complete advantage of the skirmish, made several prisoners, and convinced the Austrians that the Prussian hussars were not to be played with. At length perceiving reinforcements pouring in on every side, he began to think of making a retreat, and conceived he had nothing to risk as he depended on finding the colonel at the entrance of the defile.

That officer, however, was no longer there; he had insidiously retired to a neighbouring village without feeling the least concern for Zieten or the squadron under his command. The latter now aware of his commander's perfidy and his own danger, was indebted for his safely merely to his presence of mind and intrepidity of conduct. He called back his flankers, closed the ranks, and while a part of his troops passed the defile he charged the enemy, who had not yet collected their forces, at the head of the rest, and gained sufficient time and ground to make good his retreat. It is likewise worthy of remark, that he did not lose a single man, and carried away every one of the prisoners he had taken.

As soon as he had gained the village whither his colonel had withdrawn he demanded satisfaction for his cowardly desertion and for the danger to which he had wilfully exposed him. M. de Warm, confounded and ashamed, or rather exasperated at seeing Zieten escaped from danger and crowned with success, made no reply, but drawing his sword, fell furiously upon him. Zieten likewise drew, and in the scuffle wounded his antagonist slightly on the head. An *aide-de-camp* interfered and separated them. This affray made much noise in the army, and an engraving has handed down its memory to the present time.

The colonel, whose wound, or rather whose anger and shame confined to his tent, was unable to attend the headquarters to receive the parole of the day, and Zieten, as next in command, appeared in his stead. He was about to make report of the late expedition, when the king the moment he perceived him, cried out, "Where is Wurm?"—"He is indisposed, sire"—"Make your report then," added the king. Zieten obeyed and His Majesty was well satisfied.

During the pretended indisposition of the colonel, Zieten was charged with the command of the hussars and received orders to repair with the whole corps to headquarters on the business of an expedition then in agitation (between the 12th and 14th of July). Here Frederick reviewed one squadron after all another, and found both men and horses in the excellent order; and in testimony of his regard for Zieten forthwith named him lieutenant-colonel.

It is impossible that the king had not heard of what had lately passed, and more than probable that he was induced in consequence to recompense in this manner the bravery of an officer whose conduct he had secretly been pleased with, though he was obliged to refrain from all public testimony of approbation. The commission with which His Majesty charged him was the recovery of a transport of provisions and money lately fallen into hands of the enemy, and the newly appointed lieutenant-colonel acquitted himself to the entire satisfaction of his sovereign.

Some days after this (22nd of July), the king determined upon dislodging the enemy from the post of Rothschloss from whence they had made frequent excursions and laid the country under contribution. He intrusted the enterprise to Colonel de Winterfeld, his adjutant-general, who put himself at the head of some battalions of grenadiers and the hussars of Wurm and Prussia under the command of Zieten. The enemy was strong and their position almost impregnable. Before them they had a deep and extensive marsh crossed by a long and narrow causeway that lay in the face of a battery. Zieten began the onset, advanced at full speed along the causeway, and under a quick fire forced the passage, threw the enemy, who little expected to be attacked in front, into disorder, repulsed them after a vigorous resistance and drove them close to a mill, along the side of a rapid stream, the bridge of which had been broken down.

All retreat was thus cut off from the Austrians while Colonel de Winterfeld was still engaging the infantry, and Zieten made a whole regiment of cavalry prisoner. But how great was his surprise as well as his triumph when he discovered he had been coping with the celebrated General de Baronay, his former preceptor in the art of war! The scholar not only surpassed the master but had likewise taken him prisoner had he not crossed the stream by the timely assistance of a plank and immediately betaken himself to flight. The general the next day carried his justice and generosity so far as to write the most obliging letter to his conqueror, in which he confessed himself vanquished, and observed that the master was but too happy in having been able to escape at all from so formidable a scholar.

Colonel de Winterfeld, in a report he made of this brilliant expedition to the king, did proper justice to Zieten and his troops. This first, exploit of the hussars made a universal sensation in the camp, and the king not satisfied with testifying his approbation of Zieten in the most flattering terms, appointed him to the rank of colonel.

Too little of a patriot to exult in the glory of another, M. de Wurm was the only person who did not share the common effusion of joy which prevailed upon this occasion. Tormented with envy he resumed his command the day after the affair of Rothschloss, and was resolved at all events to distinguish himself. On the following day an occasion was offered, and he availed himself of it; but so incapable was he of turning it to any advantage, that had it not been for the timely support of Zieten, he and all his men would have fallen victims to his ignorance and cowardice. The latter fell upon the enemy in their rear, released the prisoners, took several himself and after having re-established a desperate affair, at last terminated it gloriously.

The king was pleased to dismiss Colonel de Wurm from his service and to grant him a small pension, and afterwards to place him in a battalion of garrisoned invalids; and in order to recompense Zieten for having saved the hussars, he named him their chief officer, after having united the six squadrons of Berlin and Prussia into one sole regiment. About this time Zieten was likewise decorated with the order of military merit, though it is not known on what particular occasion it was conferred. All these events took place in the month of July, and a few days after the Battle of Rothschloss.

So rapid an advancement was an extraordinary phenomenon in the Prussian Army. In the course of one month, Zieten was raised from the rank of major to that of colonel and head of a regiment created in his favour. Independently of the personal merit which acquired him these distinctions, they; are likewise to be attributed to the high idea his successful expeditions had just given His Majesty of the importance of the hussars and of their great utility in seconding the operations of the troops of the line. This is sufficiently illustrated by two original instruments, namely the colonels commission sent to Zieten and the articles of stipulation relative to the new regiment. The preamble of the former is couched in these terms. (Bearing date the 22nd of July, 1741.)

> Having had occasion to be convinced from our own observation of the assiduity and talents which our major, John Joachim de Zieten, has hitherto exerted, in our service, we afford him a, proof of our particular satisfaction and royal favour in; naming him colonel, etc.

In the second instrument, among other particulars, we find the following.

> Having thought proper to make an alteration in our Life-guard-hussars and to dismiss Colonel de Wurm from the command of the same, we have taken the faithful services which our major, John Joachim de Zieten, has hitherto rendered us into consideration, and in order to recompense the said worthy officer, who on many occasions has given splendid proofs of conduct and intrepidity, we name him our colonel, and confer upon him the new regiment which: we have formed of three squadrons of Life-guard-hussars and of three other squadrons, etc.

The circumstance of Zieten's being styled major in these two commissions has occasioned it to be generally believed that without being appointed to the intermediate rank of lieutenant-colonel he was instantly raised to that of colonel. In a letter from the king, however, His Majesty calls him "My dear Lieutenant-Colonel de Zieten;" the omission must therefore be ascribed to an error in the war-office, whose dispatches frequently betoken the hurry and confusion of the times. Another letter to Zieten proves the above in a more detailed manner. A camp of observation being formed at Brandenburg sometime after this period under the command of the Prince of Anhalt, an acquaintance of Zieten's (M. Gerlach, postmaster at Belitz), wrote him word that having been to visit it, the prince had remarked him in the crowd, and asked him if he knew of his friend's being appointed colonel; when having replied that the gazette mentioned his advancement to the rank of lieutenant-colonel only, the prince had added:

> He held that commission but two days. Wurm is dismissed and Zieten commands in his stead.

We are now come to the period in which Zieten was enabled to make a full display of his talents and love of glory. The corps into, which, eleven years before, he had obtained admission in quality of lieutenant as by favour, now saw him at their head, and were themselves rapidly advancing to the era of their most brilliant career. The name of Zieten and that of the hussars now began to be mentioned with respect throughout the whole army. The enemy though long familiarised to this kind of soldiery observed its formation in the Prussian service with alarm, and foreboded how fatal it would one day prove to them. Zieten had the merit of being the father of all the heroes who succeeded him in this line of duty, as his regiment had that of being the model of all that were formed after him.

And if Frederick the Great in his posthumous works has not nominally done justice to his general, he speaks with eulogium of the services the hussars had rendered him in the various desultory war in which they were employed, and makes particular mention of the affair of Rothschloss.

A short time after that affair the regiment of Zieten had the first occasion of displaying the bravery of their new commander. The king who was become still more sensible of the necessity of increasing the number of light troops had commissioned Colonel de Nazmer to form a corps of *Uhlans* in Prussia and to march them into Silesia. Being arrived at the camp of Strehlen the whole army was struck with the fine appearance of the men and the goodness of the horses. The king in particular was highly pleased on the occasion, and declared that he expected more from them than from the hussars themselves, at the same time adding, that he should soon furnish them with an opportunity of making trial of their prowess.

These were, however, for the greater part, young men newly-raised, ill-exercised, and withal much encumbered by their long pikes. The king, nevertheless sent them upon an expedition near Grotkaw, taking at the same time the precaution to direct Zieten to lie in ambuscade near them, and to remain a mere spectator of the battle as long as it should go on in their favour in order to secure them the glory of their success, but in case of a repulse, to support and rescue them. The event shewed the propriety of this measure.

The *Uhlans* began the attack with impetuosity. The enemy, who soon discovered with whom they had to cope, received them with such vigour that their ranks were immediately broken, and themselves put to flight, and being hemmed in on all sides they began to give themselves up for lost. These raw troops, who even had they preserved their ranks would have been but little formidable to the Austrians, as they were unpractised in the use of their arms, ceased entirely to be so the moment their ranks were broken. Their pikes, which were of no use in action, now tended to impede their flight. They wounded one another in the disorder into which they were thrown; or in bearing their arms too low, the point stuck into the ground, the rider was unhorsed, and his steed stumbled and fell with him.

Zieten leaving his ambuscade hastened to the relief of the *Uhlans*. The enemy struck with surprise, halted, and forming themselves into order of battle made vigorous resistance against this unexpected attack. The brave hussars, however, soon changed the face of the battle and delivered their comrades, and after having recovered a great part of the prisoners, they forced the enemy to retreat. The *Uhlans*, who had now regained their former courage, rallied themselves and joining the victorious squadrons, completely routed the Austrians. Zieten who returned with them to the camp had to regret the loss of one of their officers who had been killed at the beginning of the action. (The brave Captain de Kladowsky). He presented to the king the regiment he had just saved, and which without his assistance would have been annihilated almost at its very birth.

The loss, however, which the *Uhlans* sustained and the bad success of their first enterprise induced the king to transform them into hussars. They were then in their own element, and, with the aid with their sabres, they were soon able to efface the memory of the unfortunate day of the pikes.

The Austrian hussars observed with an evil eye their young rivals disputing the palm with them, and in almost every instance bearing it away. They were impatient to take revenge, and were particularly irritated against the regiment of Zieten. Yet though this regiment consisted at that time but of six squadrons, they nevertheless resisted the superior force of the enemy, and always came off with honour. The bravery of each individual, the able dispositions made by their officers, rendered this little corps as formidable in their attack as they were invincible on the defensive.

Of this we shall only state a single instance. Sixty hussars being posted at Ulmendorf were surprised by a numerous detachment of the enemy and were in the greatest danger of being made prisoners, when their principal officer (Captain de Ritter), disposing them in a masterly manner formed such a front as enabled him to keep the enemy aloof till a reinforcement arrived under the command of one of his comrades. (Captain de Ledivary, who was killed in the action). Scarce were these two squadrons united, when falling upon the Austrians, in their turn, they repulsed them with great loss. Zieten, moreover, distinguished himself personally at Freywald, as well as on many other occasions, about this time, of which no particulars are handed down to the present day.

The Royal Army, as the reader may see at large in the posthumous works of Frederick, (*The History of My Own Times*), passed the rest of this campaign in marches and counter-marches without coming to any decisive measures. Breslaw was taken by stratagem, Neisse was besieged for the sake of form, and given up on the twelfth day in consequence of a secret convention which had been negotiated by the English minister. In virtue of this convention the two armies withdrew from each other, and the Prussian troops remained unmolested in the winter-quarters which they had taken in Silesia and Bohemia. The hussars under the command of Zieten were stationed at Hermstadt, Guraw, and in several other small towns in Silesia.

The energy which had distinguished the troops of Zieten and the glory they had acquired with him rendered them doubly dear to him; he was, therefore, highly gratified when the king, during the winter-quarters set about reinforcing the hussar regiments, and his in particular, which from six squadrons was increased to ten, and divided into two battalions, the second of which was commanded by Major de

Soldan. Zieten employed himself during the present inaction of the army in the organisation of his new recruits, and he was careful that among the great numbers that offered themselves to be enlisted, none but men of good appearance, active spirit, and sound constitution should be admitted. The king, moreover, had enjoined him to engage as many Hungarians as he could find; His Majesty being persuaded, that, on account of their intrepidity, their dexterity on horseback, and their manly and distinguished deportment in general, that nation was peculiarly fitted for such kind of service.

The attention which Zieten was giving to the organisation of his regiment was soon interrupted. He received an order from Potsdam, dated the 15th of January, 1742, to leave his winter-quarters and immediately join the army of Marshal de Schwerin which lay before Ollmutz. He began his march at the head of such of his troops as were ready for service, leaving those only behind as had been newly raised and some officers to provide them with horses. The frontier was the general rendezvous of the regiment, but he had scarcely passed it before he heard that Ollmutz had surrendered.

At this time all the armies destined to operate against the queen of Hungary were embodied in Bohemia and Moravia. Ollmutz was in the hands of the Prussians, the Elector of Bavaria had taken Prague by surprise, and all the military posts were occupied by French, Saxon, Bavarian or Prussian troops. The Austrians, too weak to cope with these combined operations, had fallen back upon their own frontiers as far as Tabor and Budweis. Vienna was now in danger, and while the queen's reinforcements advanced in hasty marches in order to save the capital, the inhabitants were alarmed by a report that Zieten was already at their gates.

The king, in fact, having ordered fifteen thousand men belonging to Count de Schwerin's army to advance as far as Znaym, the vanguard of this corps (of which Zieten made part) had pushed still farther and penetrated into Austria. Zieten's regiment occupied Stockeraw, two German miles from Vienna and spread a general alarm. His hussars were dreaded even at a distance, their approach created new terror, and that terror was now at its height. The capital, however, suffered no farther mischief than what this panic had inflicted. The king being ill supported by his allies, found himself obliged to give up acting on the defensive; the siege of Brunn did not take place, and Zieten received orders to withdraw with the rest of the troops. Before he quitted his post, he was enabled to procure out of Austria abundance of provisions for the army, and in this expedition, he had acquired the glory of having penetrated farther into that country than any of the Prussian generals did after him.

A short time after these transactions (the beginning of March), a body of eight thousand Hungarians being formed at Skalitz on the frontiers of Moravia and appearing to advance into Silesia by the way of Jablunka, the king sent Prince Diederich of Anhalt to disperse them and destroy their magazines. Zieten at the head of his regiment, which composed the vanguard, met the enemy at Gedingen, and after a brisk engagement took between two and three hundred prisoners. Having put the rest to flight he advanced on to Skalitz (in Hungary.) The only road that led to that place was over a long dike which crossed a marsh traversed by several canals, the bridges of which had been broken down. Zieten caused them to be repaired, and advanced with his hussars and two regiments of dragoons against the enemy who were posted near the dike. The latter being, as it seemed, discouraged by the unhappy affair of Gedingen fell back, after having fired a few cannon, the moment they saw the Prussians marching towards them.

The magazines were burnt or thrown into the water, and the town which the inhabitants had hastily abandoned was pillaged by order of the commander in chief.

The next day the detachment marched to Ungarisch-Brod, where another magazine lay which was defended by three hundred volunteers. Zieten surrounded them, and after having taken them all prisoners burnt the magazine.

A body of Hungarian *chasseurs* had marched to Meseritz under the command of Count de Scherotin with a view of surprising and carrying off the Prussian baggage. Zieten received information of this, and having discovered their design, marched against them and had the good fortune to drive them into a wood, where he kept them shut up till the arrival of Posadowsky's dragoons, by whose assistance he dislodged them, and killing part he made the rest prisoners of war.

After these fortunate expeditions he received orders to rejoin the corps of the Prince of Anhalt, which the king had left under the walls of Ollmutz, while he himself returned into Bohemia with the Grand Army. Prince Charles of Lorain taking advantage of this movement penetrated into Moravia to attack the Prince of Anhalt with superior force. The situation of the Prussians was very critical. They were not only the weaker party, but the enemy had taken new courage under the auspices of the able general who had just been placed at their head, and who was impatient to distinguish himself by new and brilliant exploits. The Prussian general, however, displayed so much talent and shewed himself so worthy of the army he commanded, that by skilful marches and the choice of strong and well-chosen positions, he was able to keep the enemy at a distance and prevent them from undertaking anything of moment; nor was it before he had consumed his last barrel of meal that he had recourse to retreat.

It was then that Zieten approved himself of the greatest service to him, and it is well known that ever after the prince entertained the highest esteem for him and bore him the strongest attachment. Zieten, moreover, who covered the baggage and led the vanguard in this splendid and victorious retreat, acquitted himself with so much vigilance, ability and success, that when the Prussian Army arrived in Upper-Silesia, they had scarcely sustained any loss.

As soon as the corps had evacuated Moravia, Prince Charles entered Bohemia, where the king gained a victory over him on the 17th of May between Zachaslaw and Chotusitz, without having waited the arrival of the reinforcement which was hastening to his assistance under the command of General de Derschau, and which did not join him till the battle was won. Zieten and his regiment shared the honours of the day.

Soon after this the preliminaries of peace were signed at Breslaw, Charles VII. was acknowledged emperor, and the perpetual sovereignty of the Duchy of Silesia ceded to Prussia.

This splendid and important acquisition was the work of the two first years of the reign of Frederick. A genius like his was, indeed, necessary for the conception and execution of the plan, but in order to second it, the brave generals his father had left him were likewise necessary. The king, who felt the extent of the obligations he lay under to them and all the utility which he could afterwards derive from their talents, knew how to value their services, and never forgot that it was to his army he owed the first increase of his power and the first advancement he had made in the career of glory. His posthumous works remain in that respect an eternal monument of his gratitude.

Zieten was of the number of those who contributed to consolidate the strength and power of Prussia. Several enterprises, ably combined and vigorously executed, owed their success to him and concurred in promoting the fortune of the two campaigns. His principal merit, however, consisted in his having furnished his country with a new art of attack, a new kind of soldiery, the usefulness of whom was soon felt and experienced; and who aspired to the honour of protecting camps, securing marches, covering transports and retreats: in a word, of sacrificing themselves for the common cause with the most ardent and noble devotedness.

In a short space of time, he inured his brave disciples to danger, to combat, and to victory. He accustomed them to overcome every obstacle, and he was himself convinced that with their aid he might undertake everything and ensure success. His merit, therefore, procured him the esteem and consideration of the monarch, and the singular honour of returning, at the end of two years, a colonel and commander of a regiment into the capital he had quitted in the capacity of a major at the head of a single squadron.

His liberal ambition and the enthusiastic love he bore his country must have found their noblest recompense in what he had done for it, and in what it had done for him; and the more so as his enjoyment was unembittered by the slightest reproach.

He could look back upon the past without a blush; and, without having, like many other great characters in the career of arms, sullied the name of hero by acts of cruelty or weakness, he could feast his memory on deeds of justice and humanity.

It is no wonder, therefore, that with principles like these he should return from the two campaigns as poor as when he set out, and consequently still unable to complete his favourite plan of embellishing the seat of his ancestors. Occasions of enriching himself had not been wanting during that active period. He had overrun Bohemia and Moravia at the head of his light troops and had penetrated, as the reader has seen, into Austria and Hungary. The king, moreover, had repeatedly hinted to him that he had it in his power to make his fortune; yet his heart and his principles would not allow him to employ the arms he bore for the purposes of self-interest, which often transforms the protector of the country into the persecutor of defenceless humanity.

Among other letters which he received from the king on this subject while he was carrying on the-war upon the frontiers of Hungary, we find the following one:

My dear Colonel de Zieten.
I order you by the present letter to enjoin all your captains, etc. As to the sums to be furnished to the officers during their winter-quarters, the annexed tariff will direct you. If your officers, however, should be able to procure any extraordinary emolu-

ments, I shall not examine the matter very nearly, provided they take care not to push things too far, that they have recourse to gentle means, and provoke no complaints nor applications for redress.

Znaym, February 20th, 1742. Frederick.

The tariff of which this letter makes mention probably indicated the sums only, and not the objects on which they were to be levied, since Zieten who did not, or who probably would not understand His Majesty, applied for farther information, and received the following answer.

My dear Colonel de Zieten.

My intention is that during your cantonment on the frontiers of Hungary, you levy by way of contribution one thousand *rix*-dollars for yourself, and three hundred for each captain, which sums are destined to the purpose of defraying your winter-quarters. You will, however, only make your levies upon such places as lie immediately along the frontiers.

Solonitz, March 30th, 1742. Frederick.

It is evident that in the execution of commissions of this nature it depended solely on Zieten to amass considerable wealth. Not only the most favourable opportunities fell in his way, but he had likewise the king's permission to avail himself of them; for His Majesty's express indulgence to the officers in general must be considered as a tacit allowance of the like favour to their chief. Yet notwithstanding all these advantages, he quitted the country with empty hands, generously sacrificing the improvement of his fortune to the love and esteem of the inhabitants; nor did he in the subsequent course of his life ever deviate from those principles.

Endowed with such firmness of character, it was not likely that Zieten, whose conduct under the pressure of untoward events had always been irreproachable, should be corrupted by any change of circumstances. The storms of his life had subsided, and he was now happy to, the full extent of his wishes; yet averse to all pretentions, however conscious he must have been of his own deserts, he continued to live just as he, had lived before the war, and divided his time between his family and the duties of his profession.

In this manner passed away the two first years after the conclusion of the peace. Notwithstanding his advancement in rank and the increasing celebrity of his name, he never swerved from the former simplicity of his life any farther than occasional circumstances required, and being persuaded that he had still a more splendid part to act, and higher services to perform, he prepared for his task in silence, and held himself ready to obey the first call of honour and his country.

Zieten employed all the interval between the first and second Silesian war in improving his regiment and introducing such reforms therein as he considered expedient and necessary. The king having recommended to the principal officers of his light troops the different modes of evolution which he had observed in the practice of the Austrians, Zieten without admitting them indiscriminately examined and made trial of them all, and impartially adopted such as appeared the best to him.

Not satisfied with these improvements the king was desirous to furnish the hussar-officers, during the leisure the interval of peace allowed them, with opportunities of giving proof of their talents in the military art.

For this purpose, Zieten and the chiefs of his squadrons were required to make dispositions in writing on subjects the king had given them, which His Majesty afterwards revised in order to ascertain to the extent of their scientific acquirements. Hence, he was enabled to recognise the superiority of those of Zieten, which perhaps he had hitherto not sufficiently acknowledged and which he afterwards, in consequence of false insinuations, again misjudged and undervalued for a season.

The error into which the monarch fell was but too well calculated to mislead, the public likewise; and, by way of correcting their judgment, to that error we must refer such ill-informed declaimers as will not allow Zieten to have been versed in the science of tactics, but ascribe all his merit to courage and good fortune. A prejudice established on such false grounds is, however, refuted in an unanswerable manner by the contents of the following letter from the king:

My dear Colonel de Zieten.
I received, with your letter of the 9th, your disposition upon the subject laid down, together with those of your principal officers. I am in general satisfied with them, and particularly with yours and Captain d'Ostrowsky's. You will inform your officers that I consider this occupation as far from being unimportant, since the exercise of the mind in times of peace essentially facilitates the operations of actual service. I remain your affec-

tionate king,
Charlottenburg, 12th July, 1743.                                    Frederick.

Yet while the king was thus bestowing his care and approbation on the regiment of Zieten he gave great chagrin to their chief as well as to the other officers in having named several veteran sergeants of the infantry lieutenants in the hussars, on the recommendation of the Prince of Dessau. (They had served in his regiment.) These soldiers, it is true, were brave and experienced men, and as officers in the infantry would have been an acquisition to the army, but having never been accustomed to ride, and being too far advanced in age to learn the evolutions of the light cavalry, they could not be of the least service in the regiment into which they were transplanted.

This mortification was soon followed by another which effected Zieten in a more sensible manner. The king having invited several Hungarian officers into his service and incorporated them into the light troops, named some of them generals and commanders of regiments the better to secure their attachment. At this Zieten could not refrain from taking umbrage; he was the oldest colonel and yet was superseded in favour of strangers. In all probability he had applied to the king to be invested with the title and at least to receive the pay of a general officer, since he received the following letter from His Majesty:

> My dear Colonel de Zieten.
> In reply to your letter of the 12th, I exhort you to have patience till I shall judge proper to think of you. You have only to recollect with what rapidity you have been advanced; a circumstance which could not have taken place had you served in the heavy cavalry or in the troops of the line. You would, in such cases, have hardly attained the rank of lieutenant-colonel, and have been much worse off in point of emoluments. I am your affectionate king,
> Potsdam, January 14th, 1743.                                    Frederick.

The reasoning of the king was correct enough. Zieten as a dragoon would have remained at a great distance from Zieten as a hussar; but in the latter capacity, it might be said, he had brought that kind of soldiery to a high degree of perfection, and had strong claims upon the gratitude of His Majesty; yet no one chose to enter into explanations with that prince, and Zieten submitted with good grace to what he was unable to redress. He had, however, soon after the satisfaction of seeing the regimentals of his hussars reformed and embellished. The fur-mantles of the troopers were garnished with white borders, and those of the subalterns with brown ones. Their felt-caps, which they formerly wore in all seasons, were now worn during summer only, and replaced in winter by caps of martin for the officers, and of bear-skin for the private men.

Zieten, moreover, was gratified about the same time in a manner more noble and more worthy of him. He received the royal mandate, directing him to exert his care and vigilance in favour of other regiments in the service. The letter is dated Potsdam, May 16th, 1743, and is couched in the following terms:

> My dear Colonel de Zieten.
> You will see by the enclosed the order I gave to Captain de Steusting of the black hussars now garrisoned at Copenick. My intention is that during their residence at Berlin you should exercise them and put them into such order as will fit them: for actual service with all possible diligence and attention. I am your affectionate king,
>
> Frederick

About this time an incident furnished Zieten with a fine opportunity of displaying the goodness of his heart and the general humanity of his character. In the king's letter of the 14th of January, allusion had been made to the time in which he served in the dragoons, and this had awaked his feelings and renewed the painful story of that period. Soon after this the remembrance of the same period was retraced in deeper colours. The reader will recollect the captain who had persecuted him in so illiberal a manner in Prussia and so far, depreciated him in the mind of Frederick William as to have induced His Majesty to cashier him. This captain now made his appearance again; but how changed! His cowardice, which the late war had exhibited in its true point of view, had occasioned him to be expelled the regiment, and the baseness of his conduct had caused him to be everywhere considered as an outcast of honourable society.

Tormented by conscience and feeling himself universally despised, he led a wandering life without any certain means of support, and being now at Berlin and in the lowest degree of misery, he had at length recourse to Zieten. He presented himself one morning, with a pale countenance and in ragged attire, before his old comrade. Our hero did not at first recollect his person, but how great was his surprise when he recognised in the stranger his former senior officer, and when he saw him on his knees imploring for pity and relief; All sense of injuries gave way to kinder emotions; he raised the wretched man from the ground, assured him he would forget and pardon the past, and required no farther reparation than the mere detail of the intrigues and cabals to which he had formerly been a victim. At the close of the shameful recital Zieten repeated the assurances which his distressful plight had extorted, and from that moment he became his avowed benefactor.

The writer of these memoirs can never forget the manner in which Zieten, in one of the last years of his life, spoke of this incident to her. While he was relating it, she forgot with him his former enemy, his rancorous persecutor, and considered him merely as the object of his kindness and noble beneficence. She marked the tear in the eye of the venerable old man, but observed at the same time that his eye beamed with delight, and betokened his gratitude to God who had inspired him with such generous sentiments and had given him power to pardon injuries;—"for," continued he with honest exultation, "it was from the beneficent doctrines of religion that I drew such principles."

This period of Zieten's life was one of the most felicitous of any he had hitherto experienced. For this he was chiefly indebted to the cares and foresight of his excellent lady. Her singular economy and orderly management of all domestic concerns contributed essentially to their common happiness; for the income of Zieten, though ill-proportioned to the generosity of his disposition, yet surpassed his wants. He divided it among the necessitous, and gave away, without troubling himself with any thoughts of the future. The cultivation of his lands and the care of their produce neither contributed to his amusement nor engaged his attention; and to his wife, who, he was happy to find, had a turn for such occupations, he committed the whole administration of the farm and dairy.

Not that he imposed this task upon her with any view of making the most of his estate; he was only fond of seeing her engaged in a business in which she appeared to take so much delight. Fair from being influenced by sordid views he remained voluntarily unacquainted with the improvements of his lands, and never inquired into the profits he derived from them.

In the year 1743 his lady bore him a son, the only one he had by this marriage. He embraced the infant with extreme delight, he had long wished to be a father, and he considered children as a gift from heaven and the supreme felicity of the conjugal union. The birth of his son did not, however, engage him to pay more attention to the improvement of his fortune.

Riches were not his aim; his principal ambition, his ruling passion, was to be serviceable to his country whenever it stood in need of his sword.

The political horizon of Prussia now became obscured. The repose the country had of late enjoyed was nearly at an end. The system of the neighbouring powers, too inimical to the aggrandisement of that state, convinced the king and his ministers of the necessity of a new war to enable him to secure the acquisitions he had already made. During the two years of peace which Prussia had enjoyed, her example had not been at all imitated by the other powers. Austria elated with her better fortune forgot her losses and began to put forth her strength. Already the emperor Charles VII. was humbled, and deprived of the greater part of his hereditary dominions.

The empire, torn by factions, was, no longer one compact body and the balance of power was in favour of the house of Austria, which on its part again aspired to the imperial sceptre. Old alliances were broken, and new treaties were concluded. All the cabinets of Europe were in motion, and every political intrigue was played off to favour the interests of each respective court, and each court endeavoured by the assistance of its ministers and emissaries to pry into and discover the secrets of the others.

In this manner Frederick was apprised that the cabinets of Vienna, of London, and of Dresden had entered into a secret alliance against him. As soon as he was well assured of the existence of such union, he resolved to avert the effects of it by immediate preparation for war, and, in conjunction with the French, to direct his operations against the Queen of Hungary in order to prevent the entire subjugation of the emperor, and to support the weak against the strong.

The following order was issued in consequence of the plan of war which the king had secretly formed.

My dear Colonel de Zieten.
I hereby order you to inform the officers of your regiment in my name that I should be glad if they would take *chasseurs* into their service instead of other domestics, or at least such persons as may be used as *chasseurs*, as such measure would not only be more becoming, but likewise in many respects more useful and

more convenient to your officers. I am your very affectionate,
Potsdam, March 9th, 1744  Frederick.

The order to march found Zieten ill and confined to his bed. The state of his health, indeed, had been very infirm from his early youth. The wrongs, the vexations he had undergone contributed very much to impair it, and the fatigue of the service, to which he submitted like the lowest hussar, was ill-adapted to restore it. During the campaigns he inflexibly forbore to indulge himself in any of the comforts and conveniencies of life, nor could the tender instances of Mad. de Zieten prevail upon him to alter his plan. In all her letters she conjured him to take care of his health, spoke of the rheumatic complaints to which he was subject, and expressed her apprehensions of his being eventually attacked by a stroke of the palsy.

She gently chid him for sleeping on the ground, exposed to the cold damps of the night, and intreated him, as the greatest proof of love he could shew her, that he would henceforth be more careful of himself. She furnished him with beds and matrasses, and would likewise have sent him a provision of tea, had she thought he would have made use of it. These particulars are sufficient to shew to what degree Zieten could sacrifice his ease to his duty.

While he was in garrison and at leisure to pay some attention to himself, he had been less unmindful of his health. He had even taken medical advice, but without effect. A general relaxation of body, attended with continual attacks of the headache, threatened to affect his intellects as well as to bring him to the grave. He had at last recourse to violent and desperate remedies which not only proved inefficacious, but likewise rendered his condition still more alarming.

He grew worse daily and his recovery was at length despaired of. His country now called for his assistance, and at that animating voice his spirits revived, and making a strong effort, he quitted his sick-bed and marched with the army, (June, 1744.) It was, however, generally supposed he could never reach the place of rendezvous, and his disconsolate wife in particular, as appears from the letters she wrote her friends, was of that opinion. But either the effect of some new remedy, or the empire which the strong mind of Zieten had over his feeble body, or some incident not to be accounted for, enabled him to arrive in due time at his post.

Frederick, whose maxim it was to be always first in the field and to act on the offensive, suddenly entered Bohemia and marched directly to Prague. His army moved in three columns. The first, of which Zieten made part, and which the king commanded in person, traversed Saxony, either in a hostile or friendly way, along the eastern banks of the Elbe, and arrived upon the frontiers of Bohemia towards the middle of August. The king having caused the army to be preceded by a body of grenadiers and hussars in order to cover their march and secure provisions, Zieten was the first who met the enemy.

He found the regiment of Esterhazy on his way, and having fallen upon them unexpectedly, he killed a considerable number, took many prisoners, and still preceding the king's column, harassed the retreat of the rest. Several other rencounters, which he had with this corps, terminated in favour of the Prussians, and when they arrived before Prague almost every hussar wore the sabre-pouches of the regiment of Esterhazy. These pouches were very handsome and showy; for which reason the first who had gained them wore them by way of ornament. The other hussars soon began to covet them, and they were now considered as trophies. It was inglorious not to have them, an honour to possess them; and this trivial circumstance acted as a powerful stimulation with Zieten's hussars and caused them to begin the present campaign with as much ardour as they had displayed in terminating the preceding one.

The three columns being united before Prague on the 2nd of September, the king immediately began the siege of that place. On the 16th of that month the city surrendered, and the garrison, which consisted of twelve thousand men, were made prisoners of war.

This happy opening of the campaign induced the king to penetrate farther into Bohemia in order to expel General de Bathyani, and force Prince Charles to evacuate Bavaria and fall back upon Austria. On the 17th he began to march, and Zieten resumed his post in the Vanguard, which was commanded by General de Nassau, and consisted of twenty battalions and forty squadrons.

The greater part of the towns of Bohemia, which were ill-fortified and ill-guarded, opened their gates to him. Tabor alone made some resistance. On the 23rd of September a severe engagement took place between the Prussian and Austrian hussars. Zieten avenged the death of one of his brave officers (Captain de Wicklow), who fell therein; the next day the town surrendered.

On the 30th the advanced guard appeared before Budweis, a town situated nine German miles from Lintz, upon the Austrian frontiers, and naturally very strong. It is surrounded and defended by a great marsh, extensive inundations, and the rivers Muldaw and Mutsch. This fortress was provided with a good garrison, and the commanding officer, far from surrendering, began to prepare for a vigorous defence. The Prussian general, desirous of taking the place by storm, made his attack on both sides at once. The attempt was not at first successful. Six hundred Croats, posted between the ramparts and the suburbs, and covered by the Muldaw, prevented the infantry from advancing along the causeway. Zieten was thereupon sent to reconnoitre the enemy, and while he skirted the Muldaw, the Croats killed and wounded several of his men; which rousing his resentment, immediately induced him to decide upon the part he had to take.

Three of his boldest hussars, under the appearance of watering their horses, tried the depth of the river, and having found it fordable, informed their commander thereof. The order was instantly given, and the whole regiment plunged into the stream and crossed it, while the yellow hussars, who had accompanied Zieten, remained on the other side to cover the enterprise. The Croats being thus cut off behind, lost courage and betook themselves to flight. The hussars pursued them, and, having killed a great number, made prisoners of the rest. Budweis surrendered the same day. The infantry having been thus enabled to advance unmolested, the hereditary Prince of Hesse-Darmstadt, at the head of his battalion, was the first before the gates, and the garrison obtained an honourable capitulation. On the 1st of October the castle of Frauenberg surrendered to Zieten on the same conditions.

The king's division followed close upon the corps commanded by General de Nassau. Nothing impeded their progress, and after a march of fourteen days, they arrived and encamped at Budweis.

It was then that the king, desirous of doing justice to the merit, and rewarding the recent services of Zieten, advanced him to the rank of major-general (October 3rd), and, as a particular favour, and by way of reparation for the refusal he had given him in the year 1745, His Majesty was pleased to order the commission to be antedated eight months, and to announce his advancement to him in the following letter.

My dear Colonel de Zieten.

In consideration of the faithful and distinguished services you have rendered me on every occasion that called for them, I have appointed you major-general of hussars, which rank will be dated from the first of February of the present year. I have accordingly given directions that the commission should be of such date, and I have the satisfaction to give you information thereof. I have likewise ordered the keeper of the army chest to pay you the salary of a major-general on the war establishment, as well as for the allowance of an *aide-de-camp* in particular, from the aforesaid date, and I am your affectionate

Frederick.

In this manner Zieten recovered in part what he had lost, and he had in fact no reason for complaint, as the foreigners, who had been preferred to him in time of peace, remained far behind him soon after hostilities had begun, and were besides totally eclipsed by him. It was not without the most urgent reasons that at the siege of Budweis two regiments, as we have seen, were put under his command; and if the writer of these memoirs has not been more explicit, it was owing to certain restrictions she has thought fit to lay herself under.

Hitherto everything had succeeded to the king's desire, and even surpassed his expectations; but the sequel did not correspond with this brilliant commencement. That great commander fell into the snare which the Austrians had laid for him.

Giving way on all sides to superior force, they had allured him into the pursuit of them in order to expose his army to all the horrors of famine. The Prussians had nothing but abandoned villages and desolated countries to traverse, and the light troops of Bathyani, together with a body of ten thousand Hungarian hussars, impeded the arrival of provisions, and cut off every communication. The Prince of Lorrain had left the banks of the Rhine, and marched with great rapidity towards Bohemia. On his way he had met with twenty thousand Saxons, with whom he reinforced himself. In this embarrassing situation the king had no hopes but in the issue of a battle. He endeavoured therefore to come up with the combined army, but being led astray by treacherous guides, he was unable to effect his purpose, and being pressed on all sides was at last obliged to abandon offensive measures and to strive to regain the city of Prague.

This retreat, which began the 8th of October, was extremely toilsome and distressing. It was made in the sight of the enemy, and Zieten, who was stationed in the rear with his light-horse, was incessantly harassed and annoyed. It is inconceivable that this division of the army remained unbroken, and suffered only partial losses, when its destruction seemed to be inevitable; yet while General de Janus and his regiment gave way to the enemy, Zieten was enabled to cover the retreat, and the king happily arrived at Bechin on the evening of the 9th of October, and there formed his camp.

His Majesty had left Zieten behind him at Tein, a small town situated on the banks of the Muldaw in order to guard that position till the camp-ovens and baggage were in safety. Besides his own regiment, the king reinforced him with that of Ruesch's hussars, and with two battalions of grenadiers drawn from the regiments of Saint-Surin and Jeetz. Zieten was not ignorant that the neighbouring woods were filled with light troops commanded by the famous partisans, Nadasty, Ghilany, and Trenck; and being likewise aware of their design to attack him, he took his measures accordingly, and chose the most advantageous position the nature of the ground afforded.

He stationed the battalion of Saint-Surin in the town, apposite to the bridge; and in the redoubt which commanded the extremity thereof, on the other side the stream, he posted a company of grenadiers. Two companies of the regiment of Jeetz were stationed without the town close to a dike and the rest remained within with the cannon by which the dike was covered. Himself, with his regiment and that of Reusch, took post out of the town, which then lay on his right, while he had the river full before him.

Scarcely had he effected this hasty disposition when two columns of the enemy came out of the wood. Their advanced guard took the road to the Muldaw, and the flankers approached the bank of the river and began to fire. A young hussar belonging to Zieten's regiment, giving way to the impetuosity of his courage, plunged his horse into the stream and swam across it. His comrades followed his example, and two squadrons of the same hussars, stationed on the right wing, likewise plunged therein, imagining that such was the general's order. Zieten apprehended the consequence of such movement, and considered this part of his corps in a very perilous situation.

He observed them make their onset with intrepidity; he then saw them give way to superior numbers, and at last fall back upon the infantry who were posted on both sides of the bridge. He had therefore no other part to act than that of hastening to their relief, and he accordingly ordered his hussars to cross the river, and then falling upon the enemy with great fury he repulsed them, and drove them again into the woods.

After having brought back his two squadrons Zieten had no sooner taken possession of his first post, than two new columns came out of the wood and divided themselves into three bodies. One of these marched directly to the redoubt with drums beating and colours flying, and attempted to carry it by storm. The grenadiers who defended it, received the enemy with great coolness, and, keeping up a continual fire, quickly repulsed them. In the meanwhile two other divisions had passed the river, above and below the town, the infantry having either mounted behind the troopers or taken advantage of the fords; and Zieten's corps, being dispersed on either side of the Muldaw, were in danger of being entirely cut off. A body of ten thousand men, of every kind of soldiery and of different nations, surrounded his troops, whose sole resource now lay in the intrepidity and experience of their leader. Nor did their hopes prove fallacious.

As soon as Zieten had observed the movement of the enemy and discovered their design, he made his dispositions in order to counteract it. To Colonel de Ruesch he gave orders to pass over the bridge, to traverse the town at the head of the black hussars, and to receive the enemy's column which was approaching on the right. Having himself passed the river, he resumed his former position in order to oppose the enemy who were drawing near on the left. The two battalions of grenadiers, after having nearly consumed their ammunition, and finding themselves unable to defend the town, evacuated it and joined the hussars, in conjunction with whom they formed a triangle, of which they themselves composed one side, while the two regiments of hussars constituted the two others. In this position they awaited the enemy.

In the meanwhile, the column, which at first had uselessly attacked the redoubt, perceiving that it was abandoned as well as the town, followed close upon the two battalions, and scarcely had the latter taken their post in the midst of the hussars, when the Croats, arriving by a hollow way, fell upon the regiment of Ruesch with loud shouts, and made a general discharge, which was sustained with singular courage. The regiment was then about to charge in return, when Zieten, the better to secure success, suspended the moment of attack, dispatched three of his squadrons to the left in order to flank the enemy, and then fell upon them on all sides.

While he broke their ranks, and, notwithstanding their superiority in numbers, put them to flight; while thirteen squadrons fought with intrepidity, the infantry formed themselves into a square battalion under cover of seven other squadrons on the left, and engaged the column which operated on that side. Prodigies of valour were now displayed, and this handful of Prussians remained masters of the field, after having repulsed the enemy and made great slaughter. The exasperated hussars refused to give quarter; the greater part of the Croats were killed, and a few only were made prisoners,

The battle had begun at noon, and it lasted till near nine o'clock in the evening. The artillery had consumed all their ammunition; and out of sixty cartouches each grenadier had only six remaining. Three of Zieten's squadrons had sustained a continual fire; a hundred of his hussars lay dead on the fields and about seventy were wounded. He availed himself of the night and the retreat of the enemy in order to continue his march, and he encamped at the distance of half a German mile from Tein, upon the highway to Bechin, where the king had his headquarters. He procured waggons for his wounded soldiers, and they were safely removed to Tabor.

As soon as the king had been informed of this battle, he had detached a body of near twelve thousand men from the main army to hasten to the relief of Zieten. This corps, notwithstanding the diligence of their proceedings, did not join the rear-guard till late in the night of the 10th, after the engagement had been happily terminated; and they could only, applaud the success to which they had not the glory to contribute.

On the next day Zieten and his troops gathered the fruits of their recent toils. Lieutenant de Belling had been sent to report to the king the advantages obtained over the enemy, and His Majesty, in spite of the ill-humour into which his disagreeable situation had thrown him, forgot his chagrin for a moment and gave himself up to joy. (Lieutenant de Belling since that time one of the best generals of hussars in the Prussian service).

Delighted at this splendid defence, and charmed at the deliverance of his rear, he instantly mounted his horse, and proceeded to meet Zieten and his brave soldiers on their way. He applauded their valour, spoke of their leader in terms of consideration and gratitude, and placing himself at their head, led them in triumph through the whole camp. Every man rushed out of his tent to see them pass by, and the camp resounded with "Long live the king! Long live Zieten and his troops!"

Frederick, indeed, possessed in an uncommon degree the art of rewarding and encouraging the soldier, and this secret alone, without his other accomplishments, had been sufficient to gain and secure the affection of his army. He assumed for a moment the immediate command of Zieten's regiment, and the whole regiment was more than ever devoted to him; and, at the same time, he inspired with new ardour the rest of the army, who, on account of their present critical situation, stood in need of such encouragement.

Zieten's care was now to make severe inquiry in order to discover the hussar who first passed the Muldaw and drew the two squadrons into such a perilous situation. His emissaries could not, or rather, with the connivance of the general, would not discover the valiant offender; and he contented himself with publishing a proclamation, prohibiting such daring feats in future, on pain of death, and rendering the commanders of squadrons responsible, in that respect, for the conduct of their troops.

★★★★★★★★★★

Nothing at the present day can render it improper to name him. It was the brave Colonel de Lenz of the regiment of Zieten, a veteran to whom the writer of these memoirs is indebted for much historical detail. He it was likewise that first tried the depth of the ford at Budweis.

★★★★★★★★★★

The Royal Army by insensible degrees approached the city of Prague, and encamped between Beneschaw and Konopisch, and the Austrians, who followed at some distance, formed their camp on the 15th near Chlumetz. By this movement the Prussian garrisons at Budweis, Frauenburg, Tabor, and Muhlhausen, where the sick and wounded lay, were exposed to the mercy of ten thousand Hungarians, who were scouring the country, and by whom they were all successively made prisoners. The king thus lost three thousand men; the regiment of Zieten thirty troopers at Budweis; and, at Tabor, all the hussars who had been wounded at Tein.

The Prince of Lorrain, whose aim, it seemed, was to turn the king and cut off all communication with Prague, had encamped at Maschowitz. This alarming situation forced the Prussians to act on the offensive. The king made the necessary preparations on the 20th, and having passed the night under arms, and discovered, the next day, that the position of the enemy was inaccessible, he began to manoeuvre in order to draw them from it. For this purpose, he passed the Zasawa, and having encamped on the 25th at Pischeli, he continued his march towards Collin. On the abovementioned day Zieten was detached, under General de Nassau, to Kammersbourg for the purpose of dislodging the Austrians and Saxons.

The corps, which consisted but of ten battalions and thirty squadrons of horse, had a painful march to perform, as the country was mountainous and devoted to the interests of the adverse party. A detachment of three hundred hussars, that preceded the corps, supplied the want of better intelligence by the information they procured either by force or gentler means, and, in this manner, directed the progress of the march.

This detachment, under the command of two able officers (Lieutenant-Colonel de Billerbeck and Major de Wippach), lost their way one night for want of proper guides, and suddenly found themselves in the midst of woods and rocks, from whence there appeared to be no issue. At length they discovered a path which led to a village in the neighbourhood of Kammersbourg, and the detachment proceeded thither with extreme caution.

The enemy had neglected to occupy this post, and the hussars immediately took advantage of their oversight. They surrounded the village, and, securing the persons of the bailiff and his nearest relations, compelled the former to conduct a patrol in the most private manner to Kammersbourg for the purpose of procuring information respecting the force and position of the Austrians. They likewise threatened to punish: him in the persons of his family and relations in case he should prove treacherous or fail in leading them in a proper manner; and the more effectually to intimidate him they shewed him the implements of the punishment that awaited his misconduct.

The danger the bailiff found himself in, and the distress of his relations, made him readily promise everything that was required at his hands, and he was accordingly intrusted with a subaltern officer, six hussars, and a led-horse. Thus accompanied he stole through the advanced posts of the enemy and arrived at the cottage of a shepherd, whom he had mentioned as an intelligent man, and one who was perfectly acquainted with the country for many miles round. This man, they found, had taken the precaution of barricading himself in his hut, and it was nevertheless necessary to make sure of his person in haste and without noise.

The patrol occupied the door, the bailiff tapped at the window in order to awake him; but the shepherd, although he recognised the bailiff's voice, grew distrustful and positively refused to let them in. Being repeatedly assured by his countryman that he had nothing to fear, he at last ventured to open the door, when two hussars suddenly laying hold of him, mounted him upon the spare horse and the party returned in full speed to the village. The bailiff and his family were released and the shepherd was taken to the camp, where he furnished the Prussians with every necessary information. General de Nassau having thus learnt all he wished to know, attacked the enemy the next day at Kammersbourg and dislodged them with very inconsiderable loss.

In consequence of this expedition, the success of which had been owing to the detachment of Zieten's troops, the corps of General de Nassau entered Collin on the 30th of October, and thereby got the start of the enemy in the occupation of that important post.

The king, on his part, continued his retrograde march, and arrived with the main body of the army at the above town on the 4th of November, being closely followed by the Prince of Lorrain, who during the march had always encamped in sight of the Prussians upon heights which effectually secured him from being attacked by them. His Majesty was therefore naturally impatient to give him battle in order to extricate himself from his present embarrassing situation. His army had suffered extremely by the fatigues of a long retreat; his provisions were exhausted, the communications almost impracticable, and the season much advanced. The troops, hitherto full of ardour and activity, had displayed prodigies of courage and perseverance, but famine and sickness now oppressed them, and they were obliged to give way and retreat.

To evade still greater evils, and to procure some relaxation for his troops, the king resolved to station them in cantonments though the enemy still kept the field; and on the 9th of October the Prussians passed the Elbe near Collin. Nassau and Zieten covered the passage, and the former remained at Collin, while the latter accompanied the main army.

Collin and Pardubitz were become two places of great consequence, as they had served as communications between Prague and Silesia. The king, who felt the importance of securing their possession, furnished them with strong garrisons, and established a chain of posts along the Elbe, behind which the rest of his army were cantoned. At the distance of every German mile, His Majesty stationed a battalion of infantry and three squadrons, of hussars. Zieten, with a detachment of three squadrons from his own regiment, was posted at Fladop, at that time famous for a very numerous stud of horses. The king had taken his headquarters at Turnow, near Pardubitz. The Austrians, under the command of Prince Charles, and the Saxons, under that of the Duke of Weissenfels, were encamped on the other side the Elbe at Kuttenberg and Choltiz.

The enemy made several feigned attacks upon Collin with a view of masking their real plan. This plan was to cross the Elbe (the Austrians at Przelautisch, and the Saxons at Pardubitz) and to drive the Prussians entirely out of Bohemia. It is was not, however, attended with success. General de Nadasti and General de Trenck, who commanded the enterprise, being discovered in due time by a party of hussars, and repulsed with considerable loss by the garrison, were under the necessity of abandoning it, and the Austrian Army encamped in sight of that of the king at Brelock between Collin and Pardubitz without having been able to pass the river.

Although the position of the enemy, as well as the general state of the two armies, did not encourage the Prussians to expect to keep them in awe during the winter, yet the king had not relinquished his hopes. Resolved to trait the event to the latest moment, he flattered himself, that when the enemy had taken their winter quarters between the Elbe and the Zasawa, he should be able to fall upon them, to disperse them, and to become master of the two circles of Bohemia which lay in the neighbourhood of Moravia.

But the enemy, who plainly perceived the king's intention, feared him too much to risk exposing themselves to the issue of it, and in order to get rid of so formidable a neighbour, they were obliged to abandon the idea of acting merely on the offensive. For this purpose the queen of Hungary, regardless of the fatigues the troops had already undergone and had still to go through, gave positive directions to her generals to force the passage of the Elbe, whatever loss of men it might occasion, for the purpose of cutting off the king from Prague, and forcing him to evacuate Bohemia.

Prince Charles, in consequence of the above orders, took his measures with equal prudence and address. He caused a quantity of scaling-ladders to be prepared by way of mask, and ordered such marches to be undertaken as might appear to explain and confirm the letters he had fabricated and sent off for Vienna, but which he knew would be intercepted on the road. From this coincidence of circumstances His Majesty therefore calculated with much apparent propriety, that the enemy would make an attempt either on Prague or Collin on the 18th of November. With a view of counteracting this supposed design the king reinforced his garrisons, and especially that of Prague, with several thousand men.

The real design of the enemy was wholly unknown to him and he thought himself perfectly secure on the other side of the Elbe, where the chain, of posts was distributed in such manner as to warn him of the slightest movement that took place in that quarter. In effect, if Prince Charles, on the night previous to the attack, had not succeeded in dispatching a body of hussars and *Uhlans* across the river and concealing them in the wood, whence they were enabled to intercept and fire upon such as were dispatched from the advanced posts, his motions could not have remained so profound a secret. Nor is it possible to clear the hussars of Zieten from the imputation of negligence in the execution of their patrol-duty at this time; yet this is perhaps the only misconduct of which the regiment was guilty during the two first Silesian wars. But their general, was inconsolable on account of its immediate consequences, as it was but too probably the principal cause of the enemy's success in an expedition that proved so disastrous to the Prussians.

While the king and his generals thus considered themselves in perfect security, the enemy were secretly preparing to surprise them; and, in the night of the 18th of October, the combined army approached the Elbe with such caution and with so little noise, that the pontons arrived at Teinetz upon the banks of that river before the Prussians had the least intimation of these proceedings. At the moment in which the passage began, the patrols perceived a movement and gave the alarm. Zieten and Lieutenant-Colonel de Wedel with three squadrons, and a battalion of grenadiers consisting of four companies, hastened to impede the progress of the enemy; and the former dispatched one of his officers (Cornet de Panko), to make report of their situation to the king as well as to solicit a reinforcement; and, in full expectation of speedy succour, they marched to attack them.

Being arrived on the banks of the river, they found a bridge already thrown across it, and the troops defiling thereon. All the Austrian and Saxon grenadiers had been chosen, and distributed into battalions, for this enterprise, and the rest of the infantry, supported by a numerous artillery, had occupied the heights on the opposite bank, from whence they kept up a heavy fire upon the Prussians as they approached the Elbe. Notwithstanding this, the battalion of Wedel thrust back the column that were passing the river, and immediately took post before the bridge, where they lay secure from the fire of the artillery, which could not play upon that spot without killing their own troops, while the fire, of the Prussians, being directed towards the bridge, did great execution. Zieten remained at some distance at the head of his troops who were drawn up in order of battle to impede the construction of new bridges or to flank the enemy in case the battalion of Wedel should be unable to maintain their ground.

The Austrian batteries continued to fire on the Prussians without effect, and at length all their grenadiers being drawn out, an attempt was made to storm the bridge and force a passage. The Prussians waited for them with cool intrepidity, nor did M. de Wedel give the word to fire till the bridge was thronged with the enemy. A well-directed discharge then threw them into confusion, and they were for a second time driven back.

The third attempt proved more fortunate; the Austrians being continually reinforced by fresh troops at length were able to repulse the battalion of Wedel, weakened by the loss of men and the long duration of the encounter; and they began to form on the other side of the river. Zieten now marched against them with two of his squadrons, and charged them with such vigour that they were soon obliged to abandon the ground they had gained, and to seek for shelter on the opposite bank of the Elbe. The rout was so great that many of the grenadiers were thrust by their comrades into the river. The Prussian infantry, in the meanwhile, rallied and resumed their former position.

The Austrians, who little expected to meet with such opposition, seeing a handful of men, a battalion and three squadrons only, cope with a whole army, were both astonished and disconcerted. They kept up a terrible fire, but without the effect they had looked for. Their artillery had been pointed too high. The Prussians, however, lost a considerable number of men.

Zieten himself had been exposed to the most imminent danger. His horse being shot under him, a subaltern of the name of Forkard, the moment he observed the disaster, dismounted; and without any consideration of the peril to which he himself would be liable, presented his horse to his general. Zieten thanked him in the kindest terms, and, instead of accepting his offer, had the generosity to say "Keep your horse, comrade; you are an Austrian deserter; and if you are taken you will be hanged. Make haste to remount."

During this transaction another subaltern (Puschel), having offered him his, he accepted it, and assured him, that in case the want of the horse should throw him into the hands of the enemy, he would take proper steps to procure his liberty. The hussar, however, did not give him an opportunity of making good his promise; he had recourse to an expedient that did equal credit to his sense and his bravery;—having joined the ranks of Wedel's battalion, he fought as a foot soldier, and fortunately regained his squadron.

The above-mentioned feature in the life of Zieten was indeed worthy of him, and exhibits him in an interesting point of view both as a hero and a man. It were to be wished that such like instances of generosity, which frequently occurred during his long career, could be collected and preserved for his own honour and the instruction of posterity. But no one could be more sparing than he was in communications of this kind. Those even whom he most honoured with his confidence, notwithstanding all their solicitations, could never draw such secrets from him. He did good by stealth; he was conscious of its value, and loved to practise it, but he always knew how to elude the eye of observation.

This unequal engagement was carried on during the space of five hours. The Prussians continued undismayed, but their ammunition was spent, their loss of men increased, and no succour arrived. Several hussars had been dispatched to the king to inform him of the danger, and not one of them reached the camp. They had been all killed or taken by the enemy's pickets, who had concealed themselves the day before in the neighbouring woods; and the officer who was first sent off must certainly have perished, as he never was heard of afterwards. All hopes of succour being now lost, the commanders of this small corps began to think of an honourable retreat in order to avoid the unnecessary sacrifice of their men; but they did not come to this determination till the Austrians and Saxons had already passed the Elbe in several places and were making preparations for a general assault. The Prussians, however, retreated in the face of the enemy, and in such good order that they reached the forest of Wischonowitz without being broken, and caried with them all the wounded that were capable of being removed.

After having attained his end and forced the passage of the Elbe, the Prince of Lorrain established his camp on the other side of that river. Of these disastrous events the king was not informed till it was too late for redress. The cannonading indeed had been heard at the headquarters and along the banks of the Elbe; but His Majesty persisted in the belief that the attack was directed against Collin. He had not thought it at all necessary to send a reinforcement to a quarter which he did not suspect to be menaced; whereas had he afforded timely relief, the enemy must have been repulsed with considerable loss. Yet, whatever might have been the result, the king himself in his posthumous works speaks of this encounter with great eulogium:

The Battle of Teinitz will be ever memorable in the annals of Prussia. In this splendid defence M. de Wedel has emulated the name of Leonidas.

A portion of this praise falls to the share of Zieten, and His Majesty could not but tacitly allow it, when he adds:

The Prince of Lorrain surprised that a single battalion of Prussians should dispute the passage of the Elbe for five hours together, observed to those who surrounded him, that the Queen of Hungary would be peculiarly happy to have officers in her army worthy of being compared with such heroes.

This memorable day decided the fate of the campaign. The king found himself compelled to take up his winter-quarters in Silesia. The army began to march after having recalled the detached parties, and, among the rest, that of General de Nassau. The evacuation of Bohemia was executed without any loss and the troops marched in two columns, one of which the king commanded in person. The frontier was passed at Braunaw, and Zieten was the last that quitted it.

Winter-quarters being now established, the king returned to Berlin, and the campaign appeared to be closed, when the Austrians made a sudden irruption into the county of Glatz, and Upper Silesia. Persuaded that the Prussian Army, which had considerably suffered, would be too weak to make much resistance, they had promised themselves a sure and easy triumph, and in this opinion, they had been further confirmed by observing the well-timed retreat of the advanced-posts, which on the arrival of the enemy, as has been already said, had fallen back upon the main army. The king apprised of this unexpected expedition, took the field, and soon made the Austrians repent of their inconsiderate conduct.

After having concerted with the Prince of Dessau, he sent three bodies of troops against them, commanded by Dessau, Lewald, and Nassau. Zieten and his regiment were under the orders of the first of those generals, who. having formed at Neisse, marched forthwith to Jägerndorf with a view of dislodging the enemy. The Austrians were, however, no longer there. At the approach of the prince, they had retired into Moravia with much precipitation and suffered great loss on the way through the inclemency of the weather, desertion, and the attack made upon their rearguard by Zieten. Their retreat indeed resembled a flight. They passed several nights without provisions and tents, exposed to all the rigours of winter. The troops of Lewald and

Nassau met with more opposition, though not of long duration, and Silesia was soon cleared of the enemy.

After this short but important expedition, Zieten returned to his winter-quarters near Neisse, and enjoyed a repose, of which, on account of his late fatigues, he stood in great need. His regiment had suffered essentially during the campaign. Almost continually exposed to the enemy either in the rear or the van, he had lost a great number of his men, and it was necessary to supply their place by fresh recruits against the ensuing spring; a task to which he now betook himself with his usual attention and despatch. Nor had the king waited for the expedition of Upper-Silesia to give Zieten new proof of his approbation. Scarcely had His Majesty arrived at Berlin when he was pleased to grant him an augmentation of his income to the amount of twelve hundred dollars, and wrote the following letter on the occasion, bearing date the 30th of December, 1744.

My dear Major-General de Zieten.

As a mark of my satisfaction and good will, and by way of further rewarding your faithful services, I have determined and given orders, that you shall enjoy the pension of seven hundred dollars vacant by the death of Colonel de Varenne, together with the five hundred dollars which he received on the Gueldres establishment. I enclose you a copy of the order, and remain your affectionate

Frederick.

Besides this flattering token of his sovereign's favour, Zieten had the pleasure of seeing a great princess eager to testify the esteem she bore him. His reputation had reached the capital of the Russian empire; and though at the present day, in which the art of war is brought to a higher degree of perfection, his exploits would not make the same impression on the public, they were then of so astonishing and extraordinary a nature as to induce the empress, notwithstanding the principles of neutrality which she had adopted, to make his regiment a present of three hundred valuable horses. Yet, however flattering these distinctions and marks of esteem must have been to him, they made no alteration in his manner of thinking. If misfortunes and ill usage often rendered him inflexible and haughty, the favours of fortune never produced any other effect upon him than that of redoubling his zeal.

On the opening of the second campaign, which had become inevitable by the refusal of the Queen of Hungary to listen to proposals of peace, the political system of Germany had, in consequence of the death of Charles VII, taken a new form. The league of Frankfort was dissolved; the empire became more and more favourable to the interests of the house of Austria, to which the imperial crown now seemed to be clearly destined. The Bavarians had disarmed, and their new elector had recently made peace with Maria Theresa.

The Saxons, who had long been the secret enemies of Prussia, now no longer strove to disguise their sentiments, and their vicinity created new disquietude. The French, the only allies that remained true to Frederick, began to grow cold in his cause. The theatre of the war was now to be transported from Alsace into Bohemia and Silesia, and the enemies of the king had stirred up one half of Europe against him. A formidable league had already taken place, and Prussia's sole defence consisted in her king and her army.

Frederick profited by the errors he had committed, and the experience he had gained, during the last campaign. They had taught him, that to draw the enemy into the defiles of Silesia was more advisable than to venture himself too far into those of Bohemia. Devoted to this plan and having taken his measures accordingly, he waited the arrival of the Austrians and for the favourable moment of giving them battle in the open country. A body of Hungarians (the same that had entered the Upper-Silesia the preceding winter) again made their appearance there in the month of March for the purpose of creating a diversion. The king had recourse to no other expedient than that of uniting under the command of Colonel de Winterfeld all the regiments of hussars cantoned in those quarters, and despatching them against the enemy. The effect was so sudden, that in a few days the country was completely cleared of them, and tranquillity again restored. In a short time, scenes of a more serious and sanguinary nature were destined to take place.

The king's main army and the regiment of Zieten which made part of it embodied at the beginning of April between Patzkaw and Frankenstein. The Margrave Charles, at the head of a corps of nine thousand men, covered the Upper Silesia and occupied Jägerndorf and Troppaw. These two divisions in forming had left a vacuity which extended from Jägerndorf to Neisse. A body of Austrians, consisting of twenty thousand men, took advantage of this error; and dividing into two parties, the one encamped between the king and the *margrave* and occupied all the posts of communication, whilst the other, encamping along the bank of the Oder, environed the latter.

Thus situated the *margrave* found himself cut off both from a part of his baggage which lay, under a small escort, at Neustadt; and, what was far more alarming, from the army of the king. The enemy's aim was not solely to menace the division that occupied the Upper-Silesia; it was principally to draw the king's attention to that quarter, and after inducing him, to send a reinforcement to the *margrave*, to take advantage of the naked state of the frontier and proceed with a powerful army to Landshut. The king, who guessed the intention of the Austrian general, kept his own position as the most important one in the present state of things, but seeing himself on the verge of a general engagement, and being desirous of opposing the enemy with as much force as he could collect, he resolved to recall the margrave. But to communicate his orders to him was a matter of no common difficulty. Every avenue was guarded by the Austrians; nothing escaped their vigilance;—couriers, *chasseurs*, and even spies, were immediately discovered and taken.

Thus embarrassed, the king ordered a detachment of Zieten's regiment to attempt to force their way to Jägerndorf; and a hundred and twenty hussars, under the command of Captain de Probst and three other officers, set off on this daring expedition. (M. de Belling, at that time lieutenant, was of the number.) Scarcely had they arrived in the neighbourhood of Rosswald on the other side of Neustadt, when they met with two regiments of cavalry, who immediately charged them. Numbers were too disproportioned to admit of an engagement; the Prussians therefore retreated in good order, regained the town of Neustadt without the loss of a single man, and brought with them three prisoners they had taken, who were presented by Lieutenant de Belling to the king.

From these prisoners, information was obtained respecting the force and position of the enemy; but to elude the vigilance of their pickets and impart the king's orders to the *margrave* still appeared as impracticable as before. Unless an express detachment could be sent to Jägerndorf all attempts seemed to be useless; and such movement might give a false direction to the whole campaign. Yet the position of the Austrian Army rendered the junction of the *margrave* every hour more necessary, and the king was in want of the reinforcement the more effectually to strike the great blow he had meditated; nor was the *margrave*, in the critical situation in which he found himself, to be abandoned to his own resources, nor deprived of the instructions of his sovereign. The question was how to communicate the latter to him, and the choice of the king fell upon Zieten. His Majesty therefore sent him the following orders by the hands the officer who had brought an account of the affair of Neustadt.

> You will do all in your power, my dear Zieten, to push your regiment as far as Jägerndorf, where you will deliver my orders to the Margrave Charles to march without loss of time; to destroy such part of the magazines of Troppaw as cannot be removed; not to engage with the enemy in any serious affair; and to gain Frankenstein by forced marches in order to operate a junction with me.

At the same time the king enjoined Zieten to proclaim this order to the whole regiment, that in case they should not be able to make their way sword in hand through the Austrian posts, each hussar that escaped might inform the *margrave* of His Majesty's intentions.

Zieten had a presentiment of receiving this commission, and indeed he began confidently to expect to be honoured with it. Even before the order arrived, he advised his lady, who had followed him to his winter-quarters, to prepare for her return to Berlin, adding that something of a very important nature was about to take place. Mad. de Zieten was the more astonished at this declaration as none of the wives of the staff-officers in general had received any such intimation. But Zieten had spoken with the officer who came from Neustadt with despatches, for the king. He was well apprised of the present state of things, and foresaw that His Majesty would not leave the margrave without either information or succour.

Mad. de Zieten seemed much disinclined to follow her husband's advice; he urged her, however, with the tenderest importunity, and prevailed on her to leave at an early hour a company with whom she had dined. She made ready for her departure in the course of the evening; the king's order arrived in the night, and she set off.

The commission with which Zieten was charged was in fact of a very delicate nature. He was fully sensible of its importance, as well as of the uncertainty of its success, of which the king himself had likewise doubted as appears by the supplement he had thought necessary to add to the order. The declaration contained in the supplement, and which he was commanded to make known to the regiment, was far from meeting with his approbation. He was averse to damp the ardour of his troops by the communication of the precaution His Majesty wished to take; he therefore concealed the supplementary part of the order, and ventured in that instance to counteract the will of his sovereign. Instead of following the line that had been traced out to him, he adopted a new plan, founded indeed on a circumstance trifling in itself, but which proved of admirable use to him.

During the course of the last campaign, and even during the winter-excursion in Upper-Silesia, his regiment had worn their summer-dress which consisted of red mantles and felt-caps. Their fur-accoutrements had not arrived from Berlin before the campaign had already closed: Hence the Austrians were not as yet acquainted with that part of their regimentals, which moreover greatly resembled those worn by the hussars of Spleny, at this time making part of the division posted at Leobschutz. Zieten, who was aware of the latter circumstance founded upon it his hopes of deceiving the enemy, by making his own hussars pass for theirs, and leading his Prussians in broad daylight through their army. It must be confessed that few instances have happened of an attempt so boldly conceived and so happily executed.

The success of this plan depended on the secrecy with which it was to be conducted. After having drawn out his regiment, Zieten began his march without informing anyone of his intentions. He passed the Neisse at Ottmachaw, half-way to Neustadt; from whence making an inflection into a wood, he commanded his men to dismount, and their horses to be fed. He afterwards ordered his troops to proceed deeper into the wood and to take some rest. His officers could not at all comprehend this new kind of manoeuvre, and hearing a heavy cannonading on the side on which Neustadt lay, ventured to ask if it would not be more advisable to repair thither and reinforce the division garrisoned in that town. Zieten replied;

> No, gentlemen, our march must remain a secret to the enemy. We are not strong; we must have recourse to stratagem. The garrison of Neustadt is composed of men who are well able to defend themselves.

With this answer they were obliged to remain contented, though it left them as much in the dark as ever. As soon as the firing had ceased the general continued his march and proceeded to Neustadt, where he had the satisfaction of finding the garrison safe although the enemy had endeavoured to surprise and carry them off. The officer (Oesterreich), who had the chief command, seconded by another officer (Captain de Probst, of Zieten's regiment), with a detachment of hussars, had repulsed and driven them back. Of this victory the latter informed Zieten on his entrance into the suburbs.

The general being arrived at Neustadt, drew out his regiment in the market-place, where they took a hasty refreshment and likewise fed their horses. He himself went to the top of the steeple to observe the retreat of the enemy; and from whence he saw them entering their camp in two distinct columns. The discovery of this induced him to avail himself of the opportunity it afforded him of following one of those columns under the appearance of making a part of it. He was well enough aware that this was a very adventurous, and even desperate expedient. Should he be discovered he was certain of being surrounded, carried off, or cut to pieces. But the magnitude of the danger seemed rather to stimulate than repress his courage; and besides, it was the only practicable means of obtaining his end.

He marched forthwith at the head of his regiment, and took the same route that one of the columns had taken. He advanced with great apparent negligence and security. The regiment had neither vanguard nor patrols; it was distributed into squadrons, and each squadron into unequal divisions. Express orders were given neither to draw their sabres nor fire before they heard the word of command. A few straggling hussars, who were natives of Hungary, preceded the rest, and in the language of their own country carelessly saluted the posts established at the entrance of villages or along the high-road. The others quietly followed without betraying any signs of mistrust or apprehension. A regiment of dragoons observed them file along without entertaining the least suspicion concerning them; and, persuaded that they were all returning together from the expedition of Neustadt, they followed the same direction which they remarked the hussars had taken.

Between the hours of two and three Zieten found himself in the middle of the camp. The sky was clear and the whole country appeared covered with red-mantles on account of the great number of Croats that were straggling in various directions in those quarters. In order to keep the highway, it was necessary to cross a mountain. In the plain, on the left, lay Leobschutz; on the right, several lakes, and a wood which swarmed with Croats. At the top of the mountain the whole camp lay fully exposed to view, and the most trilling operations therein were easily to be observed. The further the squadrons advanced the more particularly they were ordered to keep close together the better to force their way in case they should be discovered. Hitherto, however, they had not been suspected.

The colonel of the regiment which followed them, deceived like everyone else by appearances, pushed forward his horse to salute the general and inform him that his dragoons were close behind. Zieten, without giving him any answer, was under the necessity of making him a prisoner of war. Overwhelmed with astonishment he could hardly persuade himself of his error, and unable to make his escape although in the midst of his own camp, he was obliged to accompany the Prussians on their adventurous march.

Zieten still advanced in the most tranquil manner. His route lay parallel to the enemy's camp and within a thousand paces distant from it. The Croats passed by his regiment in all directions without discovering what they were. The dragoons, however, suddenly wheeling to the left for the purpose of gaining the camp, and Zieten still continuing his march forwards, the double movement betrayed the designs of the latter. A post endeavoured to check his farther progress and were quickly overcome and dispersed. The alarm spread over the camp; and "Zieten! The Prussians!" re-echoed on all sides. Zieten availed himself of the sudden confusion into which the army was thrown, and, making the best of his way, gained considerable ground. In the mean while the whole camp flew to arms. The dragoons with some other regiments of cavalry that had not yet unsaddled their horses set off in pursuit of the Prussians, and the infantry made ready to follow them.

Zieten continued to gain ground upon them, still skirmishing, and never quitting the highway. At length finding that several regiments had arrived he turned to the left to gain a swampy meadow in order to cover one of his flanks, while the other remained exposed to the enemy's fire. One of his best officers (Colonel de Billerbeck), was wounded. The regiment still advanced, and even made several prisoners.

One of these prisoners was snatched from imminent destruction and set free by Zieten. It was one of his old comrades in the campaign of the Rhine. Struggling on the ground and trampled upon by the horses, his death seemed inevitable; but Zieten at this instant passing by, was recognised by him, and the officer calling him by his name, implored his assistance. The general recollected him immediately and ordered a hussar to extricate and set him at liberty, and likewise to protect his escape.

Further difficulties were yet in store for Zieten. A considerable body of hussars were encamped on the heights of Peterwitz, between Leobschutz and Jägerndorf. He might have continued his march without being perceived by them, and they lay too far off to be at all formidable to him; but the inconsiderate ardour of a regiment of *cuiras-*

*siers* belonging to the *margrave's* division had nearly ruined the whole enterprise. On the news of his approach, this regiment, with a view of facilitating his junction, marched between him and the Austrians, gave the alarm to the latter, and sustained their attack in spite of the superiority of their numbers. Being quickly repulsed and driven upon the regiment of Zieten, they involved them a while in their hasty retreat.

The brave hussars were, however, too far spent to be able to keep pace with them, and remaining at some distance behind they alone supported the assault of the enemy; and, still fighting as they went on, they made their way sword in hand through them, and at length arrived at Jägerndorf with a loss not at all proportioned to the dangers they had encountered.

They were received with all the joy and admiration due to their courage and good fortune. Their entry was a triumph. The *margrave*, whose embarrassments had been daily increasing, saw himself suddenly relieved from suspense, and could not sufficiently express his thanks to Zieten for the service he had done him in having made him acquainted with the king's orders. The whole corps participated his gratitude, and were eager to testify it in the most cordial and feeling manner.

Zieten has always spoken of this reception with proper sensibility, and of the expedition itself with that keen and honest exultation which the success that crowned it inspired, and with the flattering consciousness of having eluded the most renowned of the Austrian partisans, and foiled the Esterhazes, the Festeretz, the Splenys, the Corolys, the Ghilanys; all of whom had taken part in opposing his memorable march.

The moment the *margrave* had been apprised of the king's intentions, he took his measures in consequence; and having broken up his camp, he began that brilliant and victorious retreat which has rendered his name so celebrated. His division marched in the following order. The hussars of Brunikowski, Rochow's regiment of *cuirassiers*, and Bock's infantry composed the vanguard. Four hundred waggons laden with flour, the baggage, with the main body of the army, followed; and the *cuirassiers* of Gessler, the dragoons of Wurtemberg, and the hussars of Zieten brought up the rear.

The Austrians, who had anticipated the *margrave's* march had taken every precaution in their power to impede it. They had erected a battery in the neighbourhood of Jägerndorf, and the heights of Peterwitz were planted with several pieces of cannon. Their principal force lay concentrated on the Hullberg, and consisted of a strong detachment of infantry supported by thirty-two pieces of ordnance. Further on, at a village called Brelsch, were posted a body of Croats together with a formidable artillery. They were covered by the dragoons of Saxa-Gotha; and from the Hullberg to the causeway that leads to Neustadt, the rest of the cavalry, with the hussars of Festelitz, Kalnocky, and Spleny were stationed, along the route which the Prussians had to take. The infantry remained on the left upon the heights which extended from Peterwitz to Mokker.

Scarce had the margrave passed through the gates of Jägerndorf than the report of two cannons was heard from the Hullberg, and the signal was repeated on the heights of Peterwitz. The fire of the batteries and small arms now began. The Prussians returned it in a slight manner, and still continued their march. Their advanced-guard, being arrived at the foot of the Hullberg, received orders to halt and engage the enemy while the baggage filed behind the line. The Austrians now redoubled their fire, and did more mischief to the baggage than to the troops who escorted it. The latter forced to remain in a state of inactivity, burned with impatience to fall upon the enemy.

The commander of the regiment of Bork (Colonel de Gravenitz), twice sent an *aide-de-camp* to the *margrave* to ask permission to make an attack on the mountain. He undertook to carry it by storm with his own regiment only, with support in case of need, and to be answerable for the consequences. The margrave applauded his courage, but each time replied, that the king's orders enjoined measures conducive to the general safety of the troops, and positively forbad all avoidable encounters.

While the vanguard and the centre of the enemy advanced in a parallel line with the waggons along the foot of the Hullberg, a train of artillery, and part of the baggage, suddenly found themselves impeded in their passage through a defile, and were besides unprovided with a sufficient escort. The enemy perceiving this, immediately took advantage of it. They poured down the Hullberg in great force in order to disperse the rear-guard and carry off all that came in their way. Zieten and Schwerin, however, checked them in time and prevented the execution of their purpose.

The enemy had their infantry in the centre and their cavalry were posted in the two wings. General de Schwerin, who commanded the dragoons of Wurtemberg, began the attack, and having charged the regiment of Ghilany, broke their ranks and took two standards. He then met with the regiment of Esterhazy, and having sustained their fire, fell upon them sword in hand. In the meanwhile, the Austrians had nearly flanked him; and Zieten who had anticipated this movement came up, and charging them both in flank and rear, threw them into a general disorder, dispersed them, and did Schwerin this important service at the very moment in which his regiment was beginning to fall back.

While he was engaging the dragoons, the Austrian hussars attempted to turn him. He, however, kept them off with a division of his hussars, and was quickly supported by the *cuirassiers* of Gesslar; and the enemy being now repulsed on all sides, were compelled to resume their former position, and give up all further attempts upon the baggage. The rest of the troops destined to harass the march of the Prussians having observed the unfavourable issue of the engagement, took shelter in the utmost disorder in the neighbouring forests.

In this manner did the bravery of the soldiers and the ability of their commanders rescue the artillery and baggage without any assistance on the part of the infantry, whom the *margrave* had ordered to halt; for, scarcely had he observed and admired the stand his rearguard had made, then without stopping and exposing his troops agreeably to the king's orders, he resumed his march, and consigned the task of covering it and following him to the hussars. The troops moreover were not further harassed during the rest of the march, as the enemy thought fit to continue aloof.

Besides the two standards taken from the Austrians, they lost in this encounter fourteen hundred men. From the report their prisoners made, the regiments of Ghilany, Esterhazy and Saxa-Gotha had principally suffered. The loss on the part of the Prussians was proportionably great; and the day cost Zieten a considerable number of his hussars and three of his officers.

As soon as the margrave had made his way through the enemy, he gave information thereof to the king, and the junction took place on the 28th of May at Frankenstein. The more difficult this operation had been considered by His Majesty, the more agreeable was the impression which the success of it made upon him. He received the *margrave* in triumph, and decorated with the order of military merit all the staff-officers of the regiments of Zieten and Wurtemberg, and even the captains of the latter corps.

It will be naturally asked, why Zieten's captains were not allowed to share the like distinction. The regiment had not only courageously supported that of Wurtemberg in the attack at the foot of the Hullberg, but had besides in their march to Jägerndorf acquitted themselves of an important commission and encountered the most imminent dangers. We must therefore conclude, that the modesty of Zieten had prevented his displaying the expedition in its proper point of view, and that the king had been very inaccurately informed of the detail.

However, that may be, General de Schwerin was more fortunate. His sovereign was lavish in the praises and favours he bestowed upon him; and likewise assured him in his answer to an acknowledgement of thanks which the general had made, that whatever he or his family might hereafter have to request of him, nothing more would be necessary than to shew the letter in order to obtain everything that equity would allow him to grant. An occasion soon presented itself. The general's daughter had placed her fortune in the hands of one of the principal manufacturers of Berlin, who failed. She stated her case to the king, and though he himself had heavy claims upon the bankrupt's effects for sums he had advanced for the encouragement of the manufactory, he ordered the first payments to be made to this lady, who in consequence recovered all her capital.

After the junction of the *margrave* with the king, the whole army were eager to measure with the Austrians, and Frederick, who was desirous of giving them battle, soon turned this ardour to advantage.

Everything was now ready for the purpose of striking a great blow. As soon as the Austrians, with the Saxons, their allies, had entered Silesia by the way of Landshut, the king broke up his camp at Frankenstein, formed it on the 29th of May at Reichenbach, and passing through Schweidnitz on the 1st of July, he distributed his army in different encampments, which extended as far as Jauernick. The enemy advanced to Gross-Hennersdorf, and fell into the snare that had been laid for them. The king marched to meet them on the 2nd of June as far as the brook of Strigaw, and beat them on the 4th at Hohen-Friedberg.

Hitherto Zieten had not been engaged in any pitched battle; he had rendered himself, illustrious by mere desultory war. At Mollwitz he had guarded the baggage, and in the present engagement we find him at the head of a corps of reserve consisting of twenty squadrons. He was stationed behind the centre of the second line to be ready as occasion might call for his assistance.

A particular description of the battle would be superfluous: the reader whom such detail interests is referred to the account which the great commander who gained the day has given in his posthumous works, and which he will find to be admirably well drawn up. A general sketch of it will, however, be sufficient to shew the active part that Zieten had therein.

It is well known that the king had taken his measures in such manner as to approach the enemy without their having been at all aware of his march. The first act of this murderous tragedy was opened by General Dumoulin in the defeat of the Saxons. He surprised them as they were attempting to take possession of Strigaw, and obtained an easy victory. During the engagement the Prince of Lorrain drew out his army in order of battle. The Prussians, who had been beforehand with him, attacked and repulsed his left wing.

To render the victory complete, nothing further was necessary than to repulse the right. The king gave proper orders for such purpose; and while his right wing was to attack it in front, his left, which had no enemy to encounter, was ordered to fall upon the left flank and rear of the Austrians; his right wing, however, was entangled in the woods and marshes of Rohnstock and did not extricate itself till late. During this time the cavalry on the left wing, under the command of General de Nassau, had met with a disaster which might have changed the event of the battle.

Scarce had General de Kiow passed the Strigaw with the first ten squadrons of his brigade, when the bridge broke down. His object had been to attack the Austrian cavalry who were drawn up directly before him; and, notwithstanding this accident, he still persisted in his purpose, and nearly fell a victim to it. Already the enemy had hemmed him in; and after having taken or dispersed his troops, they would have fallen upon the left wing in the defenceless condition in which it would then have lain. But Zieten applied a prompt remedy to the evil and checked the danger in its birth.

He had calculated the accident of the bridge as a possible event; and judging that manner of passing the Strigaw as not sufficiently effective, he had tried the depth of the stream itself. This precaution rescued Kiow, and perhaps saved the army. He forded the brook with his corps of reserve, fell upon the enemy, broke their ranks, delivered Kiow, and afforded General de Nassau time to follow with the rest of the cavalry and to complete the rout.

**********

The king in *The History of My Own Times* briefly observes, that General de Zieten joined Kiow with the reserve, overcame all that opposed him, and afforded M. de Nassau, who commanded the left, time to ford his troops over the Strigaw.

**********

When the right wing had got clear of the woods and marshes and were ready to attack the enemy, the left wing had already gained considerable ground. Victory had decided in favour of the Prussians, and the well-concerted plan of their monarch had succeeded even beyond his expectations.

The hussars of Zieten were principally engaged with the *cuirassiers* of Hohen-Embs and the dragoons of Saxa-Gotha. They killed great numbers and gathered new laurels. A private trooper, the same who had given proof of his intrepidity at Tein, and Onfall occasions had been the first to brave danger, took General de Berlichengen on this day prisoner.

The fact indeed would not be of importance enough to be mentioned had it not been attended with circumstances which render it interesting, as they are at the same time characteristic of the Austrian general, of the hussars of Zieten, and of the great Frederick.

Berlichengen, who had commanded the right wing of the cavalry in the Battle of Mollwitz, and who on that famous day had gained considerable advantages over the Prussian cavalry, had no idea of the perfection to which they had attained in so short an interval as had elapsed since that time. He not only misjudged those new adepts in the art of war, but what principally struck and irritated him, was to see the hussars, whose very name was unknown to him at Mollwitz, now become formidable to his cavalry of the line. Instead of applauding, as Baronay had done, the progress they had made in their profession, he had recourse to invectives, and during the engagement expressed himself in so unbecoming a manner, that the hussar, of whom mention has just been made, was unable to contain his honest indignation.

He rushed upon him, and the stroke of his sabre would have cloven the general's head, had he not drawn it back in time at the expense of a slight wound hardly more than skin-deep. His gorgeous wig, however, did not escape with so little hurt; it lay dishonoured in the dust and was trampled upon by the horses. The bald-headed general, mentioning his name, now called out for quarter, and was made prisoned. He still continued his invectives, but the better-mannered hussars, who felt what was due to his rank, refrained from making any reply till they had brought him into the presence of the king. They then made bitter complaint against him and solicited redress. The king severely reproved the general, and made him feel that it became the vanquished to honour the bravery of their conquerors. At the same time, he dismissed the hussars in these terms;

> Make yourselves easy, my friends; you are brave men and have done your duty, I am highly satisfied with your conduct; continue always to act in such manner.

The Austrians retreated through Hohen-Friedberg, and the Saxons by the way of Seifersdorf. The one and the other had suffered great loss in their killed, wounded, and prisoners; in their artillery, and trophies. The Prussians followed them as far as the heights of Kauder, where the former halted for the purpose of resting themselves a while after the incessant fatigues of the day. The next morning Dumoulin and Zieten were detached in pursuit of the fugitives whose rear-guard was composed of the corps of Nadasty and Wallis, who had joined them after the battle in order to cover their retreat. Zieten at the head of his regiment advanced to Reich Hennersdorf to attack them in front while two regiments of cavalry took them in flank. The main body of the army had gained much ground, and the rear-guard only was overtaken. They-were driven into the defile of Faulbrück, and lost a great number of men and a considerable part of their baggage. The rest gained Bohemia, and passed the frontiers at Liebaw.

The king had nothing further to apprehend, nor, for the moment, anything more to wish for. The Austrians had dearly paid for their intrusion. Not only Silesia was evacuated, but the Prussians had entered Bohemia. The Prince of Lorrain having formed his camp between Königinngrätz and Pardubitz, the king made choice of his in the same neighbourhood, at Chulmitz, between Rusac and Dewatz. The two camps touched each other and appeared to make but one. Both armies kept this position for the space of three months;—the enemy to repair their losses, the king by way of caution.

The victor of Hohen-Friedberg, the conqueror of Silesia, could not be ignorant that the resources of the Queen of Hungary were far from being exhausted; faithful, therefore, to his plan of acting on the defensive only, he was satisfied with observing the motions of the enemy and starving a part of Bohemia; and has circumstanced kept himself in readiness to take advantage of events as they occurred.

This interval of repose took place only with regard to the position of the main army. The detail of hostilities, skirmishes, rencounters; in a word, all that relates to desultory war, went on without intermission, and rendered the campaign extremely harassing to the Prussians. The enemy had a great number of light troops at hand, while those of the Prussians were employed either in guarding passes, or keeping in awe a body of Hungarians posted behind Breslaw and. Schweidnitz for the purpose of annoying the transports of provisions which set out every fifth day from the latter place for the use of the army. The king himself records this fact (*History of My Own Times*). "Each bundle of straw cost a skirmish."

Moratz, Trenck, Nadasty, Franchini were every day out; in a word; it was a school of petty hostilities.

Notwithstanding the superior force of the enemy, the Prussian officers neglected no opportunity of harassing them. Their courage indeed not infrequently carried them too far: on one occasion in particular it would have proved fatal to some of them, had not the tutelary genius of Zieten interposed and protected them.

A major of his own regiment, of the name of Rohr with one of his friends, a major (Meyer), of the dragoons, had formed a plan of no common degree of boldness, consisting in an attempt to carry off a whole regiment of *Uhlans* who were encamped between Königinngrätz and Smirsitz. They had obtained the consent of their respective commanders, who entrusted two hundred horse to each of them for this purpose. Their bravery and talents were well-known to Zieten, but he was aware at the same time of the impetuosity of their tempers and dreaded the consequences of it. To prevent or repair any false step they might take he followed them with his regiment, without their privity, and lay in ambush in a wood on the highway to Königinngrätz.

What he had apprehended in fact took place. The two partisans were at first successful; they surprised a body of *Uhlans*, dispersed them, killed some, and took several prisoners. But instead of being satisfied with these advantages, they were eager to gain more, and pursued the fugitives to the very suburbs of Königinngrätz. The step was imprudent in the highest degree: they could not have been ignorant that the town was strongly garrisoned; the garrison flew to, arms in an instant, and rushed upon them from all parts. The *Uhlans* resumed their lost courage, and with the rest fell upon this handful of troops, who as they fought on uneven ground and were besides encumbered with the prisoners they had taken, were unable to preserve themselves in good order. Thus, pressed on every side, the hussars were on the point of betaking themselves to flight and trusting their safety to the fleetness of their horses, and the dragoons, not able to accompany them, of being obliged either to surrender or be cut to pieces.

This was the moment that Zieten chose for quitting his ambush. His unexpected appearance equally astonished both parties, uncertain for a moment whether he was a friend or a foe. Their doubts soon subsided; Zieten was recognised, and the mere sight of him struck the Austrians with a panic, and threw them into disorder. He disengaged the prisoners, took several himself, and not satisfied with having rescued the two majors from the distress in which he found them, he likewise terminated their expedition gloriously. Thus, in their persons he acquitted himself of a debt which he had contracted on the banks of the Rhine, when General de Baronay came to his succour as he was entangled in a defile, and rescued him nearly in a similar manner.

Soon after this expedition the regiment of Zieten was parcelled on into several divisions and stationed in detachments among the various battalions that occupied the frontiers. The general himself with some of his squadrons served in the corps of Dumoulin, who, for the purpose of protecting the transports from Schweidnitz to the army, occupied the posts of Tratenaw and Skalitz. In this interval it was that the king fought the Battle of Soor, (30th of September), and for a second time beat the army of the empress queen. That title she had just obtained in right of her consort, the grand Duke of Tuscany, who was elected emperor of Germany on, the 13th of September under the name of Francis the first.

Of this opportunity of signalising himself Zieten was deprived in spite of his inclination by the calls of duty; but when the king, on the 16th of October, broke up his camp to return of Silesia, he resumed his usual post, and covered the march, which he closed with the corps of General Dumonlin who were harassed by Nadasty and Franchini at the head of ten thousand men. In the course of this march the army being closely pressed in a defile near Schazler, owed their deliverance to the talents and bravery of Zieten, who repulsed the enemy and killed and wounded a considerable number of them. Zieten had only a part of his regiment with him; and as the small number of those who immediately accompanied him are now no more, the particulars of this affair are lost, and all that can be said on the subject must be confined to the few words inserted in the works of the king.

> An attack made by a body of cavalry on the small plain of Schazler cost the enemy three hundred men; and in this encounter Zieten lost Major de Rohr one of his best officers, whose life he had, not long before, saved.

The corps of Dumoulin were employed in forming a line of posts along the frontiers; the rest of the army, as the campaign seemed to be over, went into cantonments; and the king being set off for Berlin, they waited only for the separation of that of the Austrians to go into winter-quarters.

The Austrians, however, had no such intentions. They had concerted a plan which had it been attended with success, must have proved fatal to Prussia. The Saxons, hitherto the mere auxiliaries of Austria, who had carried their arms into Silesia for the purpose; of restoring that country to their faithful allies, now threw off the mask, and menacing the hereditary dominions of Frederick, were preparing to act on the defensive. A secret treaty had just been concluded between the courts of Dresden; in consequence of which the imperial troops were to march from Bohemia into Saxony; were to join those of the elector there, and fall unexpectedly on Berlin in the depth of winter, where they would have found the king without troops and the city without defence. It was hoped that this single blow would not only decide the fate of Silesia but, likewise of several other, Prussian provinces which the allies had parcelled out beforehand among themselves.

Of this plot Frederick was not apprised before the 8th of November; at a moment in which he had hardly terminated a ruinous campaign, and was extremely embarrassed to raise supplies for the ensuing year. Having, moreover, indisposed almost every power towards him, he found himself so circumstanced as to have no alternative left but either to conquer or perish. He then solely consulted his own genius and his courage, and conceived that bold plan which alone would have rendered his name immortal; a plan whose execution excited the admiration of Europe which waited with extreme impatience for the issue of this winter's campaign.

He gave orders to the Prince of Anhalt-Dessau to embody an army in the most private manner on the confines of Saxony. A corps of five thousand men were stationed before the gates of Berlin;—a sufficient precaution, as it was the king's intention to hinder the enemy from penetrating so far into the country. Frederick rejoined in person the main army in Silesia, and arriving at Legnitz on the 15th of November, he issued the necessary orders for attacking the Saxons both in front and rear, while he himself, at the head of his army, should fall upon the cantonments which the Prince of Lorrain had established in Lusatia, and drive him out of Bohemia.

This violent crisis called for a prompt remedy, and so desperate indeed was the general state of affairs, that it was necessary to risk all in order to save all; while Frederick, full of confidence in his own good fortune, was not less sanguine with regard to his invincible Prussians.

The situation of the two armies bore great resemblance to that which preceded the battle of Hohen Friedberg. The king had recourse to the same stratagems for the purpose of drawing the Austrians into the same snare. He carefully concealed his plan, ordered roads to be made and stores of provisions to be laid in on the way; deceived the people of the country, and consequently the enemy, and countenanced an opinion, which had been generally received, that he was preparing to cover Berlin and the electorate of Brandenburg and that he was approaching Crossen in order be beforehand with the Prince of Lorrain.

Deluded by these preparations the prince advanced his troops, and the king, whose design was to suffer himself to be overtaken by the imperialists and then to fall upon their rear and force them into action, opposed the Prince of Dessau to them, for the more sake of form, on the frontiers of Saxony. But the moment that the cantonments began to break up, he himself followed them; and approaching the River Queiss, he arrived on the 24th of November at Holstein, a strong castle in the principality of Jauer, situated a German mile from Naumberg.

The enemy still advanced towards Berlin. Their left wing touched Lauban and their right extended to Görlitz. The Queiss only separated them from the king, whom they, however, imagined to be far distant from them. His Majesty continued his march on the 23rd in four separate columns, passed the Queiss, during a thick fog, at Naumberg; and appointed, as a place of general rendezvous, the village of Catholic-Hennersdorf in Lusatia with a view of encamping there, and waiting or hastening the impending crisis of events.

The king entered Lusatia without knowing precisely what posts were occupied by the enemy: precautions were therefore necessary, and every column was accordingly preceded by a regiment of hussars, and received orders besides to sustain each other in case of necessity. The two central columns were composed of infantry, the other two of cavalry. The king led the first of the centre, and Zieten, at the head of his regiment, marched in the van.

This column was guided by a miller's servant who misled them into a marshy common grazed by cattle in the summer season but which was always impassable on the approach of winter. This disaster considerably impeded the progress of the column. Zieten, however, discovered a road through an extensive forest which led to Hennersdorf, and having taken it and arrived at. the skirts of the village, the head of his regiment came in sight of two horse-sentinels, who made a part of the enemy's advanced-guard.

The sentinels who observed but a small number of flankers come out of the wood, took them for an inconsiderable patrol only, and did not think it necessary to give the general alarm. Zieten in the meanwhile was enabled to gain information: that the village was occupied by three regiments of Saxon cavalry (Dalwitz, Obyern, and Vitzum) and one regiment of infantry (Saxa-Gotha).

The king's column with the heavy artillery were not come out of the marsh, and they were besides too far off to afford Zieten any immediate support. The embarrassment of the general was great, his resolution prompt, and similar to that he always took on such occasions; which was to attack the enemy rather than allow them to be beforehand with him. In order to give the royal column time to pass the marsh he sent an officer to inform the king, that Hennersdorf was full of troops, and that he would attack and keep them employed till succour arrived. At the same time, he divided his regiment into three bodies, put himself at the head of one of them, and ordered the two others to enter the village in the middle; to turn afterwards, one to the right and the other to the left; and to pass along at full speed without giving the enemy's cavalry time to mount and recover from their surprise.

Zieten followed these two divisions with the third, and entering the village in the same manner, found the garrison in motion and the regiment of Saxa-Gotha ready to receive him with their artillery. The hostile squadrons were likewise forming on all sides, nor was there a moment to be lost.

Zieten with his division charged the regiment and was received in a cool and resolute manner. He had then recourse to the most adventurous efforts, and those efforts succeeded; the whole regiment were cut to pieces, and all their cannon and standards fell into the hands of the conqueror.

In the meantime, the squadrons that composed the two other divisions dispersed themselves over the village to the right and the left and were engaged in continual skirmishing. The hussars of Ruesch (distinguished by the appellation of Black Hussars), now came to their support, and the enemy had no time allowed them to form into order of battle. Zieten, after the defeat of the regiment of Saxa-Gotha, remained with his division in the centre of the village. This village, which is half a German mile in length, consists of a single street only, at the extremities of which the alarm had hardly yet arrived; and as fast as the hostile squadrons endeavoured to gain the centre, where the principal attack had been carried on, they were charged and dispersed by the hussars of Zieten and Ruesch.

After the regiment of Saxa-Gotha, that of Obyern had suffered the most. Either regiment had lost four field-pieces, all their colours and standards, with five kettle-drums, before the arrival of a third regiment of Prussian cavalry and a party of infantry. This reinforcement rendered the victory complete: the village was occupied, the issues guarded, and the two remaining Saxon regiments, with all their officers and standards, fell into the hands of the Prussians.

The entry of the king into Catholic-Hennersdorf crowned this brilliant day. He established his camp there with a satisfaction equal to the magnitude of the advantage to be derived from the situation of the place. Zieten laid the trophies at His Majesty's feet, and requested for his own regiment two of the kettle-drums which he had taken. General de Ruesch solicited the like favour for his: they were granted to both, and from that time the two regiments enjoy the privilege of making use of these drums as an accompaniment to their military music. The rest of the light cavalry have not any; and every time the regiment of Zieten takes the field the two kettle-drums are deposited with great ceremony in the arsenal of Berlin.

To Zieten the victory of Hennersdorf proved the conclusion of the war and the part he had taken in it. He had the misfortune to be wounded, and for the first time during the several campaigns in which he had served. One of his hussars carelessly firing his piece in the confusion of the battle, the ball went through the calf of the general's leg. This accident obliged him to leave the army for a while and he retired on the 26th of November to Görlitz, a town in the Upper-Lusatia, which on the preceding day had been delivered up to the Prussians by capitulation.

It is not a little extraordinary and surprising that Frederick in his posthumous works speaks in a vague manner only of the service Zieten had rendered him at Hennersdorf.

★★★★★★★★★★

The passage runs thus. "While the troops were filing along the hussars of Zieten reached the village of Catholic-Hennersdorf and gave notice that it contained two battalions and six squadrons of Saxons: they added, that they would keep them employed in order to give the column time to arrive there."

✯✯✯✯✯✯✯✯✯✯

But without examining whether His Majesty's memory had been universally faithful in the composition of his history, it will suffice to observe that the exploits of Zieten were not always accurately reported to that prince, and were even sometimes concealed from him. Zieten did not possess the great art of shewing himself to advantage; malice and envy had ever full play against him. We have seen them spare him for a while, and shall erelong find them again exerting themselves, when awakened by the loudness of his renown. As long as his military achievements spoke in his behalf, he had been able to overawe his enemies, and to preserve himself in the good graces of his sovereign; but in the calm of peace the cabals that had been formed against him deprived him of them for a season.

We will not, however, anticipate this interesting part of his life, but briefly observe that from the affair of Hennersdorf the general was fully sensible that no means of doing him an ill turn were left untried, and it was perhaps his discontent rather them his wound that detained him at Görlitz, and that, at the arrival of Frederick at that place, had induced him to write to His Majesty with a view of counteracting the mischief at its birth, since we find he received the following letter in answer.

> Be assured, my dear Major-General de Zieten, it is with great concern that I perceive you have been deluded by false ideas. The tenor of your letter of the 30th implies that I have been prejudiced against your person, or at least your services. I can, however, assert with great truth, that you are mistaken, with regard to both. I esteem you as an officer of merit and am highly satisfied with your faithful and important services. If at different times I have given any particular commission to General de ———; if after having intrusted him with my secret plans, I charged him to communicate my intentions to you as often as circumstances required it, I do not see how I could have given outfence, or why I should not be allowed to act in that manner; and the more so, as this never took place but in particular cases, and that you lost nothing thereby either in point of rank or seniority.
>
> I hope this declaration will not only suffice to calm your mind,

but that you will perceive therein the proof as well as the assurance of my affection for you.

Görlitz, 3rd December, 1745,

Frederick.

(The author of the *Life of Zieten* had her reasons for not naming him. Frederick, who mentions his name in this letter, tells us it was General de Winterfeld).

This correspondence and the explanations to which it had led contributed for the moment to the re-establishment of that harmony which had formerly subsisted between the king and Zieten. His Majesty had just felt in a forcible manner the obligation he lay under to his general; and the latter, perfectly at ease during the time of his confinement at Görlitz, traced at a distance the progress of his master, and the success of the Prussian arms of which he himself had laid the foundation in the defeat of the Saxons at Hennersdorf.

Thus was the plan of the enemies of Prussia frustrated. The Saxons driven from post to post to the gates of Dresden;—the Austrians repulsed again into Bohemia;—the Prince of Anhalt conqueror at Kesseldorf (15th of December);—such were the great events that followed these first operations in Lusatia. The torch of discord and war was at length extinguished in the blood of thousands, and on the 25th of December the plenipotentiaries of the empress-queen and the King of Poland signed, in the presence of Frederick the Great, the peace of Dresden; a peace equally honourable and conducive to the interests of Prussia.

The less the expectations of Europe had augured such an issue, the more its admiration was fixed on that prince and his army. Five years before this period he had made his first appearance on the great theatre of war, and he now retired from it in the character of a conqueror and perfect adept in the military art. His first efforts even had been master-pieces; his talents were now universally acknowledged and respected; and the army, which his genius had inspired, began to be considered as invincible. The name of a Prussian and a hero were grown synonymous terms; and Silesia now conquered for a second time appeared to be for ever incorporated with the political existence of Prussia.

In this war Zieten acquired new claims to admiration and esteem. He had shewn himself able to cope with the greatest commanders of the age. Uniting wisdom with courage, rage, contempt of danger with perseverance, dexterity with presence of mind, and activity with the most perfect command of temper; he conceived his plans with the progressiveness of the rising storm and executed them with the rapidity of the thunderbolt. Unruffled in the heat of battle; singularly accurate and concise in giving his orders; foreseeing everything, prepared for everything; he was invariably able to turn the circumstances of the moment to advantage.

His military glance was correct and infallible; he was equally admirable in attack and defence; capable of the most daring enterprises, and losing every idea of personal safety when his duty called him to engage in them, he never failed to acquit himself with success. In his principles he was firm, and his probity was invincible; he was a zealous patriot, was attached to his sovereign by the indissoluble ties of affection and fidelity, and he evinced his loyalty and devotedness to him by the readiest sacrifices;—the sacrifice of everything except his honour, his principles, his religion, and his country. He abhorred all illicit means of enriching himself; he was disinterested and unassuming; ever careless of acquiring the approbation of the great or the admiration of the multitude, he was more desirous to be really good than to appear so.

Ready to do justice to the merit of another, he esteemed everyone who was recommendable for his conduct and virtues, and openly contemned such as were degraded by their vices. He was prompt to obey the orders of his prince, yet without giving up the right of consulting and availing himself of his own knowledge in the incidental execution of those orders. Incapable of bending under the yoke of fear or servilely cringing to authority, he invariably supported his dignity and character on every occasion. Such had been the general tenor of his conduct during the two Silesian wars, that he was considered as the tutelary-genius of the army, whose safety in effect was committed to his care in every march that was undertaken. Were the enemy to be attacked?—his station was in the van. Was it expedient to withdraw from action?—it was he who covered the retreat.

He had often repaired the faults of other generals, and never erred himself but in one single instance; and which, as the reader has seen, was owing to the negligence of his patrols. Hence, he possessed the esteem of the king and his brother-officers, and acquired an unbounded ascendancy over the troops he commanded; who, fully sensible of his talents and his patriotism, were persuaded he would never lead them to face destruction, but when honour and necessity required it, and when victory would crown the enterprise. His name acquired universal celebrity; he was justly ranked among the most distinguished generals of the Prussian Army, and considered as the model of a virtuous hero. The good admired him as the ornament of human nature, and his country, in reward of his merit, decorated him with the title of a true patriot.

To general admiration and esteem were joined sentiments of a more tender kind and more congenial to his nature;—the affection and confidence of his brother-officers and hussars. In the midst of the tumults of war he had ever preserved those social virtues which had marked the early period of his life. Guided and sustained by rational piety, his moral character still shone with undiminished lustre, while his talents, his faculties, His religious principles, still acquired new force as he advanced in his brilliant career. The pernicious maxim, the maxim of his day, that the duty of a soldier, superseded that of a man, was never adopted by him. The horrors of war of which he had been inured never steeled his heart to the softer calls of humanity; and such feelings he considered nor only as far from degrading his profession, but even as one of its most noble appendages.

Severe in the field and inexorable in whatever regarded the duties of the military life, (because he himself was the first to set the example, and had no errors nor neglect on his own part to call for indulgence in favour of such as were guilty of, either,) he was in all other respects remarkable for the gentleness and even the complaisantness of his manners. He was ever ready to accommodate those whom he commanded, to the utmost of his power, or to lighten with a kind word, a look, a smile, the burdens they had indispensably to sustain. His officers, his private soldiers whom he loved with paternal affection, never solicited his counsel, his interposition, his succour, in vain. Just and impartial in the extreme, he tolerated no oppression, no persecution; and though exact in the infliction of punishments, he was still more so in recompensing every noble, every liberal action.

He had always acted with feeling and equity towards the hostile nations during the various incursions he had made among them. The laws of war never induced him to overlook the sacred rights of man. Far from countenancing any kind of exactions, he was the friend, the protector, the father of the unfortunate inhabitants of the places which became the immediate seat of war. Whenever he received orders to pillage a hostile country on leaving it, his custom was to observe the mere form only; he would cause a few windows to be broken, throw down a few stoves, displace or overturn the furniture of a house or two; but was never known to deprive the inhabitant of what was absolutely necessary to him, or to commit a single act of barbarity. The soldier loved him still more than he feared him. In every place his preservation was the object of universal concern. Not only his own country but the nations who had known him as their enemy only, did ample justice to his disinterestedness and greatness of mind.

The candid reader will pardon the foregoing effusion of tenderness and esteem, and will not consider it either as exaggeration or flattery, but allow the panegyric of virtue to be uttered by the voice of truth. Of all that has been said he will find the testimonies in the breasts of the admirers of Zieten, and he will find them in the pages that precede this portrait Whoever admits the facts cannot disapprove of the eulogium, which is but the natural consequence of the other.

It may not be amiss to insert here an anecdote or two relative to the life of Zieten, which cannot be introduced in their exact order for want of due information as to the times and places that gave them birth; and which, as they serve to characterize the man and the hero, are worth preserving.

A Prussian general had a dangerous, defile to pass. On the right rose a steep, hill, on the left lay a marsh, and at the end a bridge, the sole outlet. From the hill, which the enemy had occupied, they harassed the troops, whom the general with a view of saving the baggage (part of which belonged to himself) had left in a defenceless condition. Their ranks were soon broken, and they were hurried in great disorder towards the bridge.

Zieten, who followed with the rear-guard, perceiving the confusion they were in, flew to the spot, where he found the cannon abandoned, the horses killed, the artillerymen without ammunition and on the point of surrendering. The distressed soldiers complained loudly to him of the conduct of their general, and Zieten, without making any reply, betook himself to repair his fault. Supported by the gallant *Bülow*, (afterwards general of infantry, and one of the greatest ornaments of the Prussian Army), who had just collected a small party of infantry, he attacked the enemy, dislodged them from the heights, took possession of the bridge at the moment in which they were going to occupy it; and having taken from the baggage-waggons which had been driven into the marsh as many horses as were necessary to draw the artillery, he was enabled to rescue the whole corps.

The general who had so ill performed his task obtained nevertheless all the honours of the expedition. The king publicly congratulated him on his having extricated himself in so able a manner, while Zieten and Bülow remained tacitly satisfied with the service they had rendered him without making the least display of the parts they had acted. From Zieten his friends have never been able to learn either the place in which this event had happened, or the name of the general who had commanded the retreat in so unskilful a manner. It was only in the latter years of his life that this respectable old man, made mention of the affair merely to do justice to the memory of his brother-officer.

The foregoing anecdote exhibits in the most amiable point of view the unassuming character of Zieten, and with what delicacy he acted with respect to the reputation of others. The following one will furnish an example of the good order and love of justice that directed all his actions.

In his colonel-squadron was a hussar whose bravery and intelligence had so far gained his esteem that he was desirous to advance him and to make his fortune. Before he named him to the rank of a subaltern he wished to be convinced of his probity; and one day when the hussar had returned from a foraging party, Zieten making up to him ordered him to alight, and after having examined his load, discovered two geese concealed in a bundle of straw. The general thereupon not only testified his disapprobation of such conduct in the most severe terms, but could not refrain from making him sensible of what he had lost on the occasion:

> You were on the point of being made a subaltern and you shall now remain a common soldier.

The hussar, in effect, was not advanced till a year after.

Peace being concluded the army returned to their respective garrisons. The king, who had been no stranger to the little negligences and abuses which during the war had crept in among the troops, was extremely solicitous to remedy them and to re-establish due discipline and order. The letter which His Majesty wrote to Zieten is the more worthy of the reader's notice as it shows what obligation he considered himself under to his troops, and the justice which he was pleased. to do them.

> My dear Major-General de. Zieten.
> The war is now at an end, and I take this opportunity of declaring to my brave officers that during its continuance I had reason to be perfectly satisfied with their conduct. They have done

their duty on every occasion, and crowned the Prussian name with immortal glory. On my own part I shall neglect no opportunity of giving them proofs of my satisfaction. I am moreover fully persuaded that the staff-officers and all the officers in general will do their utmost to preserve that good order and military discipline which have hitherto contributed to render the army invincible, and that they will restore them wherever they might have been relaxed. For this purpose, I recommend to you, as well as to your staff and other officers, to peruse with attention, and diligently to observe, all my military ordinances and regulations.

Potsdam, Jan. 1st 1746.                                    Frederick.

Attentive to the commands of his sovereign, Zieten strove to restore that order in his regiment which a camp-life had interrupted, and to establish that uniformity of action, that salutary restraint, that scrupulous exactness which during their residence in garrison prepares the troops for the more important duties of the campaign.

Unhappily a fit of sickness, with which he was attacked in the year 1746, interrupted the progress of what he had successfully begun. His constitution, as the reader has seen, was much impaired when he took the field; yet while the war lasted, he had as it were no time to be indisposed, nor even to pay any attention to the state of his health. Disdaining at an early period of life the farfetched cares and attentions which effeminacy bestows on the body, he had rendered himself independent of physical evils by subjecting it to the control of his mind. Yet before he could have attained this end, and inured himself to sickness as well as to fatigue, he must doubtless have frequently endangered both his health and his life; but experience has evinced the goodness of his method, as it succeeded in invigorating the one and in prolonging the other.

He was not, however, so insensible to self-preservation as to lose all concern about it, and to abandon himself up to the course of nature only; especially when medicinal aid seemed to promise him relief and did not interrupt the duties of his profession. Yet common remedies disgusted him; and after having fruitlessly tried the Hot baths of Hirschberg in Silesia, (spring of 1746), he abandoned the regular practitioners of physic and put himself under the care of empirics. He had in particular recourse to Doctor Oehm of Dresden whom he continued to commend to the latest hour of his life. Without enjoying a perfect state of health, and ever subjecting himself to the most severe regimen, the particulars of which we shall hereafter touch upon, he nevertheless attributed to the secrets of the above physician the merit of having relieved him, as well as having enabled him to grow old.

The pleasing dreams of his youth were at length on the point of being realised: his favourite plan of embellishing his estate and rebuilding his family seat at Wüstrau was shortly to be put into execution. He had now sufficient leisure for the undertaking, though his pecuniary resources were very inadequate to it. Although he had been engaged in two wars, during which he might have enriched himself; although the munificence of the king had considerably increased his income, yet the amount of his savings, at this period did not exceed the sum of eight hundred dollars.

With this small fund, and with all the inconsiderate ardour of a young man, he laid the foundation of a building on a scale that required at least thirty thousand dollars to complete;—a sum which exceeded the value of his whole estate. The king, indeed, who much approved of the undertaking, contributed to promote it, by furnishing the timber and limestone. The other expenses quickly consumed his ready money, as Zieten seemed to be building for eternity; for so solid was the construction of his house, that at the present day, (1803), after a lapse of half a century, it remains in the most perfect state of preservation.

Zieten had soon recourse to the usual methods of raising money, and procured the sums necessary for his purpose without the privity of his lady, whom, it must be observed, he had not even consulted upon the plan and estimate of the edifice. He left the care of his farm and family concerns entirely to her, and took upon himself exclusively the management of his buildings. This was, it must be owned, putting the complaisance of the most rational and sensible of women to too severe a test; nor can it be conceived how he could flatter himself that she could at all acquiesce in the security in which he fondly indulged himself, since his bad state of health must naturally create incessant apprehensions on her part for his life.

Nor could Mad. de Zieten reflect with indifference on the various sums which the building was continually absorbing, as she looked upon that business in a point of view far different from that in which her husband chose to consider it. Zieten on his part cherished the agreeable hope of enjoying this fine edifice for a length of years, of not only clearing away the encumbrances he had made himself subject to, but of making further purchases and aggrandising his Wüstrau estate; while his lady, with all apparent propriety, gave way to the dread of being involved, with two helpless orphans, in inextricable embarrassments and left, without any other inheritance than a huge mass of stones.

A prey to such alarming reflections, and not always able to disguise the uneasiness of her mind, she ventured from time to time to remonstrate gently with her husband; but all attempt were vain: he either made no reply to them or answered them very laconically and not altogether in the most courteous manner. One day in particular when his lady had just perceived that new loans were to be raised to carry on a building into which she was not allowed to have the least insight, she informed him in a note, that she trembled for him, for herself, and for the future. By way of answer, he sent her back the note after having first written at the bottom of it the following words, *Les choux étoient bons.* (This an old proverb, in other words, *Brisons là-dessus,* used in order to put an end to an argument not considered deserving of serious consultation).

This apparent harshness is in a great degree explained by the natural firmness of his character, which never allowed him to give up a measure he had once adopted, nor to listen to advice after he had once taken his resolution. To yield to his wife in a matter which solely regarded himself, was, in his estimation, unpardonable weakness; it was not, he thought, her business to take any part in such concerns, nor to encroach at all on his province. Though inflexible on this point, he shewed himself in all other respects to be the most delicate and complaisant of husbands, and never ceased to give her abundant proofs of his attachment and esteem.

Nothing in fact was more foreign to the natural turn of mind of our hero than the eager, the unremitting assiduity with which he carried on his building. It afforded a striking exception to his general rule of conduct. His own affairs, as the reader already knows, could scarcely ever command any share of his attention: yet when the public service called for his exertions, everything in that line became came a matter of importance to him. He examined, he arranged, he saw with his own eyes, and never suffered another to do what he could do himself. With regard to his domestic concerns, he acquitted himself in a very different manner: instead of entering at all into the detail of them, he was always glad to throw the burden upon others, in whom the slight notice which he bestowed on whatever interested merely himself induced him to place to most unreserved confidence.

But his building lay too near his heart to allow him to act with his accustomed indifference: it was in fact his ruling passion and absorbed all his attention and cares; he had formed the plan, he presided at its execution, entered into the minutest detail, and displayed a knowledge of architecture which he was little supposed to possess, and which excited the admiration of all who knew him. Yet the bent of his noble and disinterested disposition continued to appear through all these disguises; he always paid for the materials without cheapening them, and discharged all his workmen's bills without making the least defalcation.

Wüstrau, however, did not wholly engross either the time or attention of Zieten, who giving the preference to his regiment, consecrated solely his leisure moments to his private concerns. Conformable to this rule of conduct it was his custom to set off for his villa every Saturday evening, and, after passing the Sunday there, to return in the night in order to be at Berlin early on Monday morning. These journeys indeed were not mere parties of pleasure; on the contrary, he had often the mortification to discover that his building was but little advanced or ill executed; and too frequently he found it necessary to undo the labour of a whole week.

Happily, these disasters had no influence either upon his temper or perseverance: he bore them with patience, caused the work to be corrected, and exhorted the builders not to fall into the like errors again. Moreover, if notwithstanding his weak state of health, he made choice of the night for travelling it was merely for the purpose of gaining time, which he was always more desirous to take from his hours of rest than, from those which were due to the care of his regiment.

In one of these nocturnal journeys, having occasion for a little repose, he stopped at a village half-way on the road and asked for a bed. He laid himself down in his clothes, and stretching out his legs, he felt something moving at his feet and wrapping itself round them. He imagined it to be a serpent: any other person indeed would have sprang from the bed and endeavoured to get rid of the supposed reptile; but being much fatigued, and at the same time quite unalarmed, he left it in possession of its post, and, drawing up his feet, fell fast asleep.

When he awoke in the morning, he had forgotten the circumstance; but the landlord having asked if he had slept well, he then recollected it, and observed to him, that there were serpents in his beds, and that he would do well to be more careful in future. The terrified landlord hastened to examine the bed, and found a tame squirrel which belonged to the house, and which had taken refuge there. The danger had been imaginary only with regard to Zieten, who knew not what it was to be afraid, it had been entirely null.

In Berlin his way of life was the same as it had usually been before the war. He found but little satisfaction in company, at play, at entertainments, and even in the amusements of the chase to which he had formerly been so passionately addicted. His wife was his principal intimate: the experience of his youth had contracted his heart, had rendered it cold and suspicious, and taught him to rely on himself alone under every event that could befall him. Friendship, that supreme good of man, seemed to withhold its endearments in order to lavish them with more liberal hand upon him in the latter stage of his life: yet whenever he received company, his guests were highly satisfied with his attentions.

He did the honours of his house with peculiar grace, and was remarkable for his politeness to the fair-sex, especially when they were at all conspicuous for the amiableness of their character. Plenty and taste presided at his board; while, on his own part, he was governed by the strictest rules of moderation and sobriety. He was seldom seen in company out of his own house, and he went to court merely for the sake of duty. The farther he advanced in life, the fonder he grew of retirement, which he enjoyed unadulterated with lassitude, because it was free from ambition and intrigue.

His cabinet, where he passed those hours which he could spare from his regiment, was amply stored with plans of architecture both military and civil, with maps of all kinds, and with various authors on rural economy: and without losing sight of the glory which still awaited him, he applied his knowledge of country affairs, in the improvement and embellishment of his estate, to such purpose as to enable him one day to repose under the shades which his own hands had prepared.

His whole regiment was not garrisoned in Berlin: five squadrons thereof were quartered in a part of the dutchy of Mechlenberg-Schwerin, (the towns of Parchim, Plauen, and Lube), at that time pledged to the crown of Prussia. The distance of these quarters from Berlin, which was near twenty German miles, proved no small obstacle to the order, the discipline, and the uniformity which would otherwise have prevailed through the whole regiment. Towards the time of the manoeuvres the detached battalion always removed to Berlin to prepare themselves under the eye of their commander for the grand review; and this short residence was sufficient to put them upon a par with the rest of the regiment, as far as what related to military exercises.

With regard to discipline, it was far from being the case, as in the absence of their general they had been under the command of officers who had not universally taken him for their model. It must be indeed confessed that disorders were often committed by the hussars under the sanction of some of their new officers whose courage but too much, fomented the pride of their profession without being tempered with that moderation which is one of its best appendages. To the reformation of these abuses Zieten bestowed the most assiduous and unremitting attention, and instead of ill-timed rigour, had recourse to gentle and deliberate measures: these measures operated insensibly, and were at length crowned with success.

He knew the world in general, and particularly that part of it engaged in a military life; and without requiring from everyone a like degree of ability and good conduct, he judged according to that measure of both which he knew them to possess; commending what was praiseworthy wherever he found it, and punishing what was amiss as soon as he perceived it to be productive of disorder; ever declaring that he had rather confer favours than inflict punishments, and always recollecting past desert rather than noticing present misdemeanours, provided such indulgence was not derogatory to the laws of honour. In garrison he relaxed much from the severity he usually assumed in the field: he considered his soldiers as his pupils, his children.

In time of war, it was indeed necessary to have recourse to rigorous and even to formidable measures: the success of battles depended on such mode of conduct. Peace, however, restored indulgence and authorised gentler proceedings; and to try what use his troops would make of more liberal treatment, he was fond of softening occasionally the severity of military discipline. Influenced by humanity as well as sound policy, and desirous of stimulating the ambition and honour of the soldier, he always appeared without his cane on the parade and place of exercise. It was to show that he preferred gentle means to severe ones; it was to avoid the consequences of a sudden gust of passion; and, in fine, to, give his officers an example of moderation.

He attained the wished for end; he succeeded in conciliating indulgence with punctuality; his regiment, governed by his principles, adopted the spirit of them, and were distinguished by their orderly deportment; and the squadrons who were stationed in Mecklenberg, and who at first were not well received in that country, at length gained the esteem and affection of their several hosts.

Zieten was equally anxious to render his regiment expert in their various exercises, as to establish good discipline among them. The king after the peace of Dresden had introduced several new evolutions into his cavalry, some of which being applicable to the hussars were adopted with eagerness by their general, and attended with the fullest success. He likewise exercised his men in various feats of address; and besides the usual service of the light, troops, he accustomed them to all the manoeuvres of those of the line, in order to prepare them for every kind of attack.

Moreover, by obtaining suitable asylums for such of his troopers as began to fall into the decline of life, he was able to remove them in favour of younger and more active men. Hence his regiment never grew old, and at every review partook with their commander of the gracious approbation of their sovereign, who upon all occasions was ready to afford them the most flattering testimonies of it.

After the review of the year 1746, that monarch made Zieten a present of an uncommon as well as honourable nature, accompanied with the following letter.

> My dear Major-General de Zieten.
> I have the pleasure to send you a Turkish *scimitar*, fully persuaded that the present will meet with your approbation, and that it could not be placed in better hands. I am your affectionate king,
> Potsdam, 123rd August, 1746.                    Frederick.

Soon after this the king embellished the regimentals of his corps. During the lifetime of Frederick William, Queen Sophia Dorothea, his consort, had made the regiment a present of twelve tiger-skins by way of decoration during the grand review. The king now augmented the number and ornamented them with clasps and chains in the oriental taste. For the commanders of squadrons he added eagle's wings, which were fastened to their caps by a wand topped with a crown;— for the rest of the officers, plumes of heron's feathers. At the present day (1803), they are equipped at the general reviews in this showy manner: the spectacle is singularly striking even after the lapse of so many years, and must have been much more so when the ornaments were fresh and untarnished.

Let the reader present to his imagination for a moment a regiment, that every stroke of the kettle-drum reminded of the day of Hennersdorf, who under the command of their general were entitled to consider themselves as invincible; let him form an idea of the splendid accoutrements of the troopers, the rich trappings of their horses, and consider the majestic effect of the whole, and he must allow that such a spectacle was well adapted to inspire the regiment with courage and the beholders with admiration. Zieten himself, although superior to the false glare that strikes and dazzles the vulgar, enjoyed with a high degree of enthusiasm the triumph of his hussars and the *éclat* with which the justice of the king had honoured them.

The distinctions which the monarch conferred upon him produced, however, their common effects: they excited envy, they provoked hatred, attended with a spirit of persecution. The same officer whom Zieten, towards the close of the late campaign, had discovered to be his enemy, had now recourse to new machinations, and at length he succeeded in depriving him of the king's confidence, and in placing himself between the general and every avenue to the heart of that prince.

He laid the foundation of a series of mortifications and sorrows which continued to torment him during the space of seven years; and acted with the basest ingratitude towards a man to whom he owed his first military reputation and almost all the glory of his subsequent exploits. Zieten, however, was so much master of himself as to be able to suppress his indignation: his character appeared on this occasion, in all its dignity, both by the calm manner in which he counteracted the persecution in its earlier stages, and in the manly firmness with which he combatted it when it was afterward inflicted by a superior hand.

An attempt to prejudice Frederick against a general, whose talents and virtue commanded his esteem and affection, appears at first sight hardy and even rash. But the adversary of Zieten was the favourite of the king: his wit had captivated the monarch; he was in possession of the royal confidence, and lived with his sovereign on the most intimate footing. Zieten on the contrary never obtruded himself on his master; and instead of profiting by the experience of the past and being ever on his guard, he continued to act with his accustomed frankness and relied solely on the consciousness of his own desert. Unapprehensive of being misunderstood, and too proud to defend himself against the machinations of intrigue and cabal, he facilitated the victory of an enemy who durst not attack him openly, but who in order to ruin him had recourse to indirect measures only.

During the course of the war this dexterous and ambitious man had seized every opportunity of degrading the merit of Zieten and establishing his own upon its ruins. He made use of him and his regiment to acquire the laurels with which he ornamented his own brows. Convinced that our hero, whenever the honour of his country was at stake, was ready to undertake the most daring expeditions, he took advantage of his ardour and frequently exposed him to imminent danger, while he himself reaped all the glory of the, enterprise. Zieten commonly fought at a distance from the king; his more prudent rival generally displayed his prowess in the presence of his master. Zieten was brave without boasting of his courage: the other, less modest, was fond of assuming that character; and fearing to suffer by the parallel in case he repeatedly made mention of Zieten in his reports to the king, he was more inclined to bring forward the name of any other general who had shared the danger of the day.

He had continued from the conclusion of the war to do him every ill service in his power. At first, he merely touched upon trivial irregularities and unimportant negligences in order to prejudice him in the royal favour. At length he acted more openly and began to insinuate that since Zieten had attained the rank of general he had grown neglectful of his regiment; that he had considered it as a regiment of the line; at another time, that he had left his hussars in a state of total inaction; had never exercised his officers in patrol-duty, in the various detail of petty hostilities; that all he had done daring the two Silesian wars was merely the effect of chance and good fortune, and in no respect the result of a regular plan of operation. In line, he endeavoured to make Zieten considered not only as a bad officer, but likewise as a man incapable of forming good ones, and the king at length was led to believe that his general was even unable to make a military disposition agreeably to the common rules of the art.

It is hardly to be conceived how the monarch could have lent a serious ear to such insinuations, and the more so as it depended entirely on himself to be convinced of their futility. He had only to recollect what tasks he had laid before his officers with a view of making trial of their talents, and the manner in which Zieten had acquitted himself on those occasions (as mentioned earlier): he had only to remember the many instances, during the war and under his own eye, in which Zieten had formed his plans of operation with intuitive promptitude, and executed them with the most brilliant success.

All his exploits, however, seemed to be now forgotten: deluded in more than one respect, Frederick not only questioned the capacity, but even the zeal of the general, and upbraided him with respect to the latter in very harsh terms. In support of this assertion, we have only one of his letters to bring forward, as Zieten, who was averse to record the wrongs he had suffered, destroyed all the others a few years before his death. The letter runs thus.

> My dear Major-General de Zieten. I have just received your report on the subject of Pasch, the hussar, and I confess that what you advance in his behalf is very satisfactory: I likewise approve of your having sentenced Major de Vigh to confinement. Yet much still remains to be done; you have not suppressed the disorders which prevail among your officers as well as private soldiers; a circumstance I can only attribute to ill-timed indulgencies; as, it seems, you give yourself no trouble about anything, and suffer everyone to act as he pleases. Of this your detachment, posted along the frontiers of Saxony, furnish a striking proof: they have not recovered a single deserter; a circumstance of a very uncommon nature, and which can only be the result of radical evils; of negligence, and want of order in those who command and in those who obey.
>
> Moreover, with regard to the oath to be taken by the recruits, I cannot account for your not adopting it in your own regiment, unless by supposing you are influenced by motives of self-convenience, and are averse to give your officers a little extra trouble. I hope, however, that in future you will be less remiss, and thoroughly correct the abuses of your regiment, so that I may still be enabled to subscribe myself your affectionate king,
>
> Potsdam, March 3rd, 1750.                           Frederick.

Zieten bore these injurious censures with the fortitude of a hero: he revenged himself upon his adversary by dignified silence only; and to that silence the ignorance of the public with respect to the whole transaction must be ascribed. He was supposed to have no enemies because he did not complain of having any. To the king he still continued submissive and respectful; he loved his sovereign too well to allow himself to give way to the first emotions of resentment, and not to respect even his errors. He still trusted that the monarch would erelong open his eyes, and again receive him into favour. He had besides recourse to measures conducive to such expectations, and among other expedients he carried on a correspondence with His Majesty, which he afterwards destroyed with the rest of the papers relative to the subject.

At length perceiving that the ill-humour and the prejudices of the king daily increased, that he loaded his censures with additional harshness, and his procedure with new severities, he grew cool, complained of injustice, ingratitude; and, giving way to his natural pride, began to act without his usual restraint, and on many occasions nearly provoked his own ruin. But Frederick, at the same time indulgent and severe, caressed his general on one hand while he wounded him on the other, and was willing to pardon his inflexibility in consideration of the very merit which he was averse to allow him.

The feelings of Zieten, already worked up to a high pitch, were one day put to a severe trial at the royal table. His adversary had taken measures to expose him to undergo the examination of a scholar; and the king, who was in the secret, turning the conversation upon the late war and the achievements in which Zieten and his regiment had distinguished themselves, desired the general to give him some particulars and explanations relative to the subject. This, it must be observed, was not our hero's favourite topic: he was never fond of enlarging on his own exploits lest he should incur the imputation of vainglory, and besides he already suspected the snare that was laid for him. Observing the eyes of his adversaries fixed upon him and sparkling with malignant joy, he at length spurned the idea of reciting his lesson, of coldly analysing his glory, of spelling his military feats, and bluntly replied in the following terms:

> The moment I have reconnoitred the force and position of the enemy, I march against them, attack and beat them.

This laconic answer disconcerted the whole company. The king, however, seemed satisfied with it. He had indeed too much sense to be offended at it, yet it is probable he had not taken its true meaning, which implied, that though Zieten was able to explain, he was determined not to be driven to it; and the reply probably tended to confirm the unfavourable opinion His Majesty already entertained of the general's professional abilities.

Though Frederick thus denied him the justice due to his merit, he could not refrain from esteeming, from loving him, and giving him proofs of his affection. Two months after the receipt of the foregoing letter, the king wrote him another which we shall lay before the reader by way of corrective to it.

> My dear Major-General de Zieten.
> I have just been informed that M. de Kaiser, Canon of Gerresheim in the dutchy of Bergue, is dead. His benefice being

at my disposal, I confer it upon you as a testimony of my good will, and you have likewise permission to transfer it. I have given the necessary orders to my minister, M. de Dankelmann, and I think it proper to mention two particulars relative to this business: the first is, that the person to whom you transfer the prebend must be of the Roman-Catholic persuasion; and the second, that an offer of six hundred dollars has already been made for the benefice which, I must observe, has heretofore been considered worth double that sum. M. de Dankelmann can furnish you with all further particulars, and I remain your affectionate king,
Berlin, May 23rd, 1750.   Frederick.

Circumstanced as he was with the monarch, this present, and particularly the letter which accompanied it and formed so striking a contrast with the preceding one, mast have operated in a powerful manner upon the general's feelings.

Soon after this he enjoyed a more brilliant triumph, and which he owed to his address and good fortune. The king, in the year 1750, gave a superb tournament, and Zieten, who, among other general officers, had entered the lists, was one of the competitors who bore away the prize. This circumstance, together with the novelty of the scene in latter times, in which the spirit of chivalry seems to be almost forgotten, may perhaps render a short description of the spectacle interesting to some of our readers: it may at least be considered as an episode, and may form no unpleasing contrast to the recital of war and destruction which is inseparable from the nature of these memoirs.

Opposite to the palace and in the middle of the square called the royal garden, a tilting ground, sixty feet long and forty wide, was laid out; round which an amphitheatre was erected for the accommodation of the spectators. On either side, and over against each other, two boxes were, constructed, the one for the royal family, and the other for the court. The former, which was hung with crimson velvet, was richly decorated, and displayed the king's cypher upon a pediment supported by two marble columns. Under this box was another, of inferior size, for the princess Amelia, the monarch's sister, who distributed the prizes. Four judges of the lists; Marshal Keith; Generals Counts Haake and Schwerin; and M. d'Arnim, Minister of State, were seated on the right and the left of the princess.

The tournament opened at sunset by the light of torches and upwards of thirty thousand lamps; A detachment of the garrison occupied the avenues to the amphitheatre, and a party of lifeguards were stationed near the royal box. The two queens with the princes of the blood and all the court being arrived, Princess Amelia, in all the glare of diamonds and beauty, appeared in her box; and the king with the Margrave of Bareuth at his side, having seated himself on one of the benches destined for the judges of the lists, the four pageants, of which the spectacle was composed, began their march into the area.

The first, or the *Roman*, was headed by Prince Augustus, brother to the king (grandfather of His Present Majesty—1803), M. de Frobehn, the royal equerry, opened the procession: he was followed by a kettle-drum and eight trumpets in Roman habits, bearing streamers embroidered with eagles and inscribed with the letters S. P. Q. R.

**********

M. de Frobehn is a name of considerable celebrity. In the Battle of Fehrbellin M. Frobehn, equerry to the Great Elector, apprehensive that the white horse which that prince rode would attract the attention of the enemy, gave his own in exchange, and was soon after killed by a cannon-ball. The Great Elector ennobled his family.

**********

The prince's equerry followed next. He carried a Roman standard, and preceded four caparisoned horses, led by eight grooms in the habit of slaves.

Eight lictors on horseback, bearing fasces and shields, next made their appearance.

They were followed by eight slaves on foot, marching two and two.

M. de Schwerin, the king's first equerry, performed the office of marshal to the prince. He was dressed in a Roman habit, and bore a truncheon in his hand.

Eight freedmen followed him, two and two, and were distinguished from the slaves by blue satin caps and white plumes.

Two running-footmen.

Four pages, carrying the lance and javelin of the prince.

The prince, in the habit of a Roman consul. He wore on his breast a large eagle wrought in diamonds. On his helmet, which was tipped with an eagle, were represented Romulus and Remus suckled by a wolf. His Royal Highness was mounted on a stately white horse magnificently caparisoned.

Six knights closed the prince's pageant; Margrave Henry, Prince of the Blood; Lieutenant-Colonel Duke of Holstein Beck; Major de Chazot; Captain de Bredow; Lieutenant de Marwitz of the *gens-d'armes*; and Count Leopold de Lamberg.

The dress of the knights was distinguished from that of the prince; it was less brilliant; they wore no eagle on their breasts, and had no consular mantle.

Each knight was attended by a freedman and a slave; the former bore the lance, the latter the javelin.

The colours of the pageant were fire-colour and blue.

The second, or Carthaginian pageant, was led by Prince Henry, brother to the king, and the march was opened by a kettle-drum, two trumpets and eight Moorish *hautboys*. The black satin which composed the dress of the latter afforded no bad imitation of an African's skin; and the pearls, plumes, turbans and necklaces which they wore were exact representations of the costume of their supposed country. They had quivers filled with arrows on their shoulders, and on their bandrols was represented a palm-tree, and at its foot a lion with a horse's head, the symbol of the city of Carthage.

The prince's equerry.

Four horses, led by eight Moors.

Eight Moors on horseback, bearing lances topped with dragons by way of standards.

Fourteen Moors on foot, marching two and two.

Four pages, two of whom bearing the lance and javelin of the prince.

The prince. His Royal Highness wore a blue turban ornamented with three plumes, and a tiger's skin instead of a mantle.

The six knights of the pageant were the reigning Prince of Lobkowitz, Duke of de Sagan; Count de Schafgotsch, Commander of the Order of Malta, and grand equerry; Count Alexander Sulkowsky; Count Ahasuerus de Lehndorf, chamberlain to the queen; Baron de Wurmster, a captain in the French service; and Mr. Chung, a Scotchman.

Each knight was attended by two Moors, bearing his arms. The colours were blue and silver.

The third, or *Greek* pageant, was led by Prince Ferdinand, brother to the king.

A kettle-drum, two trumpets, and eight *hautboys* on horseback, preceded the march. The predominant colours of their dress were yellow and flesh-colour.

The prince's equerry bore his lance and buckler.

Eight Greek soldiers on horseback with spears and shields.

Six others on foot, wearing helmets, and armed with pikes and targets.

Four pages.

The prince in a flesh-coloured mantle, wearing a silver helmet, and mounted on a stately dun-coloured horse.

Six knights attended him: Prince Ferdinand of Brunswick, Lieutenant-General, and Colonel of the Guards; the Hereditary Prince of Hesse-Darmstadt, marshal; Prince Frederick of Wurtemberg, Colonel of Dragoons; Zieten; Baron de Dankelmann, President of the Regency of Minden; Baron de Montelieu, chamberlain to the Duke of Wurtemberg.

The fourth, or Persian pageant, was conducted by the Margrave Charles, Prince of the Blood.

A kettle-drum and two *janizaries* opened the march. The turbans of the latter were white and gold; which were likewise the colours of the pageant.

The *margrave's* equerry.

Twelve horses, led by as many grooms in Persian dresses.

Eight (Negro) slaves and four pages preceded the *margrave*.

The dress of the prince was Persian; it was composed of green satin lined with ermine, and fastened by diamond clasps. His turban was green; his horse covered with jewels; the whole displayed the magnificence of a Darius.

The six knights who accompanied him were Count de Schmettau, Minister of State and Master of the Hunt; M. de Blumenthal, Commander of the Lifeguards; M. de Krosigk, grand forester; Baron de Printzen, privy counsellor; Lieutenant de Kalkreuth of the lifeguards; and Lieutenant de Brocker of the *gens d'armes*. A royal equerry closed the march.

After having filed before the boxes of the king and queens, and saluted them with their lances, the cavalcade took their places in the lists which the marshal had assigned them, and waited for the signal.

The marshal having fixed the heads (made of pasteboard, and served as marks to aim or strike at), and closed the gates of the tilting ground, the trumpets proclaimed the first spectacle, and the four leaders of the pageants opened the games.

These games were divided into three distinct operations: the first was to bring down a Turk's head by a stroke of the lance; the second to hit a Medusa's head with a javelin; the third to cut down with the back-stroke of a sword a pasteboard bust praised a foot from the ground.

After the leaders had performed their exercises, the knights followed their example at six different times, and distinguished themselves in feats. of emulation and address.

After the exercise of the heads, that of running at the ring took place in the same order: the knights, however, ran but four times as the weather did not continue favourable.

The games being ended, the registers of the judges of the list were compared, and the prizes distributed. They fell to Prince Henry of Prussia, Prince Ferdinand of Brunswick, and Major-General de Zieten. The four victors alighted from their horses and received them from the hand of princess Amelia, while kettle-drums and trumpets proclaimed the triumph. To each of the princes was presented a diamond ring, and to Zieten a pair of sleeve-buttons. The pageants kept the same order on retiring as they had observed on their entry, and they paraded to the opera-house square. A masked ball, which was honoured with the presence of the king, the queens, and all the court, concluded the amusements of the day. Supper was served at seven tables, the whole night was spent in dancing, and the princes and noblemen who had composed posed the tournament, wore the dresses of the respective parts they had acted.

By the king's order the spectacle was repeated two days afterwards, and before sunset. Instead of lamps the amphitheatre was hung with garlands and festoons; the order and the pageants were the same., The prizes, which Princess Amelia likewise distributed, consisted in military accoutrements. Messieurs de Kalkreuth, de Dankelmann, de Sultowsky, and de Montelieu were the victors. M. de Voltaire, who had been present at both these spectacles, made the following *impromptu* in honour of the princess.

> *Jamais ni la Grece ni Rome*
> *N'eut des jeux si brillans, ni de plus dignes prix;*
> *J'ai vu les fils de mars sous les traits de Paris,*
> *Et Venus qui donna la pomme.*
> (Never had neither Greece nor Rome
> such brilliant games, nor more worthy prizes;
> I saw the sons of March in the guise of Paris,
> And Venus who gave the apple.)

The victory which Zieten gained on this occasion, and which he partook with the princes of the blood, shews him to have been as good a knight as an officer, and that his address was equal to his courage. The jewel which attested his prowess was highly valued by him, and is still (1803), preserved with due veneration in his family.

His triumph, however, created new envy and involved him in new persecutions. His enemies multiplied daily, and the king, still more prone to listen to their insidious representations, took every opportunity to express his dissatisfaction in the most undisguised manner. The regiment shared the disgrace of their commander, and became a standing topic of animadversion with His Majesty; and to such a point was this matter carried, that several staff-officers, encouraged by the royal example, took upon themselves the task of censuring our hero's conduct and sullying his reputation.

The army in general lamented his case, yet no one ventured to defend him. One day indeed, when the Prince of Anhalt undertook to speak a word in his behalf, and reminded the king of the services the general had rendered him and the zeal with which he had acquitted himself, the monarch harshly replied;

> It is not for his sake I would go to war again: in garrison he is not worth a straw.

About this time the adversaries of Zieten received a fresh reinforcement in the person of an Austrian colonel of the name of Nadytschzander, a native of Hungary, and who had lately made a tender of his services to the king. His Majesty, already prepossessed in favour of that nation, had given him a welcome reception, and had placed him in his own retinue. In this stranger the implacable enemy of Zieten found the man he wanted; a man he could at all times push forward, while he himself remained concealed behind the scene. This new favourite soon began to act a very conspicuous part; he had gained the royal ear by means of a specious military jargon which that prince took for real knowledge of the profession, and he at last made him believe that the hussars were nothing in comparison to what they might become under proper tuition, that they were, in fact, undeserving of the name they bore, and that new reforms were necessary to be substituted in the place of those which Zieten had introduced.

Nadytschzander proposed his own, and he began to make his first trial of them upon the regiment of Zieten. The reader may recollect that the king had formerly placed several veteran sergeants in this corps by way of recompensing their services: and now, at the instigation of the Hungarian, choice was industriously made of the rudest and most ferocious of men for the purpose of converting them into hussars.

★★★★★★★★★★

> In the Prussian infantry and cavalry, the commissions of officers are exclusively reserved for the nobles. In the hussars, the artillery, and engineers, such commissions may be obtained without the advantage of birth. Frederick the Great made much of this distinction, which at the same time served as a resource for the nobility and an encouragement to talents and bravery.

★★★★★★★★★★

If the form of these recruits was human, it was considered enough; their ferocity was a kind of recommendation. Whenever a young man was found unfit for any reputable calling, it. was usually said of him, *en Italie* he would make a good hussar, and the words at length became proverbial. The whole country was inclined to look upon this soldiery as a kind of half-barbarians; and indeed, according to the system of Nadytschzander, they were to be converted into such, to be rendered devoid of all principle, morals and humanity; in a word, to be mere centaurs. On this footing too he was always careful to treat them: "March, blackguards!" he would cry to the officers, as well, as to the soldiers, on the parade, at the manoeuvres, and everywhere.

This procedure irritated, discouraged, and disorganised the regiment. The officers who were attached to Zieten, justly offended thereat, obeyed the Hungarian with extreme reluctance; the soldiers, who at the famous Battle of Hohenfriedberg had retorted the railing of a hostile general, could ill brook that of a commander, dropt as it were among them from the skies. An alarming ferment took place, and murmurings were heard through every rank; the fine order which had been introduced with so much labour, the zeal for the service, the stubborn point of honour; all gave way to universal discontent and remissness. Zieten was overwhelmed with indignation and sorrow at these proceedings and contemplated the rapid degradation of his regiment without being able to check its progress. At length his patience was exhausted, and he resolved to lend his name no longer to such scandalous innovations, although he was well aware it must expose him to new altercations with the king.

The first that took place on this subject was at Spandaw, in the year 1753. The king had formed a camp of evolutions there for the purpose of trying and practising a series of new manoeuvres. Several principal officers of hussars, and particularly such as were of Hungarian extraction, were present at the express desire of His Majesty. Nadytschzander played the first part here: he assumed the office of tutoring the regiment of Zieten, of teaching them the very elements of the art of war, and already considered himself as their chief. The general's enemies, as well as the Hungarian stranger, flattered themselves that the Spandaw manoeuvres would close his military career and that the king would of course bestow his regiment upon the new favourite.

They knew Zieten and the warmth of his temper, but they were mistaken with regard to the king, whom they thought they equally knew, and who on this occasion shewed himself worthy of the surname that posterity had conferred upon him.

His Majesty, some days before he set off for Spandaw, having spoken in a circle of his generals of these manoeuvres, desired them to furnish him with some plans of evolution. Zieten kept aloof. He heard with pity the idle vapourings of Nadytschzander and his partisans, and remained without speaking a word. The king was struck at this, and beckoning him nearer, asked him his opinion. Zieten for the first time ventured to disobey his sovereign: he merely observed, that when he should be on the spot he should know what to do; and immediately resumed his silence. The king was obliged to content himself with this short but energetic reply; which, however, contributed not a little to raise the storm that was soon to break over the head of the general and his whole corps.

The several regiments marched to the camp of Spandaw, and that of Zieten was one of the first that arrived there. The king was waiting for him on the bridge. His Majesty was in a very ill humour that day; and of this the kettle-drummer first experienced the bad effects, "He is good for nothing" said the king, and immediately ordered him away. With him the drums were sent back to Berlin: they had perhaps too strongly reminded His Majesty of the glorious day of Hennersdorf and the exploits of Zieten. The king reviewed the regiment, found the whole corps detestable, was pleased to call the hussars country boobies, unlicked bears, and, in short, set no bounds to his complaints and reprehensions.

Zieten heard all this with respectful silence: the king, however, at last forgetting himself so far as to have recourse to abusive expressions, the general approached him, and, in the warmth of his resentment, thrust his sword into the scabbard, and exclaimed in a loud tone, "Sire, though we are good for nothing at the present day, yet there was a time in which we did our duty; as long there was any want of our services, we were, it seems, worth something."

"Yes," replied the king, "you were then worth much; but at present, you are become remiss, and good, for nothing at all."

No farther altercation at this time took place. Zieten kept silence, but still left his sword in the scabbard: and, without either declaring himself indisposed or making the least apology to the king, he remained a whole fortnight in the camp, observing the different manoeuvres as a mere spectator; and without taking the least part in the concerns of his regiment. The king, who saw himself braved, nevertheless shewed no marks of resentment, nor took any measures against the offender:—a circumstance unexampled in the annals of the Prussian Army!

In the meanwhile, the regiment had been parcelled out into several divisions, and put under the command of various colonels. This circumstance inflamed the officers and the whole corps with new resentment: they swore to wreak vengeance on their persecutors, who had now begun to consider their triumph as complete, and the ruin of Zieten as inevitable. These persecutors uniting their whole force and exerting all their efforts, at length made a general attack: they broke out in loud complaints against the regiment, accused the troopers of ignorance, and laid the most glaring imperfections to the charge of the whole corps.

The king grew confirmed in his prejudices, the favourite rejoiced at these calumnies; which were, moreover, meanly countenanced by several of Zieten's pupils, who were indebted to him for their advancement as well as for their military reputation. Prince Augustus William of Prussia was the only person who openly espoused his cause; the rest of his friends contented themselves with lamenting him in secret.

On his own part he still preserved due presence of mind and shewed an apparent indifference to everything that occurred. He attended the manoeuvres and followed up their progress, as if he had never served at all in the Prussian Army and was now for the first time a looker-on at such kind of spectacles. He was nevertheless secretly at work on behalf of his regiment, and took care occasionally to communicate such instructions to his officers as shortly afterwards enabled, them to annihilate all the chimerical projects of Nadytschzander.

Among other evolutions, the king had ordered a grand foraging-party to be executed. General de Winterfeld commanded one division of the enterprise, and the Hungarian colonel the other. The hussars of Zieten were included in either corps. Nadytschzander, who was charged with the attack, had promised to exhibit a master-stroke in the military art. He had ostentatiously undertaken to shew the whole army the manner of surprising and overcoming the enemy: his essay, however, turned out ridiculously abortive. Our partisan, who could neither form nor keep up a military disposition, being wholly unaware of the trap that had been laid for him, fell singly into it.

Captain de Reizenstein of Zieten's regiment, to whom the general had secretly communicated his instructions, and who was in Winterfeld's division, availed himself of a moment in which Nadytschzander, as he was rambling at some distance from his troops, conceived himself to be in perfect security: he rode up to him, threw his arm about him and pulling him from his horse, made him, prisoner. Scarcely had he performed this feat, when several officers and a party of hussars made their appearance, and observing the distressful plight of the man who had done them so much mischief, they were unable to set bounds to their sarcasms. They treated him, moreover, according to the strictest laws of war; he was surrounded by a detachment of hussars, and obliged to march on foot to the royal tent. Crowds of spectators accompanied him, and he was received with shouts of malicious joy. His inexpertness, his tribulation were loudly censured and laughed at, and the mob at last began to pelt him with dirt and stones.

Thus attended, the hero of the day was presented to the king, at whose hands he fully expected to find both protection and redress: but His Majesty was so struck with the oddity of the spectacle that he burst likewise into an immoderate fit of laughter. The crowd who had followed him, finding themselves thus encouraged by the king, continued their taunts in the most provoking manner, and Nadytschzander was on the point of being stoned to death. The monarch, however, in order to rescue and punish him at the same time, accommodated him with one of carriages belonging to his household, which was drawn by six mules; and, at His Majesty's special command, the late favourite was drawn in triumph to the headquarters under the guard of those who had made him prisoner.

It is probable that from the opening of the manoeuvres the king had ceased to entertain the extravagant opinion he had first conceived of this stranger's abilities. Nor was this the only disaster of the kind that befell him, as the lifeguards, it seems, had played him a similar trick. Every regiment indeed conspired against him and neglected no opportunity in their power of exhibiting his ignorance in the most ridiculous point of view. The king, whose principle it was to avoid falling into any inconsistency of conduct, still countenanced him, but no longer honoured him with his confidence; and sometime after this, having discovered that our adventurer had been guilty of various acts of perfidy towards him, he was pleased to confine him in a fortress; and thus ended his short-lived glory!

Though this enemy of Zieten had disappeared, yet the prejudices of the king still continued to operate against the latter. It was indeed remarkable, that during the interval between the second and third Silesian Wars, Frederick grew highly dissatisfied with several of his generals, and extended his ill humour even to the *margraves* and princes of the blood. At the reviews he frequently made them feel the effects of it in such a manner as to induce them to believe he had forgotten their services or was inclined to forget them.

This was, in fact, the work of that insidious, ambitious man, who aspired to the exclusive possession of the royal favour, and who had made use of Nadytschzander and such kind of men to obtain his purposes; bringing them forwards and making them act and disappear by turns. We may likewise discover in the peculiarity of His Majesty's temper a further reason for the disgrace into which several of his generals at this time fell. Frederick whose aim was perfection itself, required every one about him to acquit himself with equal elevation of mind. He had all that impatience and pretention which is so frequently attendant on genius: his claims were often unjust, of ten bordering on impossibility; and whenever he found obstacles in his way, he was more ready to blame the agents he had employed, than to reflect upon the difficulty of the task he had imposed on them: the master therefore was as often dissatisfied with his disciples as the disciples were with their master.

Of the number of the latter was Zieten. He had not even endeavoured to conceal his sentiments; and his enemies considered his ruin as certain. The boldness of his reply to the king; the manner in which he had braved his displeasure when he appeared at the manoeuvres in the character of a mere looker-on; the stubborn silence which he opposed to that which the monarch was pleased to observe;—all seemed in their eyes, to prognosticate his inevitable downfall. They were, however, much deceived in their calculation: His Majesty thought fit to act merely a passive part in this business. Zieten resumed the command of his regiment at Berlin, and set about reforming the disorders which the interregnum of Nadytschzander had introduced therein.

The king indeed at different times afforded him new cause for the exercise of his patience, but no explanations took place between them, nor any thing that looked like rupture or open war. The general followed the plan he had himself laid down. Faithful to his prince, his country, his duty; jealous of his regiment, and of the honour of the profession; feeling, in spite of the reproaches of the king, that gentleness and indulgence were far preferable to rigour, he never lost sight of them, and never caused those who were subordinate to him to share the vexations he himself experienced. He continued to treat them as his children, his friends; and though the victim of ill humour himself, no one had reason to complain of any on his part.

The enemy of Zieten at length despairing of working his ruin, had recourse to other measures, which not a little flattered his own pride. In order to prevail on our hero to humble himself before him, he strove to give him hopes of regaining by his interposition the good graces of the king. But he ill knew the general or he would not have imagined him capable of stooping so low. Was it likely that Zieten could cringe and degrade himself to such a degree?—Zieten, who, impressed with the sense of his own desert and the justice of his cause, could never be induced to yield even to the king himself, and whose becoming pride had hitherto served him as an *aegis* against all the terrors of a monarch's frown?

Of this noble pride he gave new proof at one of the following reviews. His regiment having received orders to charge, acquitted themselves, in the judgment of the king, in so disorderly a manner, that the monarch, addressing himself to the general, cried out in a tone of the utmost displeasure, "I'll see no more of this; away!" Scarcely had he uttered these words, when Zieten, who thought fit to take them in their literal sense, left the field at the head of his regiment, and marched directly; to Berlin. This movement which appeared a mere much ado about nothing to such as were not in the secret, puzzled and surprised the spectators.

The enemy of Zieten who secretly exulted in his humiliation, did everything in his power to stop him and bring him back, with a view, it may be presumed, of prolonging the illiberal delight this scene afforded him; but all his efforts were to no purpose. The general relying on the first order of the king, paid no attention to the subsequent ones, and even dismissed in a haughty manner the *aide-de camp* of his enemy who had been dispatched to recall him.

After the review it was customary for people of distinction, whether military or civil, to assemble in the great hall of the palace to pay their devoirs to the king—Zieten went there with the rest, and in the presence of his sovereign, his enemy, and the whole court, appeared with dignified assurance, and with that serenity of mind which had nothing to reproach itself with respecting the past, and nothing to fear with regard to the future. The king saw him, and remained silent.

Seven years passed away in this manner, during which time the king and Zieten seemed irreconcilable towards each other. Frederick, however, secretly preserved some remains of esteem and good will for his general, whom he must have considered of no small importance to the service or he would not have continued him in it on such conditions. Moreover, prejudiced as he was against the regiment, he still acted with proper justice towards it: the corps were never deprived of any of their rights and privileges, or of their rank in the army. One day a dispute arose between tween a captain of the *gens d'armes* and an officer of the same rank in Zieten's regiment, on the subject of signing their names to a paper. Each claimed the precedence; the one alleging the honour of the regiment, the other his long service: the king decided in favour of the seniority of the commission, and, although irritated against the corps of hussars, gave their officer the preference.

In the year 1755, a great promotion took place, in which Zieten had no share. He had the mortification to see all the major-generals of his own standing, and, among the rest, his inveterate enemy, raised to the rank of lieutenant-general, while he alone remained unadvanced. Of this he ventured to complain to the king, and he received the following answer.

> My dear Major-General de Zieten.
> I have received your letter of the 14th instant, containing representations and requests relative to your present rank and future advancement, which I am utterly at a loss to understand. You cannot be ignorant, that you preserve your rank above all the generals of hussars; nor can you either be ignorant that the hussars, having not the same rank as the rest of the army, the advancement of the other generals does no prejudice to you. I therefore hope, you will make yourself easy, and wait with patience for the moment in which I shall think fit to advance you in your turn; and I remain your affectionate king,
> Potsdam, June 30th, 1755                          Frederick.

It was in the course of the same year, that one of Zieten's officers rendered the king an essential service, and justified the choice of the monarchy whose prejudices against the regiment did not hinder him from honouring it with his particular confidence whenever his own interest was at stake. The business in question was to save the life of a Prussian officer arrested at Ulm, in the circle of Swabia, for having had recourse to coercive measures in raising recruits. A criminal process was instituted against him in that city, nor could either the repeated remonstrances or threats of the court of Berlin procure his enlargement.

To extricate him from his perilous situation, it was necessary to employ art and address on one hand, and on the other, force and violence. This delicate commission was given to Captain de Seelen of the regiment of Zieten. Everything was conducted with the greatest secrecy, and scarcely did any of the slightest particulars transpire. The fact, equally interesting and unknown, is entitled to a place in these memoirs.

Lieutenant de Heyden of the garrison of Magdeburg, was employed to raise recruits in the imperial city of Ulm for the supply of his own regiment. He had privately enlisted a tall, well-built man to whom he had given thirty florins on account, with a promise of a further sum in the course of three weeks, to be paid at Leipheim upon the frontiers of the territory of Ulm, whither the recruit had engaged himself to repair. The three weeks being expired, the man passed by M. de Heyden's house and informed one of his servants, who was standing at the door, that he was then going to Leipheim.

M. de Heyden, pleased at this intelligence, immediately ordered post-horses, followed the recruit and overtook him on the road; and having called to him, he held out his hand and assisted him in getting into his carriage, in which he had offered him a seat. The lieutenant had provided himself with a written agreement and the money which remained due to the man. The fellow at first made no resistance, hoping, as it may be supposed, to deceive M. de Heyden as he had many others, but finding himself well watched by the lieutenant and unable to make his escape, he began to cry out to the passengers and implore their assistance. M. de Heyden was then under the necessity of gagging him; and the handkerchief which he used for such purpose probably choked him; for on their arrival on the frontiers, the man was discovered to be dead. M. de Heyden, extremely alarmed and embarrassed at this accident, buried the body, with the assistance of the postillion, in a neighbouring forest.

An event of this nature was not likely to remain long concealed. A few days after, a servant-maid, to whom the postillion made love, divulged the whole affair. M. de Heyden was taken into custody by order of the magistrates of Ulm, a criminal prosecution was instituted against him, and though the tribunal could not convict him of intentional murder, he was nevertheless condemned to be hanged.

All the remonstrances made by the court of Berlin on this subject proved of no avail: the magistrates sought to amuse the king with evasive answers, and in the mean while hurried on the process in order to hasten the fatal moment. Nothing now remained to be done but to rescue the prisoner by force, and for this purpose the king desired Zieten to recommend him an able officer, whom he might dispatch to Ulm for the execution of this important business.

On this occasion Zieten shewed himself to possess a thorough knowledge of men. The exterior appearance of Captain de Seelen bespoke gentleness, politeness, and equanimity of temper, but was neither expressive of talents nor courage. An eye like Zieten's was necessary to discover such latent qualities; and the king, who disapproved the choice, was desirous it should fall upon some other, Zieten, however, persisted in that which he had already made; and although he was aware, that if the business took an unfavourably turn, the blame would fall entirely on himself, he still assured the king that he knew no other officer more likely to succeed in the enterprise than he.

His Majesty at last acquiesced in the choice, and M. de Seelen left Berlin, in the autumn, in the most private manner. His lady, whom he loved extremely, was kept ignorant of the journey, as well as its object and duration. He had taken leave of her on pretext of going to Potsdam in consequences of an order he had just received from the king. Mad. de Seelen at length not seeing him return, and discovering that she had been misled by him, gave way to the most excessive grief. She made daily application to Zieten for news of her husband, upbraided him with the cruel separation he had occasioned, and conjured him to restore the lieutenant to his unhappy family. Her affliction strongly excited his compassion, yet he could only console her in general terms: "Your husband is well," he would say; "he has nothing to fear; neither have you." This vague consolation had no effect.

Attended by six hussars in the disguise of domestics, M. de Seelen arrived at Ulm, where he appeared in the regimentals of an officer of dragoons, and assumed the name of Treskow. He lived in a grand style and was considered as a prince travelling *incognito*. His appearance engaged the public attention and commanded its respect. He made frequent excursions into the neighbouring countries the better to mask his designs, and he took an occasion of informing the Prussian resident that he expected a number of recruits from the lake of Constance and should perhaps be under the necessity of applying to him for a sum of money. In the meanwhile, he secretly watched the progress of the suit, which at first appeared to take a more favourable turn, but soon after fell into its former channel.

M. de Seelen, in consequence of this, applied to the king for a letter to the magistrates of Ulm, with leave to deliver it in person. He proposed that a categorical and peremptory answer respecting their intention towards Lieutenant de Heyden should be insisted upon, and public satisfaction and damages required proportionable to the injuries he had suffered. In case such letter should prove ineffectual, or did not meet with His Majesty's approbation, he requested to be authorised to seize upon one of the principal persons of Ulm, or, should that be impracticable, upon the Mayor of Leipheim who was son to one of the first inhabitants of that city, by way of hostage; and, provided he was allowed to strike this blow on the Austrian territory, he undertook to carry off the hostage across the Danube to Talfingen, and, by means of concealing his party in the woods during the day time, to gain Erlangen over the mountainous tract of country which lies between Talfingen and that place.

Neither of these plans pleased the king, who thereupon commissioned Zieten to suggest one that might release Lieutenant de Heyden without involving the Prussian Government in disputes with the neighbouring powers. Zieten's plan was honoured with His Majesty's approbation, and instantly forwarded to M. de Seelen. The general in forming it had relied much on the address and intrepidity of his captain: the event shewed his expectations not to have been ill founded; M. de Heyden was rescued in the night that preceded the very day on which he had been condemned to suffer.

The prison in which he was confined was a lofty tower situated on the bank of the Danube, He was kept under the guard of a sergeant, a corporal, and eighteen grenadiers, who relieved each other in parties of five; two of whom stood sentinel before his door, one at the top of the staircase, one at the bottom, and the fifth in the yard under the prisoner's window. At night the latter sentinel quitted his post, and stood at an open window that overlooked the whole court, the avenues to which were carefully made secure. These measures, together with the difficulty of bribing the guards, who were relieved every hour, seemed to render the deliverance of the unfortunate officer extremely improbable, if not impracticable.

At length, however, M. de Seelen was able to gain over a lieutenant of the town, a man indeed of shallow capacity, but zealous in the cause he had undertaken, and whose agency we shall find was not unsuccessfully employed. This person was afterwards well received in the Prussian dominions and properly provided for by the king.

Soon after M. de Seelen's arrival at Ulm, he had found means of apprising his brother-officer of the object of his mission, and had likewise been able to convey to him a bottle of *aqua fortis* for the purpose of corroding the bars of his window. He had also procured an impression in wax of the key of the prison, and a locksmith of Nuremburg had made one after that model. His hussars had prepared a ladder of ropes, and a waterman was engaged to remain at hand with a boat ready to receive M. de Heyden and to convey him to a spot where a carriage would be waiting for him. M. de Seelen had likewise made himself acquainted with the ground that immediately surrounded the prison, as well as with the streets and roads which were to be taken in the intended escape.

After having agreed upon the night and the hour, he repaired to the prison. Everything went on as he could wish. The gate was opened, the ladder fixed, the *aqua fortis* had eat away the bars; but the moment after M. de Heyden had removed them and put his foot upon the ladder, the sentinel at the adjacent window heard a noise, and, notwithstanding the darkness of the night, discovered people in motion in the court. He fired his piece, and instead of hitting M. de Seelen, the ball went through a window and killed a woman as she lay in her bed.

Before the report had drawn the sentinels together, the two Prussians had made their escape and were arrived on the bank of the Danube. But what must have been their surprise when neither boat nor waterman was to be found! The firing of the gun having spread an alarm, the man had rowed across the river. Happily, M. de Seelen preserved his presence of mind, and taking advantage of the general confusion which now prevailed in that quarter, he conveyed the lieutenant in safety to his own house, and by means of a bribe was enabled to lodge him with a poor labourer before break of day.

The magistrates gave immediate orders for the pursuit of the fugitive, and after the most diligent inquiries in the environs of the place and along the highways, they concluded he was still in the city, from whence they were persuaded he would not be able to escape. Every precaution was now taken to prevent it; the houses were searched, the gates strictly watched; every carriage was examined, and every waggon that went out of the town was unloaded: yet no discovery was made. M. de Seelen had now taken his friend under his own roof, and when he perceived that attempts were made to examine his apartments, he assumed so lofty an air, that the magistrates did not think fit to persist in their intentions.

A trifling incident, however, had nearly betrayed the whole business. In the hurry of escaping from the prison, the party had forgotten to take down the ladder of ropes. A cordmaker of the town having examined it, recognised the materials, and recollected that he had sold them to the servants of the foreign gentleman. He made his report accordingly; but the foresight of M. de Seelen had already averted the blow, by sending away such of his attendants as had been at all concerned in the enterprise, and by taking occasion to complain in different companies that some of his domestics had deserted him. Nothing farther transpired, and every suspicion at length died away.

He continued without much difficulty to conceal M. de Heyden in various places till a carriage which he had ordered to be made at Nuremberg arrived, and in which a hollow space had been contrived, sufficiently large to contain the prisoner at his ease. Everything being in readiness, M. de Seelen at length set off with his friend. When he came to the first village, he left the highroad: and it was well that he did so; for the magistrates having somehow got intimation of the affair, ordered the carriage to be pursued. M. de Seelen, however, soon gained the frontiers, and arriving safe on Prussian territory, he had soon the happiness of presenting his brother-officer, to the king.

His Majesty was highly delighted on seeing him, and received M. de Seelen in the most gracious manner. "You have distinguished yourself in a brilliant manner," said the king: and these words proved the foundation of his future fortune. The heavy expenses of the enterprise were not indeed fully repaid him; but during the seven year's war his advancement was rapid; the royal bounties were multiplied upon him, and extended even to his family after his glorious and untimely death.

Zieten shared the triumph of his friend. He had now given the king a new proof of the capacity and courage which distinguished his regiment, and rendered it capable of everything. It was hoped that this happy event would change the sentiments of His Majesty, and recall his former confidence in his general; but the moment of reconciliation was not yet arrived.

As the disgrace into which Zieten had fallen had not influenced either his public or military conduct, so neither did it at all affect the tenor of his domestic life, nor create that irritability of temper which renders those the victims of one's vexations, whose task it is but to soften or at most to share them. Too fond of his wife to allow himself to afflict her by the recital of his wrongs, he was always careful to conceal them in his own breast. His silence, however, was not the result of gloomy sorrow, which is even more distressing to love and friendship than the communications of the heart under the keenest anguish of affliction.

In the bosom of his family, he appeared serene and happy. He was ever desirous of seeing those about him cheerful and content: he would partake in the diversions of his daughter and her playmates, and sometimes seem the happiest person of the whole group. Master of his own feelings, he imagined they escaped the scrutiny of a tender wife. If indeed he had wished to deceive her, it was for the sake of her own quiet: but she was not deceived; some officious friends had from time to time given her information of everything that had happened to him. The more calm her husband outwardly appeared, the more she imagined him to be inwardly perturbated; and having less strength of mind than he, she would sometimes venture to break a silence that gave her so much pain, in order to ask him questions and to communicate her fears to him.

On such occasions Zieten with all the delicacy of an affectionate husband would either make a short reply, or smile and give the conversation a new turn. "Everything will go on well," he would say; "things will mend; you have nothing to fear; place your whole confidence in me." This was all she could draw from him; and the more she pressed him for further explanation, the more obstinately he persisted in his silence.

One day when his friends had advised Mad. de Zieten to expostulate with her husband on the too great indifference with which he treated the intrigues of his enemies, she observed, among other things, that affairs took a very serious turn, and that if the king dismissed him from his service their situation would become intolerable, as their only asylum would be the Wüstrau estate, which would then belong less to him than to his creditors. Zieten without interrupting her discourse, contemplated with a serene countenance her eyes overflowing with tears, and the more violent her affliction grew, the calmer he himself became; till at length with a smile which inspired confidence, he answered in the following words from holy writ:

*If thou doubtest in this manner, thou shalt never behold the promised land.*

New misfortunes, however, were yet in store for him, and the hand of providence seemed to inflict the blow. Too unmindful perhaps of the machinations of his enemies and the displeasure of his sovereign, he had still severer trials to undergo. He lost his only son, in the year 1751. who died of the smallpox in the ninth year of his age. With him the hopes of perpetuating his name seemed to be at an end: he was the favourite of his father, and deservedly so: nevertheless, the tender and disconsolate parent bore the loss of him without murmuring; and, hanging over the dead body, he endeavoured to comfort his wife in the language of Christian resignation; "Such was the will of good," he exclaimed, "may his name be praised, and his holy will be done."

This misfortune was succeeded by a greater, in the loss of the mother; who, in the year 1756, was snatched away from her husband's arms. Her death, which was occasioned by an inflammation of the lungs, was preceded by a series of excruciating pain. With her Zieten had enjoyed nineteen years of domestic happiness, yet at this trying moment his great mind did not sink under the pressure of affliction: he checked its effusions, and came off conqueror. Inseparable from his dying wife, continually at her bedside and witness to all her sufferings and to the last struggle that put an end to them, he maintained that calm firmness, that submissive resignation which bespeaks a perfect command of soul, which betokens and inspires courage, and imparts consolation and fortitude.

His sister-in-law partook with him in the cares of which the dying person stood in need, and from him she learnt to dry her tears and to moderate her grief. She heard him utter these words over the cold remains of the deceased;

> I have lost much;—I have lost everything; beauty, virtue, good sense, prudence, piety; for these she all possessed: the almighty, however, has taken her from me.

He then stopped while her sister gave free course to her tears; and after a short and solemn pause, he gave her his hand, and casting a consoling look at her, he said with a smile of resignation, "Come, let us go downstairs; our dinner waits for us."

This firmness of character did not result from coldness or insensibility of heart; it arose from the various trials, the sad reverses of fortune which he had experienced and the religions sentiments which he had adopted. In proof of this we need only mention the tender part he always took in the misfortunes of his friends, in the general sufferings of his fellow-creatures, and the sacrifices he was ever making to alleviate them. That stoical firmness, with which he was enabled to repel the strokes of fortune, he was far from requiring from others; on the contrary, he was ever ready to honour and applaud sensibility of disposition wherever he perceived it.

The writer of these pages borrows at the present moment from hand of gratitude the pencil she is making use of to delineate the picture of truth. On many occasions, during the trials of a perturbated life, she has experienced at his hands that indulgent goodness, that tender and compassionate solicitude which he was always ready to administer to timid and desponding affliction.

The last, the most severe blow that fate had in store for Zieten was now struck. After the death of his wife, fortune seemed weary of persecuting him; or rather the great disposer of the destiny of man, having weighed him in the balance, and being satisfied with the wisdom, the courage, the piety of which he had given such manifold proof, was pleased to reward his merit. Zieten, to use his own expression, after having wandered seven long years in a dreary and barren wilderness, had now arrived at the end of his painful pilgrimage. The prediction he had made to his lady was at length accomplished. She alas! did not live long enough to enjoy that happy period; she did not enter with him into the land of promise.

Zieten had not waited till the death of his lady ere he formed and matured his plan of retiring from the busier scenes of life. From the year 1755, on the approach of the political troubles in which he foresaw the country would be involved, he had taken the resolution to be no longer the sport of his enemies. On one hand, he was too conscious of his own desert not to be fully persuaded that at the moment of explosion the king would make advances to him and call for the succour of his arm: on the other hand, he knew mankind sufficiently to be well aware that the royal favour would be only in part restored to him; that he should be exposed to the caprice of his enemies, and, by acting under their control, he should but imperfectly acquit himself of his duty to his prince and his country.

He wished either to be free, or to quit the service: he was desirous that the bands that connected him with Frederick should either be renewed, or entirely broken. Continual vexation had undermined his constitution;—yet in any other circumstances the prospect of war would have alone sufficed to restore him to health. At this time that prospect accelerated the declaration, he made of the valetudinary state of it, and the desire he had to obtain his discharge.

This information made a deep impression upon the mind of the king. The veil dropped from before his eyes, the charm was broken, and he felt his heart resume its former warmth. He had withdrawn himself by slow degrees from Zieten, and he returned to him at a single step. To have forgotten the servicer, of his general, he must have made many a painful effort upon himself; a single moment was sufficient to recall them to his memory. The consideration of the war, together with the apprehensions of losing one of his best officers, new restored the king to himself, and to Zieten. The monarch assumed a new kind of behaviour, made every possible advance, and did not conceive he lowered his dignity by holding out his hand to the man whom he had for so long a time repulsed.

He perhaps flattered himself that a single step would be sufficient to gain his point. The smile of a monarch commonly can work miracles: but Zieten was not one of those whom a word or a look could subdue. The more assiduously the king made inquiry after his health, the worse his disorder became; the more probable the breaking out of the war appeared, the slower was Zieten's recovery. The king at length began to perceive that by such measures he should gain nothing, and had recourse to others more likely indeed to succeed, had he employed any other person to sound the general than his inveterate enemy.

This person, who had no mean opinion of his own abilities, officiously undertook the commission. He called upon Zieten, and in the course of conversation asked him, as if by mere accident, what he intended to do in case a war should break out; he likewise made particular inquiry into the state of his healthy and hoped it would not prevent his joining the army.

Zieten was not unprepared for the visit; he suspected the object of it, and received the royal emissary with suitable dignity and caution. He replied:

> It is absolutely impossible for me to undertake the campaign. Since I lost the king's favour, I have been a continual prey to vexations which have impaired my health and depressed my

courage. I cannot see in what manner I can be useful. I can neither change my tactics nor my conduct: unfortunately, both have displeased the king and involved me in disgrace. With principles like mine it is impossible to shift: I shall be an encumbrance to the army, a mere machine without spring or motion.

The emissary urged everything that he could suggest by way of counteracting this firm and precise declaration, and, on pretence of the warm interest he took in the general's welfare, he began to insinuate with all the art of a courtier, that it would cost him nothing to be re-instated in the good graces of the monarch, that a single word would remove every obstacle in his way. Zieten, however, would not accept a pardon from the king: it was justice not pardon that he looked for at his hands; nor could he condescend to owe that justice to the intercession of an enemy. He therefore remained firm in his purpose. Often too his keen and deliberate replies disconcerted the negotiator; often was the latter made to blush by the indirect and merited reproaches which were glanced at him, as well as overawed by a look of superiority that occasionally animated the countenance of the general.

At length, turning his own arms against him, Zieten assumed for a moment the language of friendship and confidence, and earnestly entreated him to use all his influence with the king to obtain the discharge he so much wished for. This last stroke drove the adversary from the field of battle; he had been confident of success, and he now felt himself ashamed to make his report to the king.

Frederick had the return of Zieten too much at heart not to determine upon making another attempt. What had been refused to the favourite, might, he conceived, be granted to the monarch; the subject, he hoped, might yield to the solicitation of his master. He therefore resolved to call himself upon Zieten, and alone.

Everything depended upon this critical moment. A yes or a no was to decide the general's fate: whether he was to give himself up to his country, or to pass the rest of his days in inglorious ease, was now to be determined. The result was happy. Zieten, his future exploits, his glory, were all preserved, and secured for the king and for Prussia.

Frederick had hoped that his irresistible eloquence would have proved a sufficient cure for the general's assumed indisposition, and he at first attempted to make him acknowledge his faults, and was desirous to persuade him, that he himself had been the sole cause of the misunderstanding which had so long subsisted between them. He closed his harangue with a promise of forgetting everything that had passed, and held out his hand in token of reconciliation.

He thought, he had done all that was necessary to do; and indeed, he had done much for a prince like Frederick the Great. But he went too far with Zieten when he required him to take upon himself the whole of the blame, to acknowledge faults of which he had not been guilty, and negligences which he had not fallen into, and to consider as a favour the recovery of the good graces of his sovereign. The wrongs of which Zieten had to complain were too deeply rooted in his memory. In the struggle that was necessary to enable him to tear himself from his king and his country, his feelings had been too deeply wounded to admit of an easy cure. He listened in profound silence to the representations of the monarch, but he heard them without yielding himself up to them, and the moment of reconciliation began to appear more distant than ever, when the good genius of Prussia prompted the king with the following words:

No; it cannot be possible that Zieten, my faithful general, on the approach of a perilous war, should abandon his king and his country, whose confidence he so fully possesses!

These few words triumphed over the firmness of our hero and found the way to his heart. He threw himself at the monarch's feet and vowed to shed the last drop of his blood in his service.

After this declaration he laid aside all further reserve, and confessed the painfulness of the struggles he had undergone to suppress his sentiments of patriotism, and which he would have been utterly unable to suppress had he not been convinced, that deprived of his master's confidence, he was nothing, and, that possessed of it, he was equal to everything.

He added, with a frankness worthy of his character and of him to whom he was addressing himself, that the persons who had injured him in the esteem of his beloved sovereign were not unknown to him; that he had marked the progressive measures they had taken to bring about his ruin; that those persons persecuted him out of mere envy; that he despised them too much to fear them, or to apprehend that they should succeed a second time in depriving him of the royal favour; that, in truth, the vexations he had suffered had considerably impaired his health, yet he should not on that account refrain from joining the army and partaking with the meanest soldier in the toils and dangers of war and the contest for victory or death. This sincere declaration touched the monarch's heart, who in order to seal that generous union, which death was only to dissolve, embraced his general with the tenderest effusion of friendship.

Zieten having from this moment recovered his native energy of mind and all the vigour of youth, was eager to begin that celebrated war, in which, for the space of seven years, both himself and his regiment were destined to display those proofs of ability, which, during as many years of peace, his enemies had not allowed them to possess. The king raised him to the rank of lieutenant-general before the opening of the campaign: his commission is dated August the 12th, 1756. The campaign at length opened. The king put himself at the head of his army, and Zieten accompanied him at the head of his own regiment. The eyes of all Prussia were fixed upon them, and their past exploits were considered as a sufficient earnest of future victories!

The interminable war which threatened the Prussian empire with devastation and rain, and in which, notwithstanding the apparent doubtfulness of its issue, Frederick was inevitably involved, began in the month of August, 1756; a short time after his reconciliation with Zieten.

The enemies of Prussia, having entered into secret alliances, had already meditated its destruction. The recovery of Silesia, in favour of the house of Austria, was not the sole object of the league; their aim was to palsy a political body which the creative genius of its sovereign had indued with such energy as to excite perpetual jealousy and alarm.

Frederick endeavoured to elude the danger with which he was menaced by striking the first blow. He collected an army, and before the powers of Europe were at all aware of his intentions, he entered Saxony; occupied the city of Dresden, and blocked up the camp of Pirna; he then marched with a body of choice troops into Bohemia; beat Marshal Brown at Lowositz; made a whole army, prisoners of war, (at Pirna, the 14th of October); and finally established his winter-quarters in Saxony.

While these events were succeeding each other with astonishing rapidity, the Prussian generals, engaged in the blockade of Pirna, had recourse to such measures as were necessary for the purpose of cutting off communications; and Zieten was of the number of those who were employed in that task.

With the first battalion of his regiment, he had joined the column under the command of Duke Ferdinand of Brunswick, while the second had reinforced the column which the king headed in person. The prince's first rendezvous was at Halle, and Aschersleben; from whence Zieten had, on the 29th of August, led three battalions and ten squadrons through Weissenfels, Zeiz, and Altenbourg, as far as Freybourg, the second place of rendezvous. After this, being charged with the command of the advanced-guard, he continually preceded the army till the duke formed his camp between Cotta and Dohna, opposite to Pirna. The other columns which arrived at the same time had taken those advantageous positions which decided the fate of Saxony.

Upon the dislocation of the army, Zieten was cantoned in the neighbourhood of Zwickaw, on the frontiers of Bohemia. He had six battalions and twenty squadrons under his command. His winter-quarters were not disturbed, and he availed himself of that interval of quiet to exercise his troops, and to familiarize them anew with the dangers and toils of war.

At the opening of the ensuing campaign, the king, after having concentrated the cantonments, distributed his army into three different bodies; that in which Zieten served was commanded by Prince Maurice of Dessau, who after several feint movements for the purpose of distracting the attention of the enemy, penetrated into Bohemia over the Bassberg; and having marched through Commotaw and Brix, joined the king at Linnai (on the 21st of April, 1758).

Zieten commanded the advanced-guard of the prince: he had likewise the command of that of the king with a more considerable body of men. On his arrival at Linnai, he was invested with the order of the black eagle.

After having collected all his columns, the king began to march, and advanced towards Prague with all possible expedition. The army of Count Brown lay before him, and several formidable detachments hovered about his flanks. Zieten was chosen to clear the route and remove every obstacle; and he acquitted himself to the entire satisfaction of the king.

It would be superfluous to make a journal of this march, and to enter into the detail of each assault. Not a day passed without an encounter, a victory, and the acquisition of prisoners. The general took possession of the magazines of Martinowes, Commotiz, and Budin. On a reconnoitring-party at Wellwarn, his regiment had the honour to have the king at their head. Count Brown having broke up his camp in order to fall back upon Prague, Zieten made an attack upon his rear-guard, and took three hundred prisoners.

During this march, and in every encounter that attended it, Zieten was accompanied by a pupil of distinguished ardour and enterprise. This was the famous Seidlitz, at that time a colonel in a regiment of *cuirassiers*, with which he had obtained the king's permission to join the advanced-guard, in order to form himself in that school. The pupil did great credit to his master, and the king had no occasion to regret his having given consent to this military novelty.

Events of higher importance were soon to succeed the foregoing transactions.

The king's army arrived on the banks of the Muldaw to operate a junction with that under the command of Marshal de Schwerin. The pontons were laid, and the troops had already begun to pass the river (at Sela); when the king received the disagreeable information, that the marshal would not be at the place of rendezvous before the following day. This disappointment rendered his situation extremely critical. In face of a hostile army of superior force, encamped under the cannon of Prague, and who, had they been duly apprized by their scouts, might have charged the Prussians with their cavalry on the bank of the river; he had nevertheless the art to conceal his embarrassment from the greater part of his generals. He had courage enough to brave the danger, and address sufficient to triumph over it.

Zieten was one of the small number of those to whom he imparted the secret, and of whom he made use to execute his plan, and to secure its success, Although he did not find the succour he had expected on the other side of the Muldaw, he refrained from giving any interruption to the passage of the troops; but in order to remain undiscovered as long as possible, he caused them to file over a single bridge; a measure which considerably retarded the march. As fast as they arrived on the other side, they encamped in the most silent manner between Trachirn and Czisnitz. Zieten was charged to cover the formation of this hasty camp, to guard the avenues to it, and to prevent anything from transpiring which might betray the arrival of the Prussians and render them liable to a surprise.

It cannot be decided whether it was to mere chance, or to the prudence of his general, that the king was indebted for the happy issue of this critical night. All that we are able to say is, that the enemy availed themselves of none of the advantages which their position might have afforded them; a circumstance either owing to their not being prepared to make an attack, or to the precautions Zieten had taken to prevent any deserter from carrying them an account of the king's embarrassment. The passage of the river and the formation of the camp could not, however, be wholly unknown to the Austrians, as from this camp their left wing was distinctly observed.

In the meanwhile, Count de Schwerin continued marching during the whole night, and his junction with the king took place on the 6th of May, at five o'clock in the morning. At the same time, and in consequence of a similar operation, the armies of Prince Charles and Marshal Brown effected a junction under the command of the former. The king was apprised that, besides these two corps, a third, commanded by Marshal Daun, was in full march, and had been reinforced on the route by that of Serbelloni and several others. This news decided the part he had to act: there was no time to be lost; the union of all these forces would have given the enemy a superiority which it would have been vain to resist.

On the 6th of May, immediately upon the arrival of Schwerin, the king fought the famous Battle of Prague, and gained a victory at the expense of slaughtered thousands.

After having reconnoitred the enemy's camp with Marshal Schwerin, and finding it advantageously situated upon the heights, and covered by swampy ground, he made the following disposition.

With the left wing, which the marshal commanded, that general was directed to attack and turn the right wing of the imperialists; their left wing being inaccessible. The king was to lead on the centre. His right wing, without acting on the offensive, was ordered to support the left. Zieten had the command of the corps of reserve, composed of ten squadrons of dragoons and twenty of hussars. He was enjoined to make no movement, unless on the express order of His Majesty.

The king considered his plan as infallible: Zieten, however, was less sanguine in his expectations, and took his precautions accordingly. He was sensible of the difficulties arising from the ground on which the left wing had to manoeuvre; he knew that the marshal had two dikes to pass before he could form his line, and, that during its formation, his flanks would lie uncovered. The danger appeared so imminent that he could not allow himself to remain an inactive spectator; and after many struggles with himself, after having duly considered both sides of the question and compared the orders of the king with the exigency of the moment, he determined upon quitting his post, yet without leaving it in a defenceless condition; and having intrusted General de Werner with the command of the corps of reserve, he took with him ten squadrons of dragoons, and stationed them along the dikes at the entrance of the defiles, wherever they might serve to cover the march of the infantry. Having made this disposition, he moved forward to assist at the attack.

What Zieten had apprehended and foreseen now took place. The marshy and broken ground, equally advantageous to the enemy as disfavourable to the Prussians, changed the attack into a flight. The heights before them, the swamps on their flanks, and the defiles and dikes in their rear, alike contributed to hem them in; and both cavalry and infantry seemed to be on the verge of destruction. Zieten immediately returned to the dikes, where he had posted his dragoons in defence of the outlets; and sent word to General de Werner to join him instantly, and to lengthen his line as much as possible in order to awe the enemy.

Without this reinforcement the left wing could not have been saved. The cavalry had charged several times, and had even broken that of the enemy; but after having lost the brave Prince of Schönaich, who was at their head, and being repulsed, turned, and put to flight, they uncovered the flank of the infantry, and left it entirely without defence. The honour of repairing this disaster was reserved for Zieten.

The Prussian infantry, who had been engaged in the pursuit of the hostile grenadiers, retreated in great disorder towards the dike of Dubatsch; and the cavalry being closely pressed by the enemy, took the road to the dike of Untermichelop. In vain the generals and all the officers endeavoured to stop the fugitives. Zieten, however, at length was able to check the infantry by drawing out a party of his dragoons in their way; and, accompanied by the rest, he threw himself before the last-mentioned dike at the instant in which the routed cavalry arrived there.

This moment proved a decisive one. He not only prevented, the fugitives from passing the dike; he was even able to rally, and inspire them with new courage. He addressed them in a calm and resolute manner, exhorted them to follow his advice, to form themselves in a line on either side of the dike; and after resting themselves a while till a reinforcement should arrive, to return to the charge and vanquish the enemy. He concluded with promising them a certain victory.

With extreme difficulty he prevailed on them to listen to his advice. A panic terror had seized upon the cavalry; and in spite of the representations of Zieten and the efforts of his dragoons, they were on the point of forcing a passage. General de Wobersnow, *aide-de-camp* to the king, who arrived on the spot during these transactions, recommended violent measures, advised Zieten to stop the fugitives by force, and to cut down some of them by way of example. Zieten, whom experience had taught to preserve his temper on the most trying occasions, begged to be allowed to proceed in his own way, and urged the expediency of waiting the arrival of succour. He promised with apparent confidence what he could only feebly hope for; as it was possible that the king might have given General de Werner orders different from those which he himself had issued.

In the meanwhile, a long cloud of dust began to arise; and, drawing near, soon exhibited a party of hussars hastening to the relief of their comrades.

Zieten pointed to them at a distance, increased their number in order to hearten his troops, and made his disposition while they were advancing. Upon the dike he placed alternately his dragoons and the hussars M. de Werner had just joined him with; and behind them, he collected and formed the routed cavalry to compose, in their turn, the corps of reserve and cover the attack.

After having formed the two lines, Zieten called the generals and principal officers about him, and addressed them in these terms.

> Gentlemen! The defeat of our comrades is a very disastrous event. Be it our task to repair the mischief, and secure a victory. To this end I shall have recourse to the following disposition.
> As soon as the fugitives are rallied behind us, General de Werner, who commands the left, will fall upon the enemy's right, and turn it. With the right wing I shall myself attack the cavalry that are in pursuit of our men. I shall rout them, make good my way to the infantry, and take the battery on the right. The rest of the cavalry will follow, one regiment after another, at equal intervals, and support us. As soon as we are in motion, the drums with beat the march.

After having pronounced these words in a loud and resolute tone of voice, he drew his sabre, and putting himself at the head of the troops, cried out, "March!" and ordering the trumpets to sound a charge, he cast his eyes along the whole line, and marked the ardour which glowed in the countenance of every soldier.

Fortune proved favourable to courage. With a handful of men, General de Warnery kept Haddick, the Austrian general, in awe, and hindered him from moving from the right and taking the Prussians in flank. The rest of the hostile cavalry had disbanded in pursuit of the Prussians: they acted without concert, and fell into disorder at the sight of the fresh troops who were advancing upon them; and who appeared more numerous and more formidable than they were in fact, on account of the clouds of dust in which they were enveloped. The Austrians now turned their backs and endeavoured to rally and form their broken regiments; but Zieten did not give them time to effect their purpose; he broke their ranks, put them to flight, and pursued them briskly.

The first he came up to was a regiment of *cuirassiers*: their commander cried out to the hussars, at the distance of fifty paces; "What! Are you all mad? Don't you see you are going to charge a regiment of the line?" The hussars made no reply; but falling upon them, they quickly overcame, and dispersed them. They overtook all the rest, whom they treated in like manner; and the dragoons of Schmettau supported the hussars of Zieten so effectually, that in this quarter the victory of the Prussians seemed complete. They performed prodigies of valour, carried away colours, standards; braved the fire of the batteries, and reduced them to silence.

While victory was declaring in favour of the Prussians; and the very regiments, who had at first turned their backs to the enemy, overwhelmed with shame and burning with emulation, were coming back to the charge to recover their lost honour; General de Werner, after, having turned the Austrians and joined M. de Warnery, had in concert with him fallen upon General de Haddick, and driven him upon the infantry of the right wing. The infantry gave way, the rout became general; Zieten cut the enemy off from Prague, and the victors took possession of the camp of the conquered.

While the well-timed application of the corps of reserve and the prompt and masterly manoeuvres of Zieten were securing success, the Prussian infantry were likewise acquitting themselves in the most brilliant manner. The colours, with which the immortal Schwerin had thrown himself into the midst of the enemy, had inspired his troops with resistless ardour. Thousands of arms were lifted up to avenge his death; and the heaps of slain bore ample testimony to the efficacy of their strokes. Zieten covered their flank, and turned that of the enemy; and, in the meanwhile, the infantry pressing forward, took possession of the field of battle.

Of the exploits which signalised the right wing and the centre, and the names of the heroes of the day, we shall say nothing, as it does not immediately belong to our subject. History has celebrated those of Schwerin, Henry, Ferdinand, Bevern: the like justice is due to others, and among that number is Zieten.

The laurels acquired by the Prussians were dearly won. The number of killed and wounded, on either side, amounted to twenty-five thousand. (In his *Posthumous Works*, the king makes the loss, on the side of the Austrians, to be 24,000 men, and on his own, 18,000.) In the midst of his triumphs, Frederick bewailed the death of his brave soldiers, and especially that of Schwerin. ("He alone was worth ten thousand men." *Seven Years' War*.) The Austrians testified the like regret for the loss of Marshal Brown, who had been mortally wounded in the battle.

The Prince of Lorrain threw himself into Prague with forty thousand of the routed army. The king determined to shut him up in that place, and took his measures accordingly. The right wing of the Austrians being cut off from Prague, they advanced further into Bohemia; still approaching the Sassawe, and Marshal Daun who had already arrived at Böhmisch-Brodt. Zieten having received orders to watch that general's motions, put himself, on the 9th of May, at the head of forty squadrons for that purpose.

Having marched towards Brandeis and Böhmisch-Brodt, he was convinced that Marshal Daun had a very considerable force with him; and which, he learnt, would soon be increased by the right wing that had been touted before Prague. His report to the king was conformable to that of General de, Manstein and Colonel de Puttkammer, who had likewise been sent to observe the enemy on the banks of the Sassawe.

In order to prevent Marshal Daun from advancing to the relief of Prague, the reduction of which by famine was shortly expected, it was necessary to oppose him with a stronger body of men,

On the 10th of May, eighteen battalions and fifteen squadrons were detached against him, under the command of the Duke of Bevern. This corps, joined to those of Zieten, Manstein, and Puttkammer, amounted to about twenty-two thousand men and they had an army to cope with, which at first was forty, and afterwards sixty thousand strong.

Notwithstanding this great disproportion of numbers, Marshal Daun thought fit to withdraw himself from the Duke of Bevern, and to march as far as Collin, Kuttenberg, and Haber. The duke camped at the first of those places; where he took possession of a magazine belonging to the enemy; he likewise detached Zieten to seize upon those of Suchdol, which were very considerable. The general put himself at the head of four battalions and eleven hundred horse; as the enemy had reinforced the post on account of its great importance in furnishing them with supplies of meal, Zieten dislodged the Cravats (Croats), who defended the heights, took a great number of them prisoners, and forced the garrison to abandon the town and magazines with very considerable loss. He afterwards made himself master of those of Kuttenberg and Neuhoff.

The duke, who followed him at no great distance, never failed to form his camp on the spot which the marshal had just occupied.

The latter had retreated as far as Haber; and although he must have had his reasons for not waiting for an enemy so inferior in force, he was nevertheless obliged to manoeuvre at the expense of his magazines; and from the 10th of May to the 11th of June, he acted a secondary part only; while the duke was covering the blockade of Prague, and Zieten (who had the corps of Nadasty to contend with) was incessantly doing him mischief.

The face of affairs changed, however, on the 18th. The right wing of the Prince of Lorrain's routed army had joined Marshal Daun, and the latter was now two thirds stronger than the duke. Strength inspires bravery; the soldiers were impatient for the onsets and the general soon availed himself of their ardour.

Zieten was the first who perceived an extraordinary movement in the hostile army. A well-timed reconnoitring-party, which with great difficulty he had prevailed on the duke to allow him to make on the 15th, had afforded him very convincing proof of that circumstance. His plan was to gain the heights of Maleschaw, from whence he would be enabled to observe the enemy. The imperialists who occupied this eminence, had filled the valley and the forests that surrounded it, with light cavalry; and, while Zieten's hussars were employed in dislodging them and clearing the circumjacent country, he himself led on his infantry to the hill; where he put a detachment of grenadiers to flight. When he arrived on the summit, he discovered what he had already apprehended; the army of the marshal lay before him; he saw the danger which threatened that of the duke, and he hastened to apprise him of it.

Marshal Daun had conducted his plan with uncommon art. In order to elude the duke, he caused his centre and his right wing to remain stationary, while the left was marching on under cover of the forests that overspread the country. This secret march could only be perceived from the heights of Maleschaw which the enemy had occupied; and without the assistance of Zieten, the duke's right wing must have been attacked, turned; and himself cut off from Collin. Thus was the plan detected; and, if not frustrated, was at least crossed, and its execution repressed. Zieten had time to inform the duke of his discovery; and the duke to take his measures in consequence.

His army was too weak to make effectual resistance, and he was obliged to fall back upon Collin. He broke up his camp; and, beginning his march, he gained the defiles which it was necessary should lie between the enemy and himself, and waited for them in the plain, where he had taken a secure and formidable position. During this time, Zieten was engaged in an encounter with Nadasty,

He had attacked him with such vigour, that the Austrian partisan was unable to make further resistance. He pushed him upon the left of the infantry, and threw the infantry itself into disorder. By thus checking the enemy, Zieten had given his general time to pass the defiles and to range his troops in order of battle. The fine resistance made by the former, and the formidable attitude the duke was now in, induced the marshal to desist from his pursuit. He contented himself with firing a few cannon, which were duly returned him; and the Prussians made good their retreat to Collin in open daylight, and without any loss.

Zieten and his detachment were the last that arrived there; after having fought, as they retreated, till sunset, and encountered difficulties of every kind. His men had been under arms since four in the morning; they had begun with forming the advanced guard, and they finished by sustaining the rear. Impeded by the artillery and baggage waggons, which it was necessary to protect; checked by the defiles and inundations they had to pass, and by the Cravats (Croats), who had concealed themselves in the cornfields, and were incessantly harassing them; these brave warriors, worn out with fatigue, at length joined their comrades. The duke gratefully acknowledged the service that had been done him, and the whole army partook of his satisfaction. The main body, however, had the greater reason to be happy; for they had lost neither tent nor waggon; while Zieten's corps had severely suffered, though their loss has never been accurately estimated.

On the next day (the 14th of June) the duke quitted his position at Collin to join the king at Caurzim, who had arrived there from Prague with ten battalions and twenty squadrons. The duke's baggage could not follow him till the day after, on account of the badness of the roads and the defiles they had to pass. Zieten, who covered it, met with scarce any annoyance on the way; and the baggage arrived in safety at its destination.

The king was apprised by the duke of the approach of the marshal, the superiority of his forces, and the necessity of yielding to numbers. His Majesty seemed to give credit to the report, and even expressed his approbation of the brilliant retreat which his general had made. On the following day, he changed both his sentiments and his humour: he maintained that Daun had not advanced his army, that the duke had been deceived by the manoeuvres of Nadasty, and that he had done wrong to retrograde. That Frederick should give way to such erroneous conclusions is a matter of no small astonishment.

Yet it should be considered, that he had hitherto been favoured by fortune in the most extraordinary manner, and now began seriously to persuade himself of the feasibility of any measure his imagination could suggest. He had resolved to attack the marshal in a position which he considered, as a bad one; and, after having beaten him, to make the forty-thousand men, shut up in Prague, prisoners of war. Reason is often the dupe of inclination, and a monarch will always find a crowd of counsellors of the same opinion as himself. In vain did the duke urge the report of eyewitnesses, the depositions of prisoners, the evidence of deserters: some of these, His Majesty considered, would not speak the truth; others, he thought, were unacquainted with it: and, as for the prisoners, they either belonged to the corps of Nadasty, or formed a part of a feeble detachment which the marshal had sent out for the mere purpose of deluding the enemy.

In a word, the king persisted in his opinion; and, according to him, Marshal Daun was stationary in his camp at Golz-Jankaw; and the duke, Zieten, and all the generals, had been deceived by false appearances. Thus prepossessed, he treated them the next day with extreme coolness, and observed repeatedly to his suite, that Nadasty had thrown dust into the duke's eyes and deprived him of his sight. He treated General de Manstein and General de Finck with still great severity;—the first of whom belonged to the corps commanded by Zieten, and the second was the head of the duke's staff. He accused them openly of having made a retreat, which, according to his representations, was useless and precipitate: and what unhappily confirmed the king in his opinion, was the disappearance of the far greater part of Nadasty's troops who had followed the duke as far as Zusmuck.

It is not the business of these pages to examine how far this error might have contributed towards the check which the king's army experienced three days after: all we shall venture to say, is that Zieten foresaw that event and even predicted it. On the 15th, he declared on the parade with much agitation of mind, that he apprehended some great disaster; as the king, he lamented, would not credit either him or his brother-officers, or the reports of the advanced posts, and obstinately persevered in his incredulity.

While Marshal Daun was still in the neighbourhood of Collin, the king made preparations for marching to Kuttenberg, to turn his right wing at Golz-Jankaw, and force him to retreat. The routes were traced out, and the 16th of June was fixed upon for the march.

A party had been detached to reconnoitre the ground. M. de Belling and M. de Gaudi, having discovered with the naked eye the camp of Marshal Daun, from the top of the steeple of Oberkrut, and plainly perceived his three lines, his cavalry and infantry, made their report accordingly. The king received them ill, asserted and maintained the contrary; and holding a map in his hand, endeavoured to make them believe that what they had seen could have been nothing else than a body of partisans belonging to Nadasty's corps. The advanced-guards, however, having confirmed the news on the evening of the 15th, and declared to have seen a line of cavalry behind the village of Stropschutz, the king detached two battalions and a party of cavalry to keep a good watch during the night.

The next day the enemy having disappeared, the detachment returned to the camp. In the afternoon, Prince Maurice of Dessau arrived with a reinforcement: the king received him in a very gracious manner and said to him, "Daun, is still at Golz-Jankaw: I shall march to Janowitz and turn his left wing. Do not attempt to dissuade me from it, if you wish we should remain friends."

In the meantime, he arranged the order of battle and made dispositions for the march; which was now no longer intended for Janowitz, on account of the position of the corps which was erroneously taken for that of Nadasty. On the 17th, the army began their march, and moved towards Suchdol and Kuttenberg. When they arrived as far as the entrance of the defile of Stropschutz, it was no longer possible to doubt of the real state of the affair. The king discovered the army of Marshal Daun posted near Krichenaw, at the distance of half a German mile from him. The veil dropped from his eyes; he now saw what the duke, what Zieten and several other generals had vainly announced. The marshal had chosen the camp and the positions already stated: his attitude clearly shewed that he meant either to attack, or be himself attacked, and that there could be no question of any retreat.

The king sent for Prince Maurice and the duke, and shewed them the position of the enemy. The latter stung with indignation at the wrongs he had suffered for some days past, observed that he had been apprised of it the night before; that he had himself seen the hostile columns occupy the field; but considered it useless to communicate it, as His Majesty, he knew, still persisted in the idea that they belonged to the corps of Nadasty.

The king's astonishment was extreme. In his writings he speaks of the appearance of Marshal Daun as an event totally unlooked for.

★★★★★★★★★★

> The king was desirous of marching the army to Schwoischitz, the environs of which were susceptible of defence; but scarcely had the troops began to move, when Marshal Daun made his appearance, and began to form his lines near the above place. This movement on the part of the enemy, caused a necessary change in the disposition of the Prussians, and the army thereupon took another direction. *Seven Years' War.*

★★★★★★★★★★

This would not have surprised him, had he taken advantage, four days earlier, of the duke's retreat and of the motives which justified it.

We now come to the 18th of June, a day fatal to the Prussian arms; and whose issue depended on an unhappy concurrence of circumstances, which at the decisive moment, operated in their disfavour.

Zieten headed the cavalry of the left wing, which was destined to begin the attack. It consisted of one hundred squadrons, including a reserve of fifteen, commanded by Colonel de Seidlitz.

Marshal Daun judging from the movements of the Prussians that his right wing was menaced, ordered his heavy artillery to that quarter, with almost the whole of his cavalry, together with the cavalry of Nadasty's corps, that of the Saxons, and a strong detachment of infantry and Cravats (Croats). The latter, with the light troops, were posted in a plantation of oaks, between the outposts of Krezor and the corps of Nadasty. The cavalry had just joined the above, and extended as far as the line of the army.

The king's plan was, that Zieten should occupy the heights of Kurtlitz with sixty squadrons; that seven battalions, under the command of General de Hulsen, should accompany him to carry the advanced battery of Krzezor, and take possession of a village and a small wood in the neighbourhood; that, in the meantime, Zieten should amuse Nadasty and hinder him from falling upon the left flank of the army.

The king's aim was to attack and turn the enemy's right wing; and to effect this, his left wing was not to leave a vacuity of more than a thousand paces broad between its own line and the troops under the command of Hulsen; it was also to turn the village during the attack of Krzezor, to move to the left in order to sustain Hulsen, or to gain the wood which would serve as a prop to it.

Zieten having met with little resistance in his attempt to occupy the heights of Kurtlitz, formed, at the same time as General de Hulsen, for the attack of Krzezor, He left him thirty squadrons to cover his flank and rear, and marched with the other thirty against Nadasty.

Hulsen's attack was attended with such success, that, before the arrival of a reinforcement of three battalions, the battery of Krzezor was carried. In the meantime, the infantry on the left wing advanced in order, and Colonel de Seidlitz, at the head of the reserve, marched between Krzezor and the heights of Koller to form a junction with Zieten, who had drawn up his cavalry there in two lines. After having stationed the reserve in a third line, Zieten marched against Nadasty, who being posted behind Kurtlitz, was threatening the king's flank.

By an able manoeuvre, attended with a prompt and successful attack, Zieten threw that general into disorder, pursued, and cut him off from the rest of the cavalry. The Saxons rallied at some distance from thence: the light troops disbanded, and fled to Collin and Radowesnitz. Zieten began to pursue them; but perceiving that his men suffered considerably from the battery erected in the wood, he halted, and took his post along the brook of Kurtlitz. From thence he kept Nadasty's troops in awe, and hindered them from regaining their former position.

In the meanwhile, General de Hulsen had taken the wood by assault, and silenced the battery. Victory now appeared certain; but from this moment, every step the Prussians took tended to impede and frustrate it. One fault after another began to be committed in various points of the army. A general (M. de Manstein), who commanded the right wing, impelled by mistaken zeal, instead of supporting the left, and remaining in the line, made an inconsiderate attack which was attended with very unhappy consequences. The wood of Krzezor being but feebly occupied, the Austrians, who perceived this, retook it, and repaired the battery. Finally, a want of union between the king and Prince Maurice brought on the loss of the battle.

The king was desirous to form a line upon the heights of Krzezor: the prince who commanded the left wing, moved towards the wood, and caused his columns to advance. The first column, which General de Penavaire covered, had arrived at the foot of the heights of Brzissli, when the attack made by Hulsen began. The king at this instant ordered the troops to halt, and was inclined to take another direction; The prince, who foresaw the danger that must attend this change, opposed the measure strongly; and a dispute arose on the subject between these two commanders, of so violent a nature, that the king was at the point of putting an end to it in an unheard of manner. During this time the favourable moment was irrecoverably lost, and the enemy regained the wood and the battery.

It was necessary, whatever it might have cost, to have retaken them for the purpose of preserving a communication with the important post of Krzezor. This was neglected to be done, merely because the generals considered themselves bound to obey literally the orders of the king, and not to change their positions without his consent.

In this day of trouble and disunion, in which a spirit of giddiness and distraction seized the best of the generals, it is not unlikely that Zieten committed faults; and the hand which is tracing the history of his life, more for the instruction of the age than for the glory of his exploits, would not hesitate to insert them, if any authentic accounts could furnish her with materials.

**\*\*\*\*\*\*\*\*\***

On the contrary, the king in the *History of the Seven Years' War* speaks advantageously of the part which Zieten acted in the Battle of Collin. "M. de Zieten had orders to oppose M. de Nadasty with forty squadrons, to prevent him from harassing the Prussian infantry in their operations: the rest of the cavalry were placed in reserve behind the lines. M. de Zieten attacked Nadasty's corps, and totally routed them. He pursued him to Collin; by which means he was cut off from the Austrians, and during the whole day, was rendered unable to impede any of the king's enterprises."

**\*\*\*\*\*\*\*\*\***

We are assured by witnesses of undoubted credibility, that Zieten's advanced-guard, which was at last commanded by generals Seidlitz and Werner, remained masters of the field of battle, notwithstanding all the efforts of the corps of Nadasty to dislodge them. Supported by a succession of fresh troops, that general had made several fruitless attempts to force a passage: the brave Prussians repelled every attack, and drove the enemy as far as Collin and Radowesnitz. Zieten was no longer at their head. The king, in order to fill up the void spaces in his army, had sent to him for two regiments of cavalry. The general being misinformed by the *aide-de-camp*, understood that he was to head them in person. On his way, he found Prince Maurice employed in distributing cavalry in the various chasms of the lines to prevent the enemy from taking advantage of their broken state.

He thought it necessary to follow his example; and he began to throw his squadrons into the gaps, and upon the enemy who were threatening them; and who, besides the advantage of ground, had likewise that of a formidable and well-served battery. As this battery was raised on the top of a steep eminence, its fire was so destructive, that, in order to get rid of it, Prince Maurice had recourse to a desperate and doubtful expedient. He engaged Zieten to put himself at the head of four regiments of heavy horse, and to attempt to carry it. The attack was made, and resisted, with equal vigour.

The assailants fell back with great coolness and good order. Their intrepid general made another effort, and was well seconded by his men. The squadrons pressed forward, and the moment of victory was perhaps at hand, when Zieten was struck with a grape shot. He was seen to faint upon his horse, and was supposed to be killed; and the troops, who a moment before had braved the mouths of the cannon, were now struck with a panic, and betook themselves to flight. Zieten was on the point of being abandoned to the mercy of the enemy.

The ball had grazed his head, and carried away his cap; the contusion it made had deprived him of all sensation, and he would have fallen from his horse, and have been trampled upon by the fugitives or buried under heaps of dead bodies, had it not been for the timely assistance of a young officer in his suite. His name is entitled to a place in the history of the man he so essentially served. The person to whom Zieten owed his safety, was M. de Berge, a cornet of the regiment of Krockow.

He flew to the general, and supported him on the saddle; and while he was endeavouring to restore him to life, the general's horse was pierced by a new discharge of grape-shot. The cornet alighted before the horse fell, and taking advantage of the moment in which Zieten began to recover, he placed him upon his own; and covering his head with an old hat which had belonged to an Austrian musketeer, he delivered him up to the care of a brave and well-mounted *cuirassier* who conducted him to the equipages of Prince Maurice, where a surgeon fortunately was procured to dress his wound. The cornet had provided himself with another horse, and rejoined his corps.

Till Zieten was in a situation to be removed, he was placed in Prince Maurice's coach, where he remained till the unfortunate issue of the day. As soon as a retreat was decided upon, the prince came in person to consult him on the direction the cavalry had to take. The place of rendezvous for the Prussians was fixed at Nimbourg. A general despondency prevailed through the army. Zieten, however, who partook of it in common with the rest, was able to conceal it in the recesses of his heart. He had now seen the laurels of many a campaign tarnished for the first time; he wept over thirteen thousand men, either killed or wounded; and he recollected with the deepest regret, the victims of the Battle of Prague and of Maleschaw: and he considered too, that much blood was still likely to be shed.

Nor is it indeed possible, even at the present day, to reflect on these accumulated disasters without shuddering; and the commander, the best practised in resources, is at a loss to conceive how Frederick was enabled to sustain, and terminate with glory, this destructive war with such disproportionate forces, and to engage in such a number of battles, undismayed by the losses he met with in several of them. At Collin, where he had only the imperialists to contend with, he had no more than thirty thousand men to oppose to double that number. The disproportion became afterwards more considerable. As the Prussians grew weak, the number of their foes increased; and instead of those brave veterans at whose head the king had opened his first campaign, he could now bring forwards raw troops only; an army of strangers, equally devoid of courage and patriotism.

In such point of view, it is, that the reader will follow up the events of this war, and judge of the talents of those who conducted it, if he would accurately appreciate the merits both of the one and the other.

The imperialists did not pursue the Prussians to the place of their retreat. Zieten arrived in safety, in the prince's carriage, at Nimbourg, where several generals and officers of rank came to; visit him and to express the pleasure they felt, on his escape from the dangers which had recently threatened him. The general presented M. de Berge to all of them as his deliverer; and the brilliant action of the young cornet excited universal approbation, and gained every heart. The whole army was thankful to him for the preservation of Zieten. The general, in token of his gratitude, made him a present of the finest horse he possessed; and, about a year afterwards, he incorporated him into his own regiment.

M. de Berge served with reputation; acquired a name at the expense of his blood; and being raised to the rank of colonel of his regiment, he died during the campaign of the Rhine, under an operation to which he was obliged to submit, on account of an old wound he had received at the Battle of Hochkirchen.

The brave *cuirassier*, who had conveyed Zieten through so many dangers to a place of safety, was not unrewarded; although the secrecy, with which the general always did his acts of kindness, deprives us of the particulars of it.

While the king, after the Battle of Collin, was withdrawing his troops by degrees out of Bohemia, and Zieten was still at Nimbourg on account of his wound, the latter had the satisfaction to hear, that his regiment had distinguished themselves on many occasions. At one time, he was informed that the king who had put himself at their head, in order to disperse a body of light troops who impeded the communications, had taken or killed some hundreds of the enemy, and had sent an account of his success to Prince Maurice; at another, he was apprized, that one of his officers had received the order of military merit for the gallant manner in which he had just acquitted himself.

This officer is not unknown to the reader, who must recollect M. de Seelen, the deliverer of M. de Heyden at Ulm.

M. de Seelen, raised since that time to the rank of major, was now commanding a party of one hundred horse at Pascopol; and the grenadiers of Kleist were defending the defiles of Wellmina, to cover the king's camp which lay exposed upon the heights of Disnova. The latter had reason to expect to be molested there; and, in fact, Colonel de Laudon, whose military talents began at this time to grow formidable, determining at all events to carry that post, attacked it, and surrounded the grenadiers; who being formed in a square battalion, sustained the shock during the space of three hours. Major de Seelen being apprised of their perilous situation, poured down from Pascopol in full speed; and falling upon the enemy's rear, delivered his countrymen at the very moment in which they were going to surrender for want of ammunition.

At this period, so disastrous to, the Prussian arms, Zieten strenuously exerted himself to revive the drooping courage of his men. 4-S soon as he recovered, he resumed his former activity; and by throwing a veil over the past, and exhibiting the future in a more flattering point of view, he imparted new vigour to his troops. He remained with Prince Maurice at Nimbourg till the middle of July, and then joined the royal army, at the head of his regiment, together with a few battalions of infantry, and repassed the Elbe at Pirna on the 29th of July. On the 30th, the more effectually to cover the march, he made a reconnoitring party of considerable importance, as it enabled him to observe the position the Austrians had taken.

General de Beck had now secretly advanced along the banks of the Löbaw as far as Weissenberg: he was discovered, and his troops put to flight. The king followed him on the next day, in hopes of overtaking, and routing him; but the general was a whole night's march beforehand with his pursuers; having, immediately after his encounter with Zieten, directed his march towards the Prince of Lorrain's army, which the Battle of Collin had delivered, and which was engaged, in pursuing of that of the king. The pursuit of General de Beck enabled the Prussians to drive the enemy from the banks of the Queiss and the Neiss, and to re-establish a direct communication with Silesia.

About this time, the king being pressed on all sides, and obliged to encounter several enemies at once, marched into Franconia to attack the French and imperialists who were now threatening Magdebourg, Torgaw, and Dresden. On the S5th of August, he broke up his camp at Bornstädel; and dividing his army into two parts, put himself at the head of one of them, and left the other under the command of the Duke of Bevern. The division of the latter consisted of forty-seven battalions and one hundred and ten squadrons; forming together a body of about thirty thousand men. With these, the duke had an army to cope with more than ninety thousand strong, under the command of the Prince of Lorrain, with whom Marshal Daun had just made a junction.

Hitherto the hussars of Zieten had ever had the honour to accompany the king on his marches, and to form a part of the corps or columns His Majesty led in person. They were now, for the first time, deprived of the exercise of a duty which the very name of hussar lifeguards seems to imply an exclusive title to. Of this innovation M. de Winterfeld was the cause: he had prevailed on the king to allow him to join Zieten and his regiment to the corps he commanded, and which was destined to act in concert with the Duke of Bevern, while the king himself was marching into Franconia.

The duke had formed his camp at Görlitz, for the purpose of being at the same time near Silesia and the magazines of Dresden, from which latter place he drew his provisions. General de Winterfeld, with fifteen battalions, encamped at Mois, in the face of Nadasty's corps. This position secured such passages to Silesia as lay between the Neiss and the Queiss. His left wing was covered by the village of Holzberg and a hill which bore the same name. The general occupied this eminence with two battalions who entrenched themselves thereon; but having neglected to take the like precaution with regard to another hill, called the Galgenberg; Nadasty, who was desirous of gaining the Holzberg, soon availed himself of the error.

Reinforced by the corps of Ahremberg, he began his march on the 7th of September in the midst of a thick fog; and giving a false alarm to Zieten's advanced posts, he turned the Holzberg, occupied the Galgenberg, and erected a battery upon the latter, from whence he began to play upon the former eminence, and to annoy the regiment of Zieten. At eleven o'clock, forty companies of grenadiers attacked the two Prussian battalions, who, after having defended themselves with singular bravery, and repeatedly driven back the enemy, were obliged to yield to numbers, and make their retreat. The unevenness of the ground, and the swarms of Austrians that covered the country, prevented the hussars from retrieving the day; and all they were able to do, was to impede any pursuit. Major de Möhring, at the head of a few squadrons, threw himself between the dislodged battalions and the Austrians, and repulsed the latter with vigour.

During the engagement, M. de Winterfeld was at the headquarters at Görlitz. The moment he was apprised of the danger his troops were in, he hastened to the camp, and putting himself at the head of a few battalions, he marched to the Holzberg with a view of recovering it, or at least of avoiding the dishonour of giving it up without making any resistance. He therefore determined to attack the Austrians notwithstanding the superiority of their numbers and the advantageousness of their position.

Zieten strenuously endeavoured to persuade him from it. He not only was aware of the danger and impracticableness of the enterprise, but he was also sensible of the folly and absurdity of it. He conjured his general not to sacrifice a crowd of brave warriors to a false point of honour. His remonstrances were vain: Winterfeld still persisted in the resolution he had taken, and Zieten's prediction was unhappily accomplished. The Holzberg, though strewed with thousands of victims, was not retaken, and Winterfeld himself received a mortal wound in the action, of which he died the next day. A great number of officers, among whom were several of the first rank, were either killed or wounded. The number of dead, with which the field of battle was covered, was so great that it was necessary to conclude a truce of forty-eight hours for the purpose of interring them.

Zieten felt deeply for the misfortunes of the day, and for the indiscretion of the man who had occasioned them. He refrained, however, from having recourse to useless reproaches: he refrained even from seeing him, lest his presence should give him pain; and he waited till he was dead, before he applied to the duke for new orders.

What further evinces the inutility of this battle and the small importance of the recovery of the Holzberg, was the circumstance of Nadasty's having abandoned it of his own accord on the 7th of September, although he had paid so dearly for the acquisition of it two days before Winterfeld's corps had joined the army of the duke.

Notwithstanding the vicinity of a formidable army, and so superior in number, that prince remained unmolested in his camp at Görlitz till all his magazines were consumed; nor did he change the theatre of war before the arrival of the last convoy. As soon as the hour for the march was collected, he called in the detachments that covered the communications; and after having distributed nine days' provision, he marched, on the 10th, towards Silesia, where he had already established his magazines.

His route lay through Lignitz: he had three rivers to pass before he arrived there, and he had, moreover, good reason to expect to meet with resistance. The main army of the imperialists lay in the neighbourhood; several detached corps kept hovering round him; and in order to check or disperse them, he had recourse to the never-failing assistance of Zieten, whom he stationed in the rearguard at the head of the division of Fouqué, lately Winterfeld's, The Austrians, instead of harassing the duke upon his march, were contended with skirting him at a distance.

After having safely passed the Neiss, the duke was on the verge of being severely harassed by a swarm of light troops which infested the circumjacent country. To rid him of this annoyance, Zieten had recourse to stratagem. He placed his hussars in ambush; and the Cravats (Croats), who considered themselves as masters of the ground, ventured too far forwards, and were suddenly surrounded and taken. In the meantime, the Prussian Army passed the Queiss, and encamped at Nauenburg.

With the like good fortune, Zieten secured the passage of the Bober. He attacked a detachment of cavalry at Bürkenbrück with such success, that out of five hundred men, of whom it consisted, a very small number escaped. During this march, he took between two and three hundred prisoners, and twenty officers. The duke arrived, with his army, first at Bunzlaw, and, on the 19th, at Lignitz.

From thence he sent a large detachment, under the command of Lieutenant-General de Fouqué, to reinforce the garrisons of Schweidnitz, Glatz, and Breslaw, which were all threatened by the enemy at the same time. For, while the Prussians were on their march to Lignitz, the Prince of Lorrain had filed through Löwenberg and Goldberg, continually hanging upon the duke's army, and at length entered Silesia with it, and advanced as far as Wahlstadt. The duke then apprehending more for the capital than for Schweidnitz], which stood in no need of succour, determined to quit his position at Lignitz, and to hasten to cover Breslaw.

In the same night in which the imperialists encamped at Wahlstadt, he moved towards Parchwitz, passed the Oder at Lampersdorf, and arrived, by forced marches, at Breslaw on the 1st of October, where he repassed the above river and formed an entrenched camp behind the Lohe. The army, for the first time since it had quitted Görlitz, was able to take some repose, and Zieten to enjoy the satisfaction of having protected it against an enterprising and more powerful enemy. His pleasure, however, was not unmixed with pain. From the past, he could derive no consolation for the future; for although the Prussians were encamped under the walls of Breslaw, they were not the less menaced; and he could perceive at a distance the storm which was soon to burst over their heads.

Prince Charles, upon whom the Duke of Bevern had gained a march by dint of able manoeuvring, arrived in the night of the 2nd of October on the banks of the Lohe at Lissa, where he encamped in the face of the Prussians. The corps of General de Nadasty, reinforced by a body of Wurtemberg and Bavarian troops, marched to Schweidnitz, and began the siege of that place on the 27th of October.

The two armies continued observing each other before Breslaw for the space of five weeks without quitting their positions; when the prince, availing himself of his superior force, soon made the duke sensible of it; and, from this moment, a reverse of fortune began to attend him, and his army, and Zieten, which the genius of Prussia struggled in vain to avert.

In these transactions, Zieten acted too conspicuous a part, not to render a short detail, relative to the division he had under his orders, an object of some importance. The eight battalions and fifty squadrons he commanded, which were considerably weakened by battles, marches, sickness and desertion, hardly amounted to eight thousand effective men, inclusive of a reinforcement he had likewise received. This motley division was equally deficient in energy and union.

It consisted of two battalions of the grenadiers of Schenkendorf and Rosenbusch; a battalion of Schultz; two battalions of Munchow; a battalion of Wurtemberg-senior; a battalion of Brunswick; a free battalion of Angenelli; of thirty squadrons, drawn from the regiments of Bayreuth, Normann, Steckow, Krockow-junior, and Wartenberg; and of twenty squadrons of the hussars of Zieten and Werner, two regiments of infantry of Lestwitz and Pannewitz, and the two regiments of cavalry of Gessler and the Margrave Frederick.

According to the duke's order of battle, this division, stationed in the left wing of the camp, extended from Klein-Mochber to the suburb of Saint Nicholas.

From hence Zieten detached General de Werner, on the 29th of October, to chase the Austrians from Klettendorf, which they had occupied with a body of cavalry, hussars, and Cravats (Croats). The expedition was fortunate: the enemy did not make long resistance; and after firing a few cannon, they began to retreat. The hussars of Zieten and Werner, having fallen upon the rear-guard, killed, wounded or took prisoners some hundreds of men.

But these slight advantages were more than counterbalanced by the alarming news, that Schweidnitz had surrendered on the 11th of August to General de Nadasty. This disastrous event entirely frustrated the plan which had been concerted between the king and the Duke of Bevern; as the latter could only cope with the enemy on the supposition that Schweidnitz would at least hold out for six weeks;—till the return of the king, who had promised succour both to the fortress and the camp. The reduction of this place was the more unexpected, as it was furnished with a sufficient garrison, and had plenty of provisions and military stores.

Nadasty leaving only a small garrison there, was enabled to join the grand Imperial Army with the far greater part of his corps; and he marched, and encamped in the prince's right wing, between Bethlem and Opperaw. It may not be amiss to remark that this single reinforcement was equal to two thirds of the duke's army, which at this time amounted to twenty-five thousand men only; including the corps under the command of Zieten.

With all the advantage which superiority of numbers could afford him, Prince Charles attacked the Duke of Bevern on the 22nd of November.

In this battle, Zieten had Nadasty to cope with again.

At break of day, the Austrians approached the Lohe, and began to prepare for three several attacks which had been concerted among them. General de Nadasty having passed the river at Hartheb, Zieten made ready for a defence. He moved to the left, to hinder Nadasty from turning the suburb of Saint Nicholas (to which place he was advancing) and likewise to cut him off from Breslaw. It was then, that the duke reinforced Zieten with the four regiments already mentioned; as, according to all appearance, the principal attack would be made on that point, Zieten now took the following positions.

The battalion of Schutz occupied the redoubt of Gräbischen, and drew up in order of battle before the village. The two redoubts on the heights between Gabitz and Gräbischen were supplied by the regiment of Lestwitz. The regiments of Gressler and the Margrave Frederick were posted in the midst of the three redoubts, to support the infantry. The village of Kleinberg was defended by the free battalion of Angenelli; and the rest of Zieten's corps were ranged in two lines, the second of which extended from Neudorf to Herdam.

General de Nadasty having formed in order of battle, detached a strong party of Cravats (Croats) and infantry to Woischowitz, to fall upon Zieten's left flank. The latter, however, had scarcely observed the head of their columns, when he received them with a discharge of artillery and fell upon them with his hussars and dragoons with such vigour, that he put the Cravats (Croats) to flight, together with the Hungarian and the Wurtemberg infantry, and took a considerable number of prisoners.

In the meanwhile, the flower of the Austrian grenadiers had attacked and carried the village of Kleinbourg, notwithstanding the glorious resistance on the part of Angenelli's battalion; who being forced to evacuate the place, formed behind a ditch; and maintained that post till the arrival of the Prince of Bevern (brother to the duke of that name) and a battalion of Lestwitz, with two battalions of grenadiers that Zieten had sent to their succour. An engagement then took place between the infantry, in which the brave troops under the command of Zieten, sustained by his own hussars and those of Werner, were conquerors.

Four companies of grenadiers, on whom the hussars made a well-timed charge, were cut to pieces, and the rest were obliged to abandon the village, together with thirteen cannon. Of these cannon, the victors, for want of horses, were unable to secure more than four, which were transported to Breslaw; the rest, with the unfortunate village, became the prey of the flames.

Such was the fruitless issue of the two first attacks made by Nadasty against Zieten; These two able commanders were, moreover, too well acquainted with each other's prowess, as well as with the art of war, to allow the flanks of their respective armies, which it was their duty to protect, to be needlessly uncovered. Satisfied with observing, with menacing, and with reciprocally endeavouring to turn one another, they deferred to a more favourable opportunity the task of measuring together and of coming to more decisive blows. Zieten, in particular, being obliged to act on the defensive, had at least the satisfaction of having kept his adversary in awe.

Although his line was much further extended than was consistent with the paucity of his troops, he maintained his post till evening; kept the corps of Nadasty in a state of inaction, and furnished him with sufficient occupation to hinder him from keeping up any communication with the main army and acting in concert with it. He had solely one untoward circumstance to combat with: the redoubt before the village of Gräbischen, whose importance was very great, as it preserved the communication between, his corps and the left, wing of the army, was, in, consequence of an unpardonable mistake, abandoned by the garrison; who, consisting of a part a regiment that was advancing upon Klein-Mochber, thought it their duty to march on along with it. The detachment not only left the redoubt naked, but even took away the artillery which had defended it. The Prince of Lorrain, availing himself of this, error, took possession of the village, which be found in a defenceless condition, and of the redoubt itself, from whence he began a heavy cannonading upon the duke's left wing, and quickly forced it to give way.

Fortune, in this battle, was in every respect unfavourable to the Prussians. In vain did their centre and right wing combat with undaunted bravery; in vain, with the duke at their head, did they dispute every inch of ground; in vain their principal officers, and particularly Prince Ferdinand of Prussia, like Schwerin in the battle of Prague, assaulted the batteries with colours in their hands; and every soldier maintained his position without giving way a single step;——the victory, as the enemy did not repass the Lobe, remained still undecided. Too feeble to drive them back to their first situation, the Prussians felt their courage decline with the declining day: they, had fought from sunrise till the approach of evening; they had been attacked upon three several points and been forced to exert themselves to the utmost of their power in making the necessary resistance.

Before them, they had a low, marshy, and uneven ground, unfitted for the manoeuvres of the cavalry. In fine, and above all, the great disproportion of numbers, of artillery, and the want of ammunition, and of everything that encourages the soldier's energy and sustains his valour, convincing them of the inutility of their efforts, and of the only part they had now to act, they gave way to such conviction, obeyed themselves only—and, without any retreat being ordered, they disbanded, and at the close of the day entered the city of Breslaw.

A single column, composed of the bravest of the army, kept aloof from this retreat. They had driven the enemy from Klein-Mochber; and the duke, who had seen them fight with such resolution and brave at the same time both the enemy and the approach of night, indulged the flattering hope that while they were repulsing the Austrians on one side, Zieten with his hussars would fall upon them and take them in the rear. He hastened in quest of him to concert upon this measure, but unfortunately on his return, the column was no longer to be found. They had yielded the field to the enemy, who had attacked them with their whole force; and being cut off from all support and unable to draw up their cavalry on account of the swamps, and the darkness which had overtaken them, they had at length followed the rest of the army. The cessation of the artillery, and the silence of the night succeeded to the tumult of arms; and the morning informed the enemy of their victory and of the advantages they had to derive from it.

Zieten, like the rest, was obliged to quit the field of battle and take shelter under the cannon of Breslaw. He was deeply afflicted on seeing the Prussians turn their backs upon the enemy; and his sorrow increased on observing them, for some time after the disaster, dismayed and chilled with terror, and their chief a prey to melancholy and despair. Zieten feelingly bemoaned this in secret; and shall now see how he acted in public, and what steps he took to repair the mischief.

The duke, after having left a garrison in Breslaw, had quitted that place on the next day (the 23rd of November) and led the wrecks of the army as far as Protsch, which lies three German miles from the above city. From thence he had attempted to reconnoitre the enemy; but being attended by a feeble escort, he had the misfortune to fall into their hands. A long captivity then interrupted the military career of the victor of Reichenberg, the hero of Prague, of Kuttenberg, of Görlitz;—of an able and experienced commander, whose recent misfortunes caused all his former successes to be soon forgotten, and whose merit was at last disowned by his sovereign, and, perhaps will be treated in like manner by posterity.

If the first and most competent of his judges had his reasons for treating him with such severity, we are too little acquainted with those reasons to acquiesce in them blindly, without becoming guilty of partiality and even of injustice. We shall therefore only observe, that the whole army lamented and loved their chief under his misfortunes, and that Zieten's grief was equally sincere and poignant.

Lieutenant-General de Lestwitz, who, in right of seniority, took the command oi the army in the duke's stead, having received at noon the account of the enemy's being in full march towards Breslaw, had given orders to break up the camp and to continue the retreat, as he was fearful that the place, which was ill supported by a garrison the duke had left in it, under the command of General de Katte, would not hold out. Every officer to whom he communicated his intention, ventured to oppose it, and to make strong remonstrances on the occasion. Among these, Prince Ferdinand of Prussia and the Princes of Brunswick and Bevern, endeavoured to cure, him of his panic, and strove to make him feel, that the danger was not so urgent, that this sudden and pusillanimous movement would tend to increase the dismay the troops were already under, and promote desertion.

M. de Lestwitz still persisting in his resolution, it was represented to him, that General de Katte might perhaps make some resistance, that he would at least amuse the enemy, and that in case Breslaw should immediately surrender, the Austrians could not undertake any thing on the same day against the Prussian camp at three German miles' distance from thence, as they would he embarrassed by the narrowness of the streets of that spacious city, in which besides there was only one bridge over which the army had to file;—all this, however, was urged in vain.

At length the generals satisfied themselves with requesting, that the order for decamping might be countermanded, and deferred to the next day. To this measure he was not only inexorable, but considering these remonstrances as so-many contradictions, he put an end to them by asking the generals, and even the princes who composed a part of them, if they had forgotten the laws of subordination, and if they wished to force him to call a council of war. This was an argument that admitted of no reply, and to which every one immediately yielded. They all withdrew, and each set about giving the necessary orders to his division.

While these preparations were making, Zieten, who had not been present at the deliberations, returned from a neighbouring village, where had been visiting a detached post. Witness to the consternation of the army, incensed at the panic which reigned through the whole camp, and seeing the preparations which were made in the headquarters for the march; he peremptorily demanded, what all that hurry and all those preparations signified.

Being informed of the order which the commander in chief had just given, he suppressed his indignation, and assuming a grave and authoritative air:

> Comrades! what are you about? Be assured there is not the least danger! Let everything alone: rely on me; we are not to march today!

In this, manner he continued to address the troops as he went on towards the general's quarters, whither he was hastening for the purpose of obtaining some explanation of what was going forwards. So entirely was his attention engrossed by this business, that he forgot to uncover himself when he entered. All other considerations, at this moment, giving way to that of repairing a capital error in judgment on the part of his commanding officer, he appeared before him with his hussar-cap on his head, and spoke to him with such force and energy, that every word seemed to be an order.

Addressing himself to the man, who had just been speaking to the other generals of subordination and a council of war, he asked him, what view he could have in ordering the troops to decamp with such precipitation. He continued:

> Would you have them lose the small remains of courage they still possess? Would you deprive the king of his army? Do you suppose that such a retreat, which it would be hard to distinguish from a flight, would not make every soldier believe his situation to be desperate? And, upon that supposition, how shall you be able to prevent desertion? how secure the artillery, the provisions, the baggage? Everything will be wantonly sacrificed without our being at all driven by the proximity of the enemy to such an extremity.
>
> For my own part, I shall never give my concurrence to such

ill-concerted measures. The army, it is true, cannot maintain its position, but must fall back. Yet what hinders us from taking that step with due reflection, and after having afforded the troops time to recover themselves from the consternation they are now under? Let us give them some rest during the remaining part of the day, and, at the close of it, issue the orders for marching tomorrow; let us then decamp at sunrise.

All the princes, all the generals, who had unavailingly urged the same advice, and had just come back to the commander in chief's quarters, were witnesses to this spirited harangue: for, the moment in which Zieten had returned to the camp, and in which a rumour began to prevail that the troops were not to march, these generals had followed him to M. de Lestwitz' tent, to learn the effect the new representations might have upon him. The affair was drawing to a crisis, when a messenger arrived in great haste with despatches for the Duke of Bevern, whose defeat and subsequent misfortune the king was yet a stranger to.

The packet was instantly opened and deciphered. Its contents announced the victory of Rossbach, the approach of the king, together with an order to pass the Oder at Lebus, and to join the Royal Army at Parchwitz. General de Lestwitz was therein named governor of Breslaw; and that officer, without explaining himself any further with regard to the march of the army, immediately obeyed the orders of his sovereign, resigned his command to Lieutenant-General de Kiow, his next in rank, and set out to his garrison.

The new commander in chief, thus furnished with the king's orders, began to execute them literally, and as if they had been addressed personally to him; and without entering into the discussions and debates which had just been agitated, he gave the order to march; when he experienced on: the part of Zieten the same opposition which had been made to the measures of M. de Lestwitz. Zieten's choler, which had long glowed in his veins, at length grew, inflamed, and inspired that becoming boldness, that irresistible energy, which, in effect, saved the army.

He first began to make General de Kiow feel that under the present circumstances, it was less necessary to abide by the letter than the spirit of the king's commands, which were given out at a time in which His Majesty not only was ignorant of the events that had taken place, but could not have foreseen them; that it was incumbent on him to confine himself to the observance of the king's principal intention in marching to Parchwitz, but that the route, the means, the detail, were the general's own concern; that the safety of the army was the first law he had to obey; that it was the business of prudence, to dictate, and of courage to execute it; that it was necessary, to put off the decampment of the troops to the next day; to pass the Oder, not at Lebus, but at Glogaw, where there, was a bridge ready to transport them over it; that the provisioning of the army was an object of the highest importance and might be better effected in the latter town; that having passed the Oder without molestation, the troops would easily arrive at Parchwitz.

This counsel was certainly worthy the attention of the general of an army, dispirited by defeat, insensible of its own force, and scarce alive to the instinct of courage. If Zieten waved for a moment the duty he owed to the laws of subordination, to seniority of rank, to example, to a commander in chief, we cannot better palliate his conduct than by laying it to the account of his love for his country, and by connecting it with the event to which it led. At this critical and decisive moment, he could not prevail on himself to take a scrap of paper for his rule of conduct; he consulted duties of superior importance, and considered the preservation of the army as the most sacred object he had in view.

To this end, as he still observed M. de Kiow hesitate and seem averse to come to any determination, he proceeded in a more resolute manner, and exclaimed; "Shall I tell you, general, what is necessary to be done? Come; let us make a disposition together."

Kiow complied in silence. It was instantly committed to paper; Zieten revised it, took up the pen, retouched it, made alterations and additions. He conducted this business with vehemence; his eye was on fire, and his whole countenance inspired terror. All this was, however, necessary; and a few days after, the king was obligated to him for the safety of the duke's army, and for the happy effects which resulted from their junction with the troops; who by the victory of Rossbach had prepared that of Leuthen and delivered their country from imminent danger.

The merit of Zieten appears in a stronger point of view, when we consider that the Prussian troops, practiced in the art of fighting and gaining victories, had not till lately been lectured in the school-of adversity, and that the duke's army would probably have disbanded and given themselves up to the enemy, had they been at all aware of any pusillanimity in the conduct of their commander. The very idea of the possibility of such an event made Zieten shudder; and to this well-grounded apprehension was joined the consideration, that a great part of the army was composed of strangers, or at least of Silesians, whom the difference of religion and the obligation of fighting against their former sovereign, rendered ill-attached to the service of a prince whose tolerance and eminent qualities they were not yet acquainted with.

Nothing, indeed, could be more likely than their taking the first opportunity that offered to desert their standards and return to their respective homes, or even to go over to the enemy. More than one instance of the kind, and to which he had himself been witness, served to increase his apprehensions. Among others. On the day in which the battle was lost, being engaged behind the army in rallying the fugitives, an officer (not a native of Prussia) passed by him in full speed at the head of thirty deserters; "Whither are you going?" demanded Zieten.

"To the Austrians," he replied.

The general, who at this moment was accompanied by his faithful attendant-hussar (Fahrenhols), calmly turned his horse's head, and said to the latter "Let us be gone, comrade, lest they should force you and me to go with them."

The deference which M. de Kiow shewed to the advice of a subordinate general on the late occasion, did him the greatest honour. He ordered the decampment for the next day, and marched the army to Parchwitz through Glogaw.

The garrison of Breslaw followed the army immediately after. Prince Charles had granted them free egress, with arms and baggage, in order to enter with the greater expedition into the town. The king did not wait the arrival of Lestwitz, Kiow, and Katte, to express his disapprobation of a conduct which he taxed with heedlessness and cowardice. He had previously ordered Zieten to put them under arrest and to convey them to Glogaw. But being soon convinced, that they had not been guilty of treason, and that their conduct had solely arisen from, the embarrassment of their situations, he ordered them to be set at liberty, and afterwards made them ample reparation.

At the time when he charged Zieten with this disagreeable commission, he had named him general in chief of the duke's army (November the 27th), till the junction which soon after took place at Parchwitz. Zieten had the satisfaction to bring him the wreck of that army, which now scarcely formed a body of fifteen thousand men; but they were all warriors, inured to danger and fatigue, and who had shewn themselves incapable of desertion; choice troops, ripe for exploits, and waiting only the voice of their prince, their country, and the call of honour, to rekindle in their breasts the sacred fire of heroism. This reinforcement, small with regard to number and appearance, but which Frederick knew how to appreciate for their courage, and shortly to turn to good account, he owed to the firmness, the preserverance, the resistance even, of Zieten.

Prince Charles being informed of the return of the king, who had marched from the banks of the Oder to Leipsic in twelve days, and calculating that, after the junction, the two corps could not amount to more than thirty thousand men, whom he considered as worn out with fatigue, quitted his post at Breslaw in order to offer battle. He passed the Weistritz, (rivulet that runs through Schweidnitz), encamped between Leuthen and Lissa, and took a formidable position. He hoped to vanquish the king, as he had vanquished the duke: he, however, experienced himself the fate which he had endeavoured to prepare for others.

Frederick began his march at the head of his little army on the 4th of December. The fortunate encounters of his advanced-guard, which he led on in person, assisted by Zieten and his hussars, were so many preludes to victory. Strong detachments of the enemy were posted at Neumark and Borna, and were successively surprised by the Prussians. Near three hundred Austrians were killed, twelve hundred were made prisoners, together with nineteen officers. Five standards and all the camp-ovens were likewise taken.

On the following day, the 5th of December, was fought that famous battle, which, on account of its consequences as well as the dreadful carnage that attended it, is deserving of a distinguished place in the annals of war. Few readers can be ignorant, that, on the evening before it was given, Frederick, with all his generals and other officers, had solemnly bound themselves to conquer or to die. An able disposition followed this awful engagement; the parts of the grand tragedy were given out, and every one acted that which was allotted him in a manner conducive to the success of the day.

The king acknowledges in his works, that he was glad to have found the enemy in a position that facilitated his enterprise; that he was necessitated, and had resolved to attack them wherever he should have found them, had it been even at Zobtenberg. He had likewise reason to rejoice at the spirited temper of his troops, who had so well seconded him, and executed with such exactness and celerity, what he had conceived with so much skill and genius. A day so memorable, and so interesting to the military reader, has a claim to particular notice, in the life of one of its most distinguished heroes, and we shall therefore add a short but accurate account of the battle for his satisfaction.

Zieten was situated in the right wing: there the attack was made, and such could not fail to be his post. He had Nadasty before him, and he beat him according to custom. Six brave battalions of grenadiers, two regiments with General de Wedel at their head, took the batteries of Nadasty's corps, and put his infantry to flight. Zieten, at the head of his cavalry, broke the ranks of the enemy's horse, pursued and hemmed in the fugitives, and completely routed them. (M. de Zieten charged the enemy's cavalry, and put them to flight, *Seven Years' War*). This fortunate commencement greatly facilitated the attack made by the king on the left wing of the Austrians, which being no longer supported by Nadasty, was soon borne down, turned, and driven upon the centre, and the centre driven upon the right. In less than six hours the whole line was in a confused heap; the colossus was broken, the disgrace of Breslaw cancelled, and victory reinstated in her former post.

From the 18th of June till the beginning of December, the army of the empress-queen had affected to give the law to the Prussians, to drive them out of Silesia, and to confine them to their former boundaries. It was now the Austrians' turn, not only to yield, to retreat, but to fly with such precipitation and loss, as to be reduced to less than half their number on their arrival in Bohemia.

The vicissitudes of fortune which abound in every situation of life and influence every event, are in no point of view so remarkable as in the chances of war.

The consternation of the imperialists, which was one of the principal causes of their defeat, began with the corps under the command of Nadasty. Zieten, who was enabled to avail himself of this, took a prodigious number of prisoners. His own regiment alone, commanded by the gallant Colonel de Seelen, took two thousand Bavarians and Württembergers. The panic was so great, that the remains of a whole regiment surrendered to a cornet and six of Zieten's hussars. The cornet conducted his prisoners to the king, who immediately raised him to the rank of captain, and invested him with the order of military merit.

The principal attack had been attended with greater difficulty. The enemy made resistance on every point, and in particular, defended the important post of Leuthen with great valour. The reduction of that place was reserved for Captain de Möllendorf, (later field-marshal of the Prussian Armies and governor of the city of Berlin), who carried it at the head of a battalion of guards, and secured the victory of which Zieten had laid the foundation. The Prussian battalions dislodged the enemy from one post after another. The regiment of Bayreuth took them in flank, and the rest of the cavalry completed the rout. Dismay succeeded to bravery; and the Austrians, being ill-officered, ill supported, and alike unable to defend themselves or to run away, yielded to the conquerors in crowds, in half-battalions, in battalions.

To shew to what degree this panic had possessed the minds of the enemy, and how far the mere presence of Frederick was formidable, we shall here mention an anecdote, which M. de Tempelhof has preserved in his excellent history of the seven years' war, and which recalls the memory of the heroic ages, in which Achilles, unarmed, put the Trojans to flight by only appearing before them. The battle was gained; night came on, and the king, desirous of following up the advantages he had acquired, marched with some battalions of volunteers to Lissa, into which the bulk of the hostile army had thrown themselves for the purpose of crossing the Weistritz.

His Majesty, at the head of the infantry, and attended by a part of his suite, entered the town, and proceeded to the castle, notwithstanding the Austrian, troops he passed on his way, who all gave him place. The generals, the officers who occupied the apartments of the castle, received him in the most respectful manner, did the honours of the house, and retired. A little while after, his battalions arrived; but they were not so civilly received, as the enemy repeatedly fired on them before they evacuated the place.

The victor of Rossbach and Leuthen terminated the campaign as gloriously as he had began it, whilst Prince Charles, awakened from the agreeable dream, into which fortune had for a moment lulled him, began to fall into a long series of disasters, which strikingly exemplified the caprice of that fickle power. His conduct after the battle served but to aggravate his loss; his retreat, which had rather the appearance of a flight, led him into the same errors which Zieten had with so much difficulty prevented the Prussian generals from falling into after their defeat at Breslaw.

Instead of taking post behind the Weistritz, which he had passed during the night, he fell back upon Breslaw; and far from expecting the king (who followed him very closely) and after having thrown a strong garrison (17,600 men), into that city, which fell into the hands of the Prussians, he hastily continued his retreat. All that Zieten had predicted of the duke's army, and which would infallibly have happened to it, had the advice of the commander in chief been followed, was now literally fulfilled in that of Prince Charles. The Austrian troops, doubly dispirited at having been beaten by those whom, they had just before overcome, stood in more than ordinary need of encouragement. Instead of measures conducive to such end, his flight was precipitated, and the preservation of the army despaired of. Hence thousands of deserters come over to the Prussians; and the more so, as Zieten, who pressed them on every side, had left them no other resource.

On the 7th of December, the king had ordered Zieten to march in pursuit of the enemy with a considerable body of men, composed of three battalions of grenadiers (Wedel, Manteuffel, Heyden), three regiments of infantry (Asseburg, Bornstedt, Meyerink), three of dragoons (Czettritz, Normann, Bayreuth), four of hussars (Werner, Seidlitz, Puttkammer, Zieten), and two free battalions, those of Angenelli and Kalben.

Notwithstanding the defeat and dispersion of the enemy, this division was not equivalent to the force which they still possessed. After having, two days before, exhibited a front consisting of more than eighty thousand men, they were now, according to the calculation of General de Tempelhof, reduced to nine thousand infantry, and twenty-eight thousand cavalry; a number, however, still superior to Zieten's detachment.

But supposing them upon an equality (as a flying army loses much when compared with the army that pursues it,) the Austrians would have been able to take post, and to cope with the Prussians, had Zieten left them time for such purpose. On this occasion it was that he displayed his knowledge of the country, and of the art of war in general. As soon as he foresaw a position which might prove advantageous to the enemy, he drove them forwards to hinder them from taking possession of it. Whenever they had any defiles to pass, he took care to occupy them beforehand; so that in order to gain Bohemia, they were not able to take the route they had intended to take, but such only as the Prussian general prescribed them.

Prince Charles had entertained hopes of being able to halt under the ramparts of Schweidnitz. He marched for that purpose through Boraw, but Zieten, who followed him over the Lohe and through

Gross-Mochber, prevented him from taking post there; and driving him continually before him, he was enabled, in the space of a fortnight (from the 7th till the 22nd of December) to recover all Silesia from the Austrians, and to compel them to repass the mountains.

It is not possible to make a just estimate of their loss in troops, artillery, baggage, and military stores. An historian of the time has calculated it at nine thousand men, and three thousand-waggons. Other writers affirm it to be still more considerable. Zieten had no leisure to make any estimate; he considered himself as having done nothing while anything yet remained to be done; and looking before him only, he kept no reckoning with the past.

To satisfy the views of the king, and to pursue the enemy to the utmost, he was compelled to put the vigour of his troops to the severest test, and to require miracles at their hands. They had been long and incessantly engaged in marches and encounters, while the rest of the army were enjoying the sweets of repose; his infantry could barely find accommodations in the villages on their route; his cavalry, ill-encamped, were exposed to all the inclemency of the season, and during fifteen days the detachment had only one day of rest. It will appear from the correspondence of the king, which we shall lay before our readers, that the general, touched at the hardships which his men underwent, had ventured to make representations to His Majesty, and the more so, as they were frequently in want of bread.

At the same time, it will be seen, that being obliged to steel his heart to the feelings of compassion, which would have retarded the progress of the operations, he at length entered into the views of the monarch; and that, exerting himself anew, he was enabled to impart fresh ardour to his troops, to reconcile them to the endurance of hunger, cold, sickness, and the most painful privations.

It were to be wished that an accurate account could be given of the various marches, posts, and dispositions of this pursuit, which the general projected and varied from day to day. But the rapidity of the operations precluded all possibility of noting the details; and the memory of those who had a part in them soon became confined to vague and confused ideas of what had passed, and unable to form any regular picture of that busy period. This deficiency is the more to be regretted, as M. de Tempelhof, in his aforementioned history, wishes for exact memoirs relative to this expedition, which, as he declares, would be equally instructive in the operations of regular as well as desultory war.

When the king at length became in peaceable possession of Silesia, and enabled Zieten's troops to partake of the general repose of the army; when he had leisure to estimate the loss of the enemy after the re-taking of Breslaw, Schweidnitz, and of the whole province, it was found to amount to sixty-six thousand men, exclusive of the garrison of Lignitz which had obtained free egress. Besides these, upwards of three hundred officers, among whom were several generals, had fallen into the hands of the Prussians. In the battle itself and during the pursuit, the king and Zieten had taken twenty-eight thousand prisoners. To the foregoing estimate may be added six thousand deserters. The number of cannon taken, amounted to one hundred and seventeen; and that of the standards and colours to fifty-one. The Austrian Army had lost, in the battle, upwards of seven thousand men, killed and wounded, and that of the Prussians, five thousand.

Such much success did not, however, satisfy the vast desires of Frederick, whose genius, superior to good, as well as to ill fortune was subservient to its own impulse only. Of this we shall find proof in the following correspondence, the notes to which, in the kings' own hand, it may be observed, are particularly valuable.

### Letters from the king to Zieten:

My dear Lieutenant-General de Zieten. I have just received your report, and I have the satisfaction to tell you that everything you have done has been well done. I, however, urgently expect you to push and harass the enemy, and not give them a moment's rest. If they take the road to Moravia, you will draw your bread from Neisse; if they turn towards Schweidnitz, the country must furnish you with that article. Above all things, I recommend you to pursue them to the utmost extremity, without allowing them time to take breath or to recover themselves. I am willing to believe your men are fatigued, and even harassed; but, do not forget that the Austrians are ten times more so, and that it behoves you to push and pursue them incessantly till you have driven them beyond their mountains. I am your affectionate king,

Headquarters at Dorian,                                                 Frederick
December the 9th, 1757.

*In His Majesty's own hand.*

My dear Zieten, at the present moment, one day of fatigue will procure us a hundred of rest. March on, general; never quit the saddle; keep continually at the heels of the enemy.      Frederick.

## LETTER 2.

My dear Lieutenant-General de Zieten. I learn everywhere, as well from deserters as from the most undoubted authority, that the Austrian Army is not only in full retreat, but in the greatest disorder. The consternation which prevails through every part of it, is owing to the vigour of your pursuit. I exhort you to follow them without the least relaxation and to drive them before you to the foot of their own mountains. Should they take shelter under the cannon of Schweidnitz, you will of course be unable to dislodge them; but the moment they resume their march, you must keep at their heels till you drive them upon their frontiers.

Colonel de Werner will assist you, and you will furnish him with a few squadrons of hussars for that purpose, together with a free battalion and a few companies of grenadiers. In a word, do whatever you consider proper to be done in order to drive the enemy beyond their mountains. Should they make a stand under the ramparts of Schweidnitz, you must nevertheless detach Werner with a party of hussars, grenadiers, and light infantry: he is acquainted with the country, and will block up the passes or force the enemy, to gain them before him. Observe, that if we push them to their frontiers, and still further; if we do them all the mischief, we can this year, and thereby totally dispirit them, we shall have so much the less business to do the next; whether the war continue, or the issue of the present campaign bring on a peace.

For my own part, after having reduced Breslaw (which will not take up more than three or four days) I shall follow you with the army, and accompany you till we come to the frontiers of Bohemia. I again recommend the contents of this letter to your serious consideration, and I am ever your affectionate king,
Headquarters at Durian,
December 10th, 1757

*In His Majesty's own hand.*

The safety of the state depends on your zeal.

                 Frederick.

## LETTERS 3, AND 4 WITHOUT DATES.

(They are both in the king's own handwritings, and shew how near he had the pursuit of the enemy at heart.)

Still keep at the heels of the Austrians. Order the regiments of Szekuly and Burnitz to advance to Freibourg: follow up the enemy beyond Landshut. Lose not a moment; pursue them incessantly. The country must furnish your bread.

Frederick.

My dear Zieten.
Press the enemy closely. If they threaten resistance at Bogendorf, send Werner, with all speed, with two battalions to the mountains. They must be driven upon Trautenaw. I will not allow them to retain an inch of ground in Silesia; and in passing the mountains, they must lose artillery, baggage-waggons, and a great number of deserters. Keep continually behind them. Occupy the post of Landshut if you are able, and, in that case, Schweidnitz and Lignitz will be insulated. *Adieu!* I trust, I shall have done here in four or five days.

Frederick.

## Letter 5

My dear Lieutenant-General de Zieten.
I received your two reports of the 14th; and, in answer to which, I observe, that it appears to be the intention of the enemy to remain some time at Freibourg, in order to allow the garrison and magazines of Lignitz time to join them. From thence, I have reason to believe, they will retreat to Schweinhaus or still further. They must, however, be turned. Situated as you now are, I do not imagine you would be able to cut off their supplies from Lignitz, or to promote desertion. Send some detachments to Strigaw, to Jauer, etc. by which means you will annoy them more effectually than you now can do. Should General de Meyer do his duty, and you be able to send him a reinforcement, I am fully persuaded, that a part of the magazines will fall into your hands, and that the garrison of Lignitz will be cut off. I am etc.

Headquarters at Durian,
December 15th, 1757. Frederick.

## Letter 6

My dear Lieutenant-General de Zieten,
I enclose you a letter written by the Prince of Lorrain to the

Governor of Lignitz, which has been just intercepted, and which furnishes us with very useful intelligence.

You will see by this letter both the plan and the disposition of the enemy. I believe you are strong enough to dislodge Bakowsky and Palasti; and I therefore desire you to give your whole attention to that object, to act with the utmost vigour, and to terminate affairs with all possible speed, agreeably to my wishes and intentions. I am, etc.

Headquarters at Durian,
September 18th, 1757, Frederick.

*Letter from Prince Charles of Lorrain, enclosed in the foregoing.*

Colonel.

The advanced season no longer permitting the army to remain encamped, and obliging me to procure it rest and security as far as lies in my power, the troops will march tomorrow to Landshut, and I shall take care, as far as it may be practicable, to maintain the communication with Lignitz, I apprise you of this, colonel, and at the same time recommend you to keep a good watch, and particularly to confer, as long as circumstances will permit, with lieutenant Colonel de Palasti, who is posted at Hirschberg, and who has informed me, that he has fortunately introduced a good provision of cattle and salt into Lignitz.

He may perhaps furnish you with other articles of consumption, if you are enabled to keep up the communication with him and facilitate the means of supplying you. On my departure from hence, I shall leave Lieutenant-General de Bacow with a considerable detachment to cover the country and maintain correspondences. You will dispatch yours by the hands, of Colonel de Palasti, who will deliver them to General de Bacow, from whom I shall duly receive them. Finally, colonel, I earnestly recommend the good defence of the post committed to your care; hoping that you will not think of surrendering it, unless circumstances, which may screen you from all military responsibility, should authorise such measure.

I am, as ever, colonel,

Headquarters at Freibourg,
December 15th, 1757. your devoted

Charles of Lorrain.

(The style of this letter, which has been preserved as far as a translation would admit of, forms a striking contrast with that of the king's letters.)

On the back of the letter from Zieten to the king, dated from Neudorf, December 17th, 1757, His Majesty had written the following lines in his own hand.

> 'Tis well.—Bacow is at Freibourg;—he must driven from thence. An Hungarian occupies Hirschberg;—he must be dislodged. As for the garrison of Schweidnitz, it must be observed by a body of cavalry.         Frederick.

## Letter 7.

My dear Lieutenant-General de Zieten. I am happy to see by your report of the 21st, that things go on to my wish, and that you continue to push the enemy, and will be able to make them evacuate Silesia. We shall be on the 27th at Strigaw, Jauer, and in their environs: we shall there see what is to be done with regard to Lignitz, I should be glad if you could let me know at Strigaw, towards that time, what progress you shall then have made. I am your very affectionate
Breslaw, December 23rd, 1757.

                Frederick.

## Letter 8

My dear Lieutenant-General de Zieten.
I am well satisfied with the manner in which you attacked the rear-guard and drove the enemy out of Silesia. All would have been still better, had you not remained so long at Reichenbach. (Zieten had halted there but one day, out of fifteen, which were taken up in continual marches). I hereby charge you with the command of the cordon along the frontiers of Bohemia. Begin to form the chain with your own battalions and the free ones. I shall instantly send you Noble's. You will detach Major de Kleist to Goldberg with Szekuly's battalion, to dislodge the enemy from thence. I have just charged Fouqué with the blockade of Schweidnitz.

The regiments of Puttkammer and Seidlitz will remain at their post. Yours and Warnerey's shall go into winter-quarters, Meyer, with the regiment of Beyreuth's dragoons, shall continue in service. Withdraw by degrees the regiments of Normann, Czettritz, and Wartenberg. Recruit your own, and render it complete. I shall furnish the horses; they are all ready. Recommend the same measure to the other regiments, The three regiments of dragoons, which you draw from the line, you will post between Hohengiersdorf, Ober-Mögendorf and Kunzendorf. I am, etc. etc.

Frederick,

*Zieten's answer.*

I humbly thank Your Majesty for having been pleased to entrust me with the command of the frontiers of Bohemia, I shall do my utmost to render myself worthy of this new mark of confidence. I beg to request Your Majesty to inform me exactly of the two points which are to begin and end the chain of posts I am to establish. I have one free battalion with me, which is that of Angenelli: de Katten's forms part of the detachment of Werner, as I formerly reported to Your Majesty, I shall begin the chain with the battalion of Angenelli, the hussars, and the two companies of *chasseurs*, unless your majesty should give me different orders. I shall station Major de Kleist at Goldberg with the battalion of Szekuly, Captain de Heinecke, of my own regiment, is at Löwenberg: I have heard no direct news of him.

With regard to my regiment as well as that of de Warnery, I wait Your Majesty's ultimate orders to send them into quarters. The regiments of Normann and Czettritz march from hence tomorrow, and will repair to Salzbrun, from whence the former will march the next day to Kunzendorf, and the latter, on the same day, to Ober-Mögendorf. I shall inform the regiment of Wartenberg, which is still at Reichenbach, of Your Majesty's commands, and that corps shall forthwith march to Hohen-Giersdorf.

I have detached General de Czettritz from hence with the regiments of dragoons, till your majesty decides whether or not General de Stechow shall remain here; which step may be speedily rectified, as the distance is no more than three miles. (*German miles, containing about 4¾ English miles each*).

General de Fouqué having disposed of the battalion of Meyerink to reinforce the garrison of Reichenbach, I beg Your Majesty will decide whether I am to recall that battalion in order that General de Wedel's regiment be united. I shall neglect nothing that is necessary for the purpose of completing my own regiment with all possible speed.

Colonel de Werner informed me on the 19th, that he had not been able to effect his purpose on account of the snows, and because General de Janus still occupies the mountains on this side of Braunaw; that, from Neisse, where he has taken post, he was on the point of marching to attack the corps of Simbschen at Neustadt; and that General de Kleist was about to give him a reinforcement of infantry. He has besides, Heyden's battalion of grenadiers with him.

Landshut, December 25th, 1757.           J. J. de Zieten.

*The king's answer, written on the back of the letter.*

We have not yet time to provide for the frontiers. Let us first see if we can do anything at Schatzler. The magazines of Trautenaw must not be suffered to subsist; they must be burnt or taken, or the enemy must be driven to the necessity of setting fire to them. As for the other regiments and what relates to the cordon, I shall settle their destination after the surrender of Lignitz. Everything at Reichenbach must remain in its present state. Werner is at Jägerndorf. He is well there; the estates he has in that part of the country are, in some measure, the cause of his march. As soon as Lignitz capitulates, I shall settle the posts. I must speak with Wedel, that I may give him the necessary detail,                  Frederick.

## LETTER 9

*In His Majesty's own hand.*

I have just learnt that the Austrians have a considerable magazine at Trautenaw. Were it in your power to take possession of it, you would crown your exploits. If you cannot effect this by force, have it set on fire, though it should cost you a thousand *ducats*. Bring this about, either by force or address; one of the two. The thing is very important, and would hinder the enemy from assembling in force in those parts the next spring. *Adieu*, Strigaw, December 25th.          Frederick.

## LETTER 10.

*In His Majesty's own hand.*

My dear General.

I am well satisfied with the news you have just sent me on the subject of the enemy. I should, however, have been much more so, had you been able to have undertaken anything against Schatzlar. All the defiles lying beyond that place, you have nothing to fear from the cavalry. Spare no expense in procuring good information or in gaining over such people as may be of service to you. You need only mention what sum you want, and you shall be duly supplied therewith. I am your very affectionate,

Strigaw, December 26th, 1757.                          Frederick.

## LETTER 11

My dear Lieutenant-General de Zieten.

I thank you for your good wishes, and in return, I wish you and your whole corps a happy new year.

As Schweidnitz is now invested on all sides, and is in want of many necessaries, I imagine the enemy will attempt to throw in succour or provisions, and I enjoin you to frustrate any such enterprises. I am told they have six thousand men at Braunaw; you will learn whether this be true. They are in force in the neighbourhood of Trautenaw; and in taking the direction of Böhmisch Friedland, they may make an attempt against Löwenberg. These are the three points which merit your attention. Your regiment will inform you of what passes near Löwenberg. If in, reality, the enemy should attempt anything, there will be a movement in that quarter; they will undoubtedly make feints, appear to advance upon other points, and mask their operations. Do all you can to discover their real views; and take care not to be deceived by false appearances. In case of an attempt, I shall give you a list of the regiments and their quarters, that you may be able to procure reinforcements whenever you may want them. The quarters of Hirschberg, Löwenberg, Bunzlau and Frankenstein, will, in particular, be in readiness to second you at the shortest notice. You will continue to give me an account of everything that passes, and, above all, should anything of this nature happen. I am etc. etc.

Strigaw, December 30th, 1757.

                                               Frederick.

Two things are observable in the foregoing correspondence; the first, that in the short space of time that had elapsed since the battle of Leuthen, Zieten had done much in the pursuit of the enemy and for the safety of Silesia; the second, that in spite of all his efforts and the efforts of the corps under his command, the king still expected and required more at his hands, and that, although His Majesty was sparing in his praises, he was far from being so in his censures, since he considered the halt at Reichenbach as a reprehensible measure. Reichenbach was, however, no Capua. It was merely twenty-four hours' interruption of a hitherto uninterrupted pursuit. It was a moment of rest, absolutely necessary to enable both men and horses to continue and complete their task.

Zieten, moreover, executed the orders of the king in their fullest extent, excepting perhaps what related to the magazine of Trautenaw, to which it is not certain that he set fire; and had he not acquitted himself of the commission, so far was it from being a matter of reproach, that it can only be said, that, accustomed as he was to look the enemy in the face, he was ill fitted for a kind of warfare, in which courage was of no use, and which, besides, savoured more of barbarity than heroism.

Zieten, as the reader has seen, had undergone incredible hardships in the course of this campaign; yet he had still more toils to encounter during the winter. He had now the command of the cordon posted over the chain of mountains between Schmiedeberg and Landshut, which was composed of nine battalions and twenty squadrons. In consideration of their services and the loss they had sustained, the king had allowed Zieten's own hussars and those of Warnerey to go into winter-quarters.

The generals, however, availed themselves but little of this interval of repose; they were almost incessantly employed in repairing the havoc which four bloody battles and a series of daily encounters had made in their respective regiments. Zieten's, among the others, was completely recruited, and, at the return of spring, the whole army exhibited a formidable front.

The rest of the winter passed away unmarked by any military event. The corps which Zieten commanded was, in the fullest extent of the term, a corps of observation. Frequent patrols and reconnoitring parties, at the head of which the general appeared in person, fully convinced him of the immobility of the enemy, and enabled him to encourage the hopes of the king relative to the blockade of Schweidnitz, which had been undertaken by M. de Fouqué. We are in possession of one letter only of the king's, written at this period, and we shall insert it, to shew to what degree His Majesty was satisfied with his general.

My dear Lieutenant-General de Zieten.

I am much obliged to you for the news you give me in your letter of the 21st. Everything you say is very much to the purpose; yet I still apprehend a movement on the part of the enemy to succour Schweidnitz, or to fall on some of our quarters. Let us therefore be upon our guard: let us endeavour to discover, and to foil their intentions. My presence will perhaps be necessary, and I shall not fail being with you as soon as I shall be able to gain further information.

In the meanwhile, it appears to me necessary, that beginning with Silberberg, you send out your patrols as. far as the defiles of Braunaw, for the purpose of reconnoitring the ground well, or at least to discover the motions of the enemy, so that General de Fouqué might receive instant information thereof. You will take care to do whatever is necessary, and to make frequent report; particularly relative to the least change on the part of the enemy. I am your affectionate king,
Breslaw, February 23rd, 1758

Frederick.

*In His Majesty's own hand*

The most essential point is to avoid being deceived by false appearances. I am of opinion that the enemy will make some attempts in the neighbourhood of Trautenaw. Of Braunaw, Friedland, and Silberberg, we must not lose sight for a moment.

Frederick

The Austrian generals came not to the relief of Schweidnitz, which after having sustained a regular siege, surrendered in the middle of the month of April. Zieten had covered the operations on the side of Pfaffendorf, Johannsdorf, and Weissbach: but before we transport the reader with him into Moravia, where, as it is well known, the king entered after the taking of the above place; we shall mention an event which occurred in his regiment, and with regard to which he acted in a manner worthy of himself, and perfectly conformable to his character.

We have already stated, that in the Battle of Leuthen, one of Zieten's cornets had taken the remains of a whole regiment prisoner, and that the king, by way of recompensing so brilliant an exploit, had given him the military cross and named him captain upon the spot This young man, who afterwards displayed considerable talents in his profession, but who being at that time very deficient in education and experience, was so intoxicated with his good fortune as not to know how to enjoy it with moderation, and he soon exposed himself to the risk of losing every advantage to be derived from it.

Considering it sufficient to be a captain of royal creation, and, without announcing himself in such capacity either to his general or to any of the officers of the staff;—without waiting to be informed in what regiment he was to exercise his new rank; he made choice of the squadron to which he belonged for such purpose, and declared to Lieutenant de Stankart, that he was now at the head of it, and that the lieutenant must give place to him, and receive his orders. M. de Stankart, inured to the service, and rigid on points of subordination, refused to consider him in any other light than that; of his cornet. The newcreated captain was much enraged at this opposition, yet put off all further discussion till after the battle, when the business degenerated into a duel.

Fortune now abandoned her favourite, and he was severely wounded. For the purpose of facilitating his cure, he was charged with a mission and despatched to Berlin, where his irregularities in a little time became the subject of complaint, and forced his general to represent to the king, that it would be proper to suspend his new commission for a while, and to degrade him to his former rank. His Majesty, in compliance with the general's advice, gave immediate orders, that, for the present, the young officer must content himself with his cross, and, that to regain his rank, he must wait his turn and the favourable reports of his general.

The affair made much noise. The example, indeed, was an instructive one. If on the one hand, such bold and decisive proceeding inspired sentiments of fearful respect for the general who had adopted it; on the other hand, the disinterestedness of his motives and the purity of his intentions secured him the love and confidence of the whole army. Nor was this all, however incredible what we have to add might appear. The young man, who certainly, as we have already seen, was not wanting either in ambition or spirit and whose self-love had been so deeply wounded, withdrew neither his respect nor his attachment from the general who had thus stopped him in his splendid career.

Instead of quitting the regiment and entering into some other corps of light horse, in which he might have made a more rapid advancement, he was not in the least inclined to throw off the authority of Zieten, and thus made ample reparation for errors into which his want of education and his ungovernable temper had thrown him. Faithful to his general and to his superior officers, he afforded an example of orderly conduct which gained him the affection and esteem of his comrades, and which afterwards caused his exploits to be attributed to personal merit, which jealousy might otherwise have considered as the result of good fortune only. Time confirmed his reputation, and cemented his generous union with Zieten. An army which produces such models, and which encourages such emulation, must force envy itself to declare it invincible.

The king having quitted Schweidnitz in order to invade Moravia, Zieten at first covered His Majesty's departure by a position which disabled the enemy from annoying him; after this, being joined by the corps under the command of Major-General de Zieten, they began their march together.

\*\*\*\*\*\*\*\*\*\*

> This general lost his life in the Battle of Frankfort in the year 1769. He distinguished himself in this march by repulsing the vigorous and repeated attacks of General de Laudon and General de Buckow at Gottesberg

\*\*\*\*\*\*\*\*\*\*

The former, on the 4th of May, arriving at Neustadt, found the army at Schmirsitz, and protected the king's quarters (at Prosnitz), during the siege of Ollmütz which was carried on by Marshal Keith.

The Austrian Army, after having hung upon the rear of that of the king, encamped in Moravia opposite to it. Availing himself of his superiority in light troops, Marshal Daun had distributed them into various detachments, which he posted round the Prussian Army to harass it; and, at the same time, he carefully avoided coming to any serious engagement. The corps of Saint-Ignon occupied a position at Preraw, extremely incommodious to the Prussians and very convenient for himself, as by affording him a communication with the surrounding divisions, it preserved one with the fortress, into which Marshal Daun was, by such means, enabled to throw two thousand men on the 22nd of May, unimpeded and even unobserved by General de Retzow who commanded in those parts. The king justly apprehending that Saint Ignon would open a direct communication with the place, and take the corps of Retzow which he was threatening, His Majesty ordered Zieten to approach Preraw, to reconnoitre the position, and to meditate on the means necessary for dislodging the enemy.

Zieten broke up his camp on the same day (May the 22nd), at

noon. He passed the Morava with three battalions of grenadiers, two regiments of cavalry, and nine hundred hussars. After being reinforced by Restow's corps, he advanced upon Preraw, through Grosser-Teinitz, Krzmann and Kockor; and, in order to secure a retreat, he left detachments of infantry in every village and in each defile. These precautions were not useless. General de Saint-Ignon, who had been apprised of his march, and whose particular orders, as well as his own advantage, required him to avoid an engagement, had left only a feeble detachment of hussars and Cravats (Croats) at Preraw; and in spite of the superiority of an almost inaccessible position, defended by dikes, marshes, and a river, he withdrew with the rest of his troops to the heights of Bichnow: he moreover sent his baggage to Kropin.

In this retreat, Zieten imagined he perceived a snare. He might have easily dislodged the Cravats (Croats), and pursued the Austrian general; he was, however, unwilling to hazard the attempt, and was apprehensive of being cut off from the main army. Had he advanced too far, he would have left the strong fortress of Tebetscha behind him; and there was a considerable garrison in it. He was, moreover, liable to be turned, on his leaving Kropin and Kremsir, by some strong detachments which lay in those quarters; and he would have exposed, perhaps sacrificed, his men to no purpose; a measure he always was averse to. His reconnoitring having been effected, the enemy dislodged, and his junction with Retzow operated, he fell back upon Ollmütz, and encamping in the plains of Bistrowa and Brezcz, he shut up the place on that side. Saint-Ignon resumed his former position which now became less alarming.

We are now coming to one of the most trying periods of the life and the various campaigns of our hero. Hitherto, properly speaking, he had been never beat; at least, the corps he had commanded, whether on particular expeditions or in pitched battles, if they had not conquered, had ever preserved their well-earned reputation, in the midst of the general defeat. For Laudon, the task of checking him in his splendid career was reserved, and, by a masterly stroke, to overcome him with superior forces. This defeat brought on the loss of a convoy consisting of between two and three thousand waggons, loaded with provisions, military stores, and arms for the king's camp, and caused the raising of the siege.

This convoy set off on the 21st of June from Neisse and from Cosel. Colonel de Mosel who escorted it, was at the head of twelve battalions, composed, for the far greater part, of raw recruits and convalescents, together with a body of twelve hundred horse. The less the enemy were supposed to be privy to the expedition, the more were they able to conceal from the Prussians the measures that were taken to defeat it. It was, indeed, almost impossible that they should not succeed in their designs against the convoy, acquainted as they were with the ground, and having mountains, rivers, and every inhabitant of the country in their favour.

Colonel de Mosel being arrived at Trappaw, passed the frontiers on the 20th of June. Marshal Daun now availing himself of the information he had gathered on his way, ordered General de Laudon to gain Hoff by a circuitous route, and to lie in ambush there, while General de Siskowitz should pass the Morava, join Saint-Ignon at Preraw, and keep himself concealed in the forest of Alt-Lieba, until the moment fixed upon for the attack. Furthermore, the marshal, with a view of diverting the king's attention to another point, made several motions with the main army. He reconnoitred the position of the Prussians, broke up his camp, and, drawing nearer to them, appeared to be making ready to give them battle, and took every necessary measure to keep them occupied.

The king being informed by Zieten's patrols, that Saint-Ignon had quitted the post of Preraw to march further on, concluded that the Austrians intended to attack the convoy. He was, however, far from foreseeing the whole extent of the plan. Ill served by his spies, as is commonly the case in a country devoted to the enemy, he was unacquainted with the march of the other columns: yet the movement of Saint-Ignon was alone sufficient to excite his apprehensions, and he did everything in his power to avert the impending mischief.

To this end, he despatched Zieten to Colonel de Mosel, and gave him two battalions of grenadiers, two regiments of *cuirassiers*. And six hundred dragoons, together with orders to reinforce himself on his way with the corps of Retzow. The evening before, Zieten had detached Colonel de Werner with a battalion and five hundred horse. Having rejoined them at Giebaw, he learnt that the colonel had not been able to advance further on.

At the same time, a heavy cannonade was heard, its smoke was perceived, and there was no longer any doubt that Colonel de Mosel was attacked by the enemy. In consequence of this, Zieten's corps halted at Giebaw; the baggage was sent back, was fallen upon by the light cavalry of the Austrians, and rescued by the valour of Seidlitz's hussars. In the meanwhile, Zieten, who had followed Colonel de Werner, at the head of a regiment of *cuirassiers*, supported him in so vigorous a manner, that they joined Mosel towards the evening, who after the encounter had advanced as far as Neudörfel. It was now the 28th of June, On the preceding day, the latter, on account of the broken roads and the slow progress of the convoy, had found himself under the necessity of making halt at Bautsch, to wait for the arrival of two thirds of the waggons, and to send back to Troppaw whatever he conceived the army in a situation of dispensing with for the present moment.

These untoward circumstances favoured the projects of Laudon. His division had time to advance, to occupy the passages, and to intercept the communications. The arrival of Werner at Giebaw, sufficiently indicating that succour was at hand, Laudon had accelerated his march, in order to post troops on the hills which commanded the defiles between Bautsch and Alt-Lieba, through which the convoy had to pass. He had likewise thrown his Hungarian infantry and Cravats (Croats) into the woods, and stationed a body of dragoons and hussars in the plain, in order to make an attack on all sides at once.

Colonel de Mosel beginning his march on the same day, found Laudon in the defiles of Bautsch. He forced the passage, formed beyond the defiles, drove out the infantry' and the Cravats, (Croats) carried a battery-with the bayonet, and after having taken two hundred prisoners, he repulsed Laudon as far as Bahr with the loss of five hundred men. When the engagement was over, M. de Mosel sent his *aide-de-camp*, de Seville, (later lieutenant-general, and Governor of Neuchatel), to the king with a circumstantial account of his success; and continuing his march, he joined Zieten at Neudörfel, as has been already mentioned.

The enemy were thrown into disorder; but the convoy was likewise in the same condition. During the engagement, the guides and their assistants arrived at Troppaw in the utmost confusion. The Austrian hussars taking advantage of the disorder, began to pillage and destroy the provisions. The Prussian cavalry came up too late to prevent the havoc; they, however, put the enemy to flight, but the mischief was already done.

The troops having reached Neudörfel, the night of the 28th was employed in collecting the wrecks of the convoy; not one half of which was recovered. The guides having abandoned their horses; the horses, which were spent with fatigue, were unable to get clear of the deep roads; the fugitives were already at a great distance from the spot. Zieten had taken the command upon himself: it was necessary to re-establish good order, to give time for repose to both men and horses; to re-organise the convoy;—and in this manner the 29th was taken up.

This new delay furnished the enemy with an opportunity of making a fresh attack. In the former one, Laudon alone had acted, as on his being informed of the approach of Zieten and the succour that accompanied him, he had been beforehand with him, in consequence of a forced march. At present, that able general being reinforced with the corps of Serbelloni, placed himself in ambush between Lieba and Dohmstädtel, in the woods that skirted the road.

The Prussians began to file along. The wary Austrian still kept his position. Already the head of the column and the convoy, under the command of M. de Krockow, began to spread out on the plain, and the centre which followed considered themselves in perfect safety; when all on a sudden, the enemy rushed between them, and occupying the outlet, began a furious engagement, which Zieten sustained with his accustomed bravery; an engagement, which, seconded as he was by the valour of his troops, would have turned out in his favour (as several hostile battalions had already given way, and lost their artillery) had not Laudon, by turning, and surrounding the rear of the convoy, changed the face of affairs and decided the victory.

The Prussians had to contend, at the same time, with the difficulties of the ground and a twofold attack. Their separate situation was, moreover, in their disfavour, as well as their having a convoy to protect, and an enemy to cope with. Their muskets too were rendered useless by a continual fall of rain, while those of the Austrians had been preserved dry till the very moment of action. Every circumstance was in favour of the latter, who did not neglect to take ample advantage thereof. The convoy was dispersed and plundered, the powder set fire to, and the military stores and provisions destroyed.

The advanced-guard of General de Krockow, consisting of two hundred and fifty waggons, solely escaped, and arrived in safety at the king's camp. Zieten had made a last desperate effort. He threw himself, at the head of a party of his troops, upon the enemy; but not being strong enough to force his way through them, and being cut off from the rest of the division, he escaped with much difficulty to Troppaw, with the remains of his small party.

History has honoured the memory of the gallant warriors who lost their lives in this encounter. We shall confine ourselves to a single instance of patriotic bravery which commands our admiration and calls forth our sensibility. Of nine hundred new recruits, all in the flower of their age and the vigour of life, who were enlisted for the purpose of completing the regiment of Prince Ferdinand, not one hundred survived the affray. The rest, together with the gallant officer who commanded them, were left dead on the spot. General de Tempelhof speaking of them in his *History of the Seven-Years' War*, (vol. 2), observes that "if they were unable to conquer, they at least knew how to die."

The conduct of Zieten has both its censurers and its panegyrists. The former blame him for having halted at Neudörfel for the purpose of collecting the scattered convoy. According to their opinion, he should have gained the defile of Dohmstädtel, have tempted the enemy to follow him, and have taken advantage of the plain in case of an engagement. The advocates of Zieten reply, that he could not have maintained his post at Dohmstädtel, even had he been able to occupy the defile; that a string of waggons, in a mountainous country, traversed by a single road, takes up a considerable line; that a convoy, liable to be attacked on every point, requires a numerous and extended escort, and that by compressing the troops, the baggage must have been sacrificed.

Should it be said, that on the day on which Zieten halted, Laudon and Seskowitz had not formed a junction, and could not have attacked him; it would not have been the less true, that by marching onward, he would have rendered the convoy incapable of following him, and thus abandoned it to the mercy of the enemy. Besides, he was unacquainted with the combined movements of the two generals; and he expected to have been, harassed by the flying troops that infested the route, against whom he conceived he should make the more effectual resistance by distributing his men along the file of waggons.

However, it might have been, it were to be wished that, impartial and well-informed as he ever was in his judgment of his own exploits and his own errors, he had himself furnished the documents necessary for the elucidation of this affair. In default of this, we must refer the dispute to such, as being the most capable of deciding it, will doubtless pass the most equitable judgment.

The consequences of this disastrous event are well known. The king raised the siege of Ollmütz; a siege which had proved the more irksome and laborious, as it had been necessary to draw all his subsistence from Silesia, and as every convoy had been in continual risk of falling into the hands of the Austrians. There is, moreover, reason to believe, that the enemy would not have allowed the king sufficient time to complete the siege of this place or to have taken due advantage of his conquest, since storms were now rising against him in various parts of his dominions, and to quell which his immediate presence was necessary. One of the most enlightened of all Frederick's critics, (this estimable writer is only known by the vague appellation of "the Austrian Veteran"), and so much the more worthy of credit in the present case, as he was one of the king's most zealous admirers, asserts, that by his expedition into Moravia, and the ill-advised siege of Ollmütz, that monarch had most assuredly furnished his enemies with arms against himself; that he had lost sight of the advantages he might have derived from the victory of Leuthen, and, in a word, that he was ignorant (of what is now no secret) that the Austrian Army, which was entirely disorganised daring the winter of 1757, availed itself of the time the king lost before Ollmütz in order to recover its former complement and vigour.

Zieten, cut off at Dohmstädtel from the rest of the convoy, arrived at Troppaw with a handful of troops, but did not long remain there. The king having taken his march through Bohemia after the raising of the siege, the general had orders to join His Majesty at Neisse.

It was about this time (the beginning of July) that the Russians, who were advancing by quick marches towards the frontiers, were expected to enter Silesia. Zieten, after having reinforced several garrisons, remained until the 24th of July at Neisse, and then rejoined the king's army at Skaltitsch.

At this place he found his regiment, whose joy at his arrival was extreme. His own was not less so when he was apprised, that during the siege, and on the retreat, that regiment had acquitted itself with its usual *éclat*, and that it was entirely owing to it, that the king had not been more closely pressed by the corps of Laudon, which hung upon his rear during the above-mentioned retreat. The regiment had suffered much; the courage of the troops had proved very destructive to them. Among a thousand instances of valour, one example of intrepid fidelity of which we shall here make mention, is particularly worthy of the reader's notice. During the siege, a private hussar, of the name of Lange, keeping sentinel, alone and unmounted, before the tent of the major of the regiment, was attacked by several troopers at once, and not only refused to yield, but began and sustained a most unequal combat with them.

When his sabre was at length forced from him, he continued to defend the entrance of the tent with his carabine. He finally remained master of the field, and though severely cut and mangled, happily none of his wounds proved mortal. His carabine bore upwards of twenty honourable marks, acquired in this singular fray. The nocturnal surprises that took place at Weissen-Kösteritz during three successive nights, had deprived the regiment of a considerable number of men, together with an excellent officer, (Lieutenant de Jurgas).

Zieten and Seidlitz, at the head of their cavalry, covered the king's retreat. Scarcely had the monarch honourably made his way through the defiles of Moravia and traversed the mountains of Bohemia, when he flew to the succour of his country to the extremity of the electorate of Brandenburg, now menaced by the Russians, who, after having burnt the town of Custrin, were proceeding on to the heart of the Prussian dominions.

This was one of the most critical situations in which the king had been involved during the whole war; yet his courage sustained, and his genius extricated him. He detached fourteen thousand men from his army, and with these, he hastened to the relief of Count Dohna, who was no longer able to cope with the more numerous forces of General de Fermor. The rest of the main army he intrusted to the command of the Margrave Charles, to whom he gave orders to cover the frontiers of Silesia.

Marshal Daun, with whom the *margrave* had to contend, was meditating the vast design of forming a junction with the French Army and with that of the circles of Germany; of attacking Prince Henry, the king's brother; of forcing him to repass the Elbe, and of making himself master of that river, while the Russians gained possession of the Oder, and the Swedes advanced upon Berlin, which he had marked out as the place of general rendezvous.

After having composed the king's advanced-guard and beat several detachments in his way, one of which he met at Politz, Zieten quitted His Majesty (who now passed the Oder) and joining the division of General de Fouqué, he remained in Silesia under the command of the *margrave*.

The Prussian Army was divided into three bodies. At the head of the first, the king beat the Russians at Zorndorf, on the 25th of August. With the second, Prince Henry disputed every foot of ground with the French, and with the German circles, in Saxony; and with the third, the Margrave Charles took so good a position, that he was able to cover both Silesia and the *marquisate* of Brandenburg at the same time.

Thus miscarried the formidable plan of the enemies of Frederick, after so many dear-bought victories, well-times marches, and skilful positions; and Prussia was indebted for its preservation to the joint efforts of its sovereign and his gallant army.

Zieten was now separated from his regiment. Both himself and that corps were distinguishing themselves in different countries. The regiment, which had accompanied the king, was of eminent service to His Majesty in the Battle of Zorndorf. After having overthrown the Russian cavalry, it made great havoc upon the infantry; and although twice surrounded by the enemy, the troops cut their way through them, and spread terror among the Cossacks who covered the retreat. On that famous day, the regiment gained new laurels at the expense of much blood, and among the killed and wounded, were reckoned twenty-one officers.

While the hussars were thus acquitting themselves in the plains of Zorndorf, their chief was engaged in Silesia, in a career, less brilliant, indeed, but in every respect as conducive to the public welfare. Of this, an intercepted letter from General Laudon to Marshal Daun, affords ample proof. Daun, who was then in the neighbourhood of Meissen, acknowledges in this letter, that Zieten, whom he always found in his way, was at one time, harassing his rear, at another, impeding his march. Laudon's report was made a short time previous to the change of operations which took place in those parts, when Daun had been prevented by the king's return from forming a junction with the army of the German circles for the purpose of attacking Prince Henry, and when Laudon had failed in his scheme of invading the *marquisate* of Brandenburg.

We shall not enter into any detail respecting the marches and counter-marches of the division under the command of Zieten, which consisted of eight battalions and fifteen squadrons. His principal rendezvous was Löwenburg, whence he kept the enemy in awe, and made such attacks as their various motions rendered necessary. At length the *margrave* and Zieten entered into a twofold plan of operation which the circumstances of the moment required. To this end, the former repaired to Silesia, and the latter to the electorate of Brandenburg; and while Laudon advanced toward the electorate, Zieten skirted the Bober, and hung upon his rear; but being obliged to halt during twenty-four hours in order to allow the provision-waggons time to keep up with him, he was not able to hinder that general from taking advantage of the delay and sending a detachment as far as Cottbus, Frankfort, and Peitz, to put the country under contribution.

The critical situation in which the king then found himself could alone give any importance to this circumstance, which at any other period would have been confounded in the crowd of events; and even now, it was far from being attended with any disastrous consequences, as after the victory of Zorndorf, the king having detached Prince Francis of Brunswick, that prince, assisted by Zieten's hussars and a single free battalion, cleared the whole country.

Zieten has been censured for having allowed the enemy to gain a march upon him. The charge is, however, more severe than just. The general had to choose between two evils, and he made choice of the lesser. What could he have expected from his troops, had he left them without bread in an exhausted country, far from the magazines of Schweidnitz, whence he drew his subsistence? The imperialists drew theirs from Zittaw, which lay at no great distance from them; and besides, they foraged in Lusatia, and their flying corps were more expeditious than the Prussians in the transport of their convoys.

As soon as Zieten was furnished with a provision of bread, he continued his march, (on the 25th of August), and advanced towards Güben, where he arrived the 29th. He dislodged the enemy from thence, pitched his camp at Lieberose on the 13th of September, and covered the *marquisate* of Brandenburg. For the space of two months, he had the satisfaction of checking the progress of the victor of Dohmstädtel.

Nothing could be more difficult than this defensive kind. of warfare; as, to the obligation of avoiding the possibility of a battle, was added the necessity of discovering the plans of the enemy, opposing their marches, throwing obstacles in their way, disputing every inch, of ground with them, and, in a word, of tiring them out without venturing to take any repose himself.

Soon after this, the king hastened to the relief of his troops in Lusatia and Saxony. He had traversed the schemes of the Russians during a period of twelve months, and with a bold and skilful arm had broken that formidable colossus which threatened his country with destruction. On the 4th of September, His Majesty had arrived at Gross-Dubritz, and forced the enemy to leave off acting on the offensive I and to reflect with regret on their having lost the only opportunity they had of laying waste the *marquisate*. Frederick found Prince Henry entrenched with his small army at Gumig, coping with a body of a hundred thousand men, and, at the same time, covering both the Elbe and the capital of Saxony.

In Silesia, His Majesty found the Margrave Charles encamped in the face of Marshal Daun. He strove for a long time to force the latter from his strong post and to join battle, nor was he able to turn him before the beginning of the month of October. Daun then took the fine position of Kittlitz; and the king, the memorable camp of Hochkirchen. The army of the German circles being already withdrawn, the field remained clear for the two great powers.

The king's camp touched that of the enemy, who considered this security as a bravado, and began to meditate vengeance. Its open position was extremely perilous; every general was apprehensive of the consequences of it, and Zieten partook of their alarms. The king placed entire confidence in the reports of a spy, which having proved true in the first instances, lulled the monarch into a false security, and brought on the disasters he soon after experienced. Daun, who had detected this spy, compelled him to continue his reports to the Prussians and to lead them astray. He therefore informed them, that the marshal was in continual expectation of a surprise, that he was making mounds and entrenchments, and, in a word, that he confined himself to defensive measures, without forming the least plan of acting on the offensive.

The king's intention being, in fact, to surprise the marshal, these reports acquired a further degree of probability in his estimation; and it was scarcely possible for him to escape being deceived by them. The 14th of October was the day fixed upon for the execution of this plan. He indulged the most sanguine hopes, and even considered the success of it as infallible. Credulity encourages expectation. The hussars of Zieten had, however, perceived on the 13th, an extraordinary movement in the enemy's camp. Colonel de Seelen, their commanding officer having made instant report, the king, by way of precaution, forthwith ordered the troops to lie under arms; but observing that everything remained quiet till the evening, and deluded by the false report of his spy, he ordered them to return into the camp.

Zieten and Seidlitz did all in their power to undeceive him. They repaired to his tent, conjured him not to allow the troops to disarm, and communicated their apprehensions and suspicions. The king remained unmoveable. Desirous of preparing the troops for the night of the 14th, he was determined they should take sufficient rest on the preceding day, and he furthermore gave orders that the cavalry should be unsaddled.

The latter order particularly concerned Zieten who commanded that part of the army. The general was now under no small embarrassment. On one hand, he considered what he owed to the king; on the other, what he owed to his country. In obeying the one, he would expose the other to danger. He was, however, able to reconcile those opposite duties; or rather, consulting his own prudence and courage; venturing further than any other would have ventured; opposing the consequences which he foresaw to the responsibility which he took upon himself; and aware that the safety of the state would justify him before the tribunal of subordination, he took his resolution accordingly, and obeyed and disobeyed at the same time:—he ordered the horses to be unsaddled for half an hour, and then gave orders for their being saddled again

This precaution saved the army. In a few hours after, the enemy fell upon the right wing of the camp, which they found unprepared for making any defence, as the troops were already asleep. A dreadful carnage ensued, and the consequences would have been fatal, had it not been for the intervention of Zieten and his cavalry, who flew to the succour of their comrades, and checked the progress of the enemy. They fought with incredible bravery, and afforded the Prussian battalions time to form in order of battle. The four regiments of Zieten, Czettritz, Schöneich, and Normann, performed prodigies of valour. They sustained the infantry, charged that of the enemy, seemed to fly, to multiply their numbers; and being seconded by a few battalions, were at length on the point of gaining the victory. But the foggy weather, the confusion, the general alarm, all of which were favourable to the Austrians, prevented the Prussians from duly recovering themselves and acting in concert.

It is not here the place to enter into the detail of this disastrous, yet glorious day; the leader will find ample information in the history of the times; but we thought it necessary to state the above anecdote, and to shew Zieten exposing himself to the anger of his sovereign, rather than to expose his prince and his country to ruin. If it was not in his power to lay the storm, he was at least able to mitigate its fury; and in acquitting himself of this duty as became a good patriot, he was enabled, amidst all the distresses and disasters of the day, to enjoy the satisfaction of having considerably diminished their number.

Frederick, though vanquished, nevertheless made that fine retreat, which will never be forgotten, and which, unique in its kind, displays the intrepidity of his soul, and the force of his genius. He quitted the field of battle, which was heaped with thousands of slain, to pitch his camp at a league distant from thence where he assumed so formidable a posture, that the enemy, although in possession of all his artillery, durst not venture to attack him.

After being joined by Prince Henry, the king marched into Silesia, relieved Neisse and Cosel, which were closely besieged, advanced forty German miles in the space of ten or twelve days, returned to Saxony with the like rapidity; and after having forced Marshal Daun to raise the siege of Dresden, compelled him to evacuate Leipsic and Torgaw, drove him into Bohemia, chased the Army of the Circles into Franconia, and at the end of the campaign of 1758, remained in peaceable possession of Silesia, Saxony the Oder and the Elbe.

In all these operations, Zieten had proved of the utmost importance to him. In the first instance, after the surprise of Hochkirchen, he covered the retreat, and effectually prevented the Austrian cavalry from annoying the army. When the king had gained Neisse, Zieten returned to the army of Prince Henry, then stationed among the mountains; and upon the movements made by Daun in order to invest Schweidnitz, he covered the march of the prince, and facilitated his junction with his brother. He preserved the communication with the fortress, and kept Laudon, Brentano, and Nauendorf in awe.

Furthermore, when the king returned into Saxony, and the prince had followed him to Lauban in order to hold a conference with him, His Majesty entrusted the command in chief of the army to Zieten, who now had Laudon to contend with. He was so well enabled to check the motions of that general, that he kept him in a state of inactivity during the rest of the campaign. On the 1st of December, both parties entered into their respective winter-quarters, and Zieten betook himself to his former position among the mountains.

He was likewise charged to cover the chain of posts between Landshut, Schmiedeberg, and Greiffenberg, at the head of seven battalions and twenty squadrons; and though he apprehended no surprise on the part of the enemy, he was not the less vigilant, and attentive to their slightest motions, nor the more remiss in making his reports to the king.

With these cares and toils, others of a different nature were combined. His regiment was now to be recruited both with officers and private soldiers.

The campaign of 1758 had made such havoc in that corps, that he was under the necessity of requesting the king's leave to make choice of such officers as he found in the several regiments of the army as were proper for the hussar service. Of all his losses, the most irreparable one had been that of Colonel de Seelen, the *commandant* of the corps. This brave officer being mortally wounded at the surprise of Hochkirchen, and left in that village on account of the impracticableness of carrying him away, was massacred the following evening by a party of Cravats (Croats). His courage and his humanity had gained him the esteem of the king, and the respect of the whole army.

Zieten, without intending it, made him a suitable epitaph. We shall state the circumstance in a few words.

Before the beginning of the seven years' war, the general had ornamented his dining-room at Wüstrau with the portraits of the principal officers of his regiment. That of M. de Seelen, was a remarkable good likeness. One day (a long while after the war) when one of the guests was looking attentively at the picture, Zieten observing him, exclaimed, "The man you are contemplating there, was worth all of us put together."

In effect, noble, modest, disinterested as he was, he deserved that flattering eulogy. His various exploits, his innumerable expeditions, rendered him dear to Frederick, whose orders were generally couched in the form of requests, and who on more than one occasion, had, in a moment of gratitude, promised to redress the wrongs of fortune, and to enrich him; a favour, which Seelen as often acknowledged to His Majesty, would be of little avail, as whatever he might thus receive, he should consider as belonging as much to his friends as to himself.

A few moments before the fatal bullet reached him, having seen Lieutenant de Probst, his friend and pupil, wounded at his side, he ordered him to be carried behind the ranks. (Since that time, *commandant* of the regiment. He fell in the Bavarian War, in the year. 1778.) While the surgeon was employed in dressing the wound, a party of hussars passed by, bearing the colonel, wrapped, up in his cloak. What an interview for the two friends! Seelen bade his pupil a last favewell, but refused his embraces, not only to spare the lieutenant's emotions, but probably to prevent himself from immediately sinking under the anguish arising from his wound. He died as he had lived. The king relieved the pecuniary distresses of his, widow and daughter, who were not only unprovided for, but much encumbered with debts.

One of the colonel's creditors behaved in the most noble manner to these unfortunate ladies. He had advanced M, de Seelen, not long before his death, the sum of six thousand dollars upon a house the latter had in Berlin. Being informed that the house was shortly to be sold for the purpose of paying off the mortgage, he immediately called on Madame de Seelen, and making her a present of the deed, declared it was far from his intention to distress the family of a worthy man, who, had he lived, would certainly not failed to have paid him. This generous creditor was M. Jacob Moses, a wealthy Jew of the city of Berlin, who died a few years ago with the reputation of great probity, humanity, and talents.

The colonel's son treads in the footsteps of his father. The king frequently exhorted him to follow the example, and at the same time, was pleased to renew his promise of taking care of him. He was first placed in the regiment of Zieten, from whence he was removed into the hussars of Anspach, with the rank of captain, in the reign of Frederick William II.

We have stated, that Zieten obtained leave from His Majesty to recruit his shattered regiment with such officers, belonging to other corps, as he should judge fit for the service; and we shall insert their names, because several of them have since succeeded him as generals. These were M. de Zettmar, M, de Hund, M. de Prittwitz, M. de Drössel, M. de Wolfrath, M. de Luck, M. de Holzen, M. de Schladen, M. de Ledevary, and M. de Rumberg.

At the same time, he removed some of his veteran, captains into regiments of easier discipline, advanced many young officers by way of encouragement (among others, M. de Lestocq, now general of a regiment of hussars, and an officer of great professional talents), raised several sergeants of merit to the rank of lieutenant, and obtained the royal approbation of all these useful proceedings.

We shall now insert some of the letters of the king and Zieten which were written at this period.

*Letter from the king.*

My dear Lieutenant-General de Zieten.
I charge you by the present letter to write to me frequently in order to inform me of everything that occurs in your quarters, and of the various motions of the enemy.
Dresden, December 15th, 1758.

*(Postscript, in the king's own hand),*

Send me the names of such officers as you think fit to fill up the vacancies in your regiment.                              Frederick.

*(Another postscript, at the bottom of a letter from the king.)*

I entirely approve of the arrangement of the quarters you have pointed out.                              Frederick.

*Letter from the king.*

My dear Lieutenant-General de Zieten.

I charge and earnestly recommend to you to procure such spies as may speedily and accurately inform you of whatever the enemy may be meditating and preparing against you. Spare no expense in this business, and particularly for spies of consequence, should it be in your power to obtain any of such description. I shall not regret the money, and shall instantly reimburse you,

Breslaw,                                                          Frederick.
December 17th, 1758.

*Letter from Zieten, without any date.*

In consequence of Your Majesty's gracious commands, I have just conferred the squadron, vacant by the death of Colonel de Seelen, on Captain de Prittwitz. I wait Your Majesty's disposal of the hundred dollars accruing from the pay in the interval. I humbly propose the following division of the five hundred dollars winter allowance for the chief of the squadron. I would give a moiety to the widow, because she is straitened in her circumstances, and that her late husband's equipments were taken at Hochkirchen; the other moiety, I would present to captain de Prittwitz. I apprize your majesty, that either party will be satisfied with such arrangement.

In the regiment-chest, there remains the sum of seven hundred and thirty-six dollars, arising from the pay of those who died and were not immediately replaced by others; and I humbly propose, unless Your Majesty should decide otherwise, that this sum be granted to the regiment, to be divided among such of the officers as lost their equipments at Zorndorf and Hochkirchen; as well as among those who are newly arrived, and have not the means of furnishing their own. I promise Your Majesty to make this division according to the strictest rules of equity, and I may venture to assure you of an increase of zeal and attachment on the part of such officers as shall participate this benefaction.

We have every reason to believe that the king gave his consent to an arrangement equally prudent and equitable, and we have inserted the letter merely to afford new proof of the upright and impartial character of Zieten. There are still extant a multitude of reports of this nature which the general made to the king during the months of January, February, March, and May, of the year 1759. They contain the military, historical, and political occurrences of the day; observations upon the prevailing sentiments of the Hungarian nation; various changes which happened in the Austrian Army, together with some curious particulars relative to Vienna. These authentic and valuable reports are not only too bulky to find a place in these memoirs, but would be at the same time superfluous, as they contain matter which has since appeared in the history of the times, and which is amply discussed in the works of Frederick the Great, and in the *Observations of an Austrian Veteran*.

For the like reason, fourteen letters, written by the king to Zieten, are not inserted in these sheets. They are dated from Breslaw, in the months of January, February, and March, 1759, and contain general and particular orders, directions relative to discipline, and details with regard to the position and motions of the enemy. In five of these letters, the king expresses his approbation of Zieten's conduct. In one, written in the month of March, His Majesty complains of the infrequency of his reports, and that the general had not apprised him of the march of the Austrians. In the following letter, of the 5th, he informs Zieten that the rumour of the above-mentioned march had been unfounded, and he likewise thanks him for a late report. Finally, in the last letter but one, dated the 15th, he desires him to repair to the headquarters at Bohnstock, to hold a conference with him.

In consequence of this, Zieten, at the beginning of the fourth, campaign, waited upon the king, who was likewise attended by all the other generals, for the purpose of receiving His Majesty's orders.

It is well known that the king, at the beginning of the year 1759, remained on the defensive, without passing the mountains, that he was satisfied with covering Silesia and endeavouring to dive into the intentions of the enemy, in order to counteract them with the more energy and success.

He at first divided his army into cantonments in the environs of Schweidnitz. Marshal Daun distributed his in like manner in Bohemia, and his quarters extended from Trautenaw to Reichenberg. Zieten's corps lay encamped in the vicinity of the latter town. It consisted of eighteen battalions and nineteen squadrons. His headquarters were at Landshut, and the extremities of the encampment the towns of Löwenberg and Greifenberg.

The enemy made no attempts against the centre, but meditated a bold stroke upon. Greifenberg with all the confidence of success, on account of the proximity of that town, and the advantages the ground afforded them. Colonel de Duringshofen was garrisoned in the above place with one battalion of grenadiers; and four squadrons of Zieten's cavalry, under the command of Major de Hund, were stationed in the adjacent villages. In the night of the 23rd of March, the corps of General de Beck quitted its post at Zittaw.

This body of men, which was six thousand strong, advanced in three columns upon Greifenberg. The Prussian *commandant*, duly apprised of their march by Zieten's patrols, had time to send his baggage to Löwenberg, and to call the garrison of that place to his succour, as well as to occupy, in the meanwhile, the strong position of Klingenberg. In this place, he waited the arrival of the enemy. The intended surprise was now changed into an open attack: the Prussian grenadiers fought with the most determined bravery; till finding themselves surrounded by three hostile columns, cut off from the post of Löwenberg, and their commanding officer mortally wounded, they were compelled to yield, and were made prisoners of war.

After having imposed a contribution of two thousand florins upon the town of Greifenberg, the Austrian general left it on the same evening, and marched into Bohemia. This assault, which had been masked by a false attack along the whole frontier, was attended with no further consequences; and though it does not directly relate to Zieten, we have nevertheless made mention of it, as a part of the corps he commanded was involved therein.

To prevent. such disasters in future, the king reinforced the posts of the mountains, altered their positions, stationed Zieten nearer to the frontiers, and having directed him to establish his headquarters at Löwenberg he furnished him with a battery mounted with twelve pounders. His Majesty covered his flank by a second corps, under the command of Lieutenant-General de Wedel. Thus, the two generals, placed as they were, had it in their power to afford each other mutual assistance as necessity should require; but their principal object was to observe Laudon, to follow up his motions, to keep a strict look-out on all points, to vary their quarters, change their fronts, gain information by sending out reconnoitring parties, prepare for attacks and repulse skirmishes. In this painful service, Zieten acquitted himself to the satisfaction of his sovereign.

Whilst he remained thus on the defensive and was checking the progress, of the enemy; and while stationed in the centre of the operations, the king was following the same plan; Prince Henry and General de Fouqué (the former, in Bohemia, and the latter, in Moravia) were proceeding with great vigour: they gained magazines, carried off garrisons, and took the Austrians in their rear. Not satisfied with these advantages, the prince had entered Franconia, dispersed the troops; of the circles, and after having deprived them of the well-stored magazines of Nuremberg, had driven them upon Bohemia and Bavaria. We mention these exploits because Zieten always spoke of them with admiration. It was soon after this, his lot to be a nearer observer of the hero by whom they had been achieved, as he was detached from the army of the king to join that of the prince.

At this period, it was, that General de Wedel was sent against the Russians. Zieten, who was his senior officer, felt himself at first aggrieved on the occasion. Reflection, however, soon came to his aid, and suggested the following consolation, which we shall give the reader in the general's own words, as communicated by him to one of his most intimate friends.

> The king prefers Wedel to me, and I forgive with all my heart. There are no laurels to be gathered in the service on which he is sent; and especially if he should take such and such positions. In such other (which he pointed out) he may cope with the enemy, may even come off victorious, and, (added he with warmth,) should Wedel have sense enough to make a proper choice, I should go half-distracted not to be in his place.

Unfortunately, the general adopted the position which Zieten had mentioned as extremely dangerous. He was beat at Kay, near Zullichaw, and the country became exposed to new danger. The victorious Russians entered the *marquisate* of Brandenberg, in order to assist the Swedes who had penetrated therein on the side of Pomerania, at the same time that the Austrians were menacing to join them by, the way of Silesia, and that the army of the circles were approaching the Elbe and the Spree.

Pressed on all sides, Frederick hastened with a part of his army, to the relief of Wedel. He gave his brother, whom he had called into Silesia, the command of the rest of the troops; and in this manner it was that Zieten was now to fight under the banners of Prince Henry.

These changes took place in the month of August. The Battle of Frankfort soon aggravated the disasters of this campaign, and plunged the country into the deepest distress. The great Frederick himself despaired for a moment of the salvation of the state.

The prince, his brother, not only did not despair; but was enabled, by his calm intrepidity, the wisdom of his measures, and his skilful manoeuvres, to re-establish the equilibrium of Prussia, and to deserve the name of the Preserver of his Country.

After this eulogy, that of Zieten will be sufficiently expressed by adding, that he exactly co-operated with the prince in defeating the projects of the enemy, in opposing stratagem to force, and able manoeuvres to superiority of numbers.

The army which the king left on quitting his brother, consisted, according to some accounts, of twenty battalions; and according to others, of forty, together with seventy squadrons. The prince was encamped at Schmolseifen, on the borders of Lusatia, and Daun was stationed over against him between Mark-Lissa and Lauban.

It was of the utmost importance to the prince to keep up a direct communication with the army, which the king commanded in person against the Russians. On the one hand, it was necessary to hinder Marshal Daun from penetrating into the electorate and placing the king between two fires; on the other, the Russians and the corps of Laudon were to be prevented from marching into Silesia and from falling upon Glogaw, which was incapable of making much resistance.

The motions of the marshal were of an alarming and unequivocal nature. He was forming a considerable magazine at Guben in Lusatia for the Russians, towards whom he had made an advance, by having marched with the main body as far as Pribus. The rest of his troops being divided into numerous detachments were posted along the Neisse and the Queisse.

As soon as the prince was informed of these movements, he ordered Zieten to hang on the enemy's flank and observe a parallel direction, and to re-establish the communication with the king who was now at Furstenwald. Zieten filed along the Queisse and the Bober, and advanced to Sagan. He reinforced himself, as he went on, with the corps posted on the frontiers, and at length found himself at the head of fifteen battalions and thirty squadrons, which might be estimated together at ten thousand men.

**********

We shall here add an exact list, for the better explanation
Brigade of Major-General de Bülow.
1 battalion of the grenadiers of de Billerbeck.
1 *ditto* of de Nimschefsky's
2 *ditto* of de Peverlng's,

2 *ditto* of de Munchow's.

Major-General de Braun.
1 battalion of de Reberdach's.
2 *ditto* of de Linstadt's.

Major-General de Sidow
2 battalions of Brunswick's the younger.
2 *ditto*, of de Stutterheim's.
2 *ditto* of Prince Ferdinand's,

Major-General de Bandemen,
10 squadrons of de Faseld's *carbiniers*.
10 *ditto* of de Scimitar's.

Major-General de Czettritz,
5 squadrons of the dragoons of Czettritz.
5 *ditto* of de Gersdorf's hussars

★★★★★★★★★★

He arrived on the 16th, at Bunzlaw, and on the 17th, at Ober-Leschen. He pitched his camp at the latter place, where he had the Bober before him, while his flanks were covered by thick forests.

He remained wholly inactive till the 27th, without being disturbed either by the marshal, who, as it has been observed, was camped at Pribus, or by General de Beck, who had re-occupied Sagan. During this interval, he kept up a free communication with the prince's army and with the fortress of Glogaw.

Alarmed at this bold posture, Daun did not venture to attack him. Soon after, the prince followed him with the bulk of the army, and marched upon Sagan, after having left General de Fouqué at Schmol-seifen for the purpose of observing the rest of the Austrian troops in the camp of Lauban.

On the 27th of August, the prince arrived at Bunzlaw. Zieten, on the same day, advanced as far as Sprottaw, where the hussars of Gersdorf had a skirmish with a party of Beck's corps. That general evacuated Sagan on the same afternoon. The Prussian advanced-guard entered the place the moment in which the Austrians quitted it. The latter having had the precaution to break down the bridge, their loss consisted of a small number of prisoners only.

Zieten arrived on the 28th at Sagan, and pitched his camp on the Galgenberg. He threw a few battalions into the town, repaired the bridge, and stationed some advanced-posts on the other side of the river to check the progress of the enemy. The latter were now meditating a retreat.

The prince followed at a small distance behind, and reached Sagan on the 29th, Zieten gave place to him, and arrived the same day at Soraw, where he seized upon a magazine, and made eighty-four hussars and three officers prisoners of war.

This slight advantage, however, did not render him insensible to the dangers that threatened him. He found himself surrounded by several hostile detachments, which the elevated situation of his camp enabled him plainly to discern. He discovered the main army of Daun with several separate divisions, together with the corps of General de Beck. The latter in particular excited his attention.

In the meanwhile, the motions of the prince and his arrival at Sagan had put an end to the projects and all the offensive measures of Marshal Daun, who not being able to gain Glogaw in due time, fell back from Triebel to Pribus, and from thence, as far as Muska on the other side of the Neisse. He gave up his plan of opening a communication with the Russians and of supplying them with flour from Guben; he was even apprehensive for the safety of that magazine, and caused it to be transported over the Neisse to secure it from the danger with which it was threatened. The different corps of his army, including that of de Beck, at length received orders to retreat.

Of these motions Zieten was informed by General de Czettritz, whom he had sent out on a reconnoitring party, and who having fallen upon Daun's advanced-guard at Triebel, had returned with seventy-three prisoners.

The Austrians flattered themselves that the Prussian general would fall into a dangerous state of security in his camp at Soraw; and though they were five times more numerous than their enemy, they suffered him to remain unmolested during the two last days of August and the first of September, the better to encourage his supposed security. After this, they made a feigned retreat with a view of secretly taking a position favourable to their designs of intercepting and carrying off the corps of Zieten. Beck was instructed to march through the forest of Soraw and take a direction to the left, in order to occupy the Buschmühle (a water mill on the rivulet which runs through Soraw), and the defile which lay on the road to Sagan. Buckow was directed to turn Zieten's right wing and take him in the rear. Daun, in the meantime, intended to attack him in front.

The whole of the 1st of September was taken up in preparations in the three several camps. Of this Zieten unfortunately was not apprized, as a strong patrol, that had been sent out towards Maska in the night of the 1st, either neglected their duty, or performed it in a very imperfect manner. A quantity of provisions and baggage waggons, moreover, arrived at the camp the same night, which increased the general embarrassment; and according to all appearances, Zieten and his ten thousand men could have no prospect of escaping out of the hands of the enemy.

Two fortunate circumstances, assisted by a bold manoeuvre, at length extricated them from their dangerous situation. A patrol of two hundred hussars, sent out from the prince's army, discovered accidentally the advanced guard of General de Beck in full march, in the evening of the 1st. They made their report to Zieten, and confirmed the truth of it by producing thirty prisoners, whom they had just taken. A second lucky incident was the arrival of the free battalion of Salemnon, which the prince had detached on the presumption that it would not prove an unwelcome reinforcement. This battalion arrived in the defile of the Buschmühle at the moment in which Beck was beginning to occupy that post. He thought himself discovered, and taking the battalion and the hussars for the advanced-guard of a corps which the prince had sent to the relief of Zieten, he returned to the forest without having taken possession of the defile.

The night passed undisturbed away. At daybreak, the vedettes gave notice that they perceived a cloud of dust arise in the environs, and distinctly heard the marching of an army. The advanced-guard confirmed their report. General de Czettritz then put himself at the head of two hundred horse, and was soon able to discover plainly the columns that were advancing upon him.

Misled by the report of the officer who had commanded the patrol the preceding night, Zieten could hardly conceive these columns to be part of Marshal Daun's troops; and great was his surprise, when after having advanced to make his own observations, he discovered the Austrian Army full before him. Fifty thousand men were in full march upon him; if they had been able to occupy the heights which commanded his present position, his little army would have been lost. To retreat was all he had now to do; but to effect this in good order was an enterprise of no small difficulty. Zieten, however, was equal to the task. He ordered the retreat, and it was immediately executed in a manner more like a military evolution in time of peace than an operation of real service. The camp was broke up; the baggage preceded the march, under the escort of the regiment of Rebentisch.

The main body began to move, preceded by the heavy cavalry and artillery. They passed the bridge and defile of the Buschmühle without meeting with any obstruction. The infantry followed, the advanced guard, which was composed of the battalions of Lindstädt, Nimschefski, Piverling, Salemnon, the dragoons of Czettritz, and the hussars of Gersdorf. The whole corps vanished from the sight of the Astonished Austrians. Their infantry was unable to overtake that of Zieten; their cavalry was checked by the bravery of Czettritz's dragoons; while the corps of Beck, which endeavoured to harass the march near the Buschmühle, and in the environs of Mansdorf, was repulsed with loss by Salemnon's battalion and those of the rearguard, each of which had formed into a square. The enemy thus frustrated in all their attempts, nevertheless could not withhold their admiration from, nor suppress their applause at, this splendid and extraordinary retreat.

To the praise due to the whole corps, a troop of Czettritz's dragoons is in a particular manner entitled. It consisted of a hundred men who were stationed, with Captain de Beauvré at their head, in the advanced-guard for the purpose of defending the defile of the Buschmühle till the army had passed through it; and they acquitted themselves with such successful bravery, that the post remained unforced. The battalion of Salemnon, which covered the bridge, behaved with: like intrepidity, repulsed the corps of Beck upon every attack, and lost no more than fifteen men.

The loss which Czettritz's dragoons suffered was still less considerable. They joined the battalion when the main body of the army had gained the forest and plain of Sagan, and arrived there without any accident. The enemy took one prisoner only; but it was a prisoner of distinction. Captain de Beauvré, the officer who had fought so gallantly, had the misfortune to have his horse shot under him, towards the end of the engagement. He was stationed in the rear of the retreat: his troops did not at first see him fall; he was instantly taken by a party of Austrian cavalry, and thus purchased with his liberty the glory he had so recently acquired.

Marshal Daun was at no great distance from the spot. The Prussian officer was presented to him, and the general's character appeared in a very advantageous point of view on this occasion. A liberal enemy and an impartial judge of merit, he launched forth in the commendation of the captain's bravery and Zieten's retreat; an encomium the more flattering and sincere, as he had imagined it utterly impossible for the Prussians to have escaped from him.

He was unable to conceive how Zieten, without having been apprised in time of the enemy's approach, had remained quiet in his camp till the very last moment. To explain this matter, M. de Beauvré was under the necessity of informing the marshal of the negligence of the officer who had commanded the patrol; and this additional circumstance tended to increase the esteem which that commander felt for Zieten, and the high idea he entertained of his capacity and courage.

Scarcely had Zieten arrived at the prince's camp, when General de Czettritz received a note from M. de Beauvré, in which the latter informed him of his captivity, the manner in which he had been received by the marshal and several other generals, whose names he mentioned, and requested him to send his equipment. This note and the names it contained convinced the prince and Zieten, that the latter had the whole Austrian Army to cope with.

On the 3rd of September, the marshal occupied the post of Soraw, and his army extended through Lower-Lusatia.

The king, in the meantime, had advanced towards Saxony. His camp lay at Waldow, and the Russians were posted at Lieberose. The army of the circles had besieged and taken Dresden. The communication between the king and the *marquisate* of Brandenburg was kept open by five of Zieten's squadrons and the free battalion of Hordt. His Majesty's communication with the prince had been interrupted by the position Marshal Daun had taken; and to re-establish it, was a very essential point.

For this purpose, the prince left Sagan, fell back upon Silesia, made a, sudden entrance into Upper-Lusatia, and having defeated several corps of observation, took the marshal in his rear, and drew all his attention to that quarter. In this fortunate expedition, the particulars of which we shall not enter upon, the exploits of Zieten were of the most brilliant natures. He continually cleared the route of the prince, took possession (on the 8th of September) of the garrison and magazines of Friedland, made himself master of a convoy of a hundred and fifty waggons, in the neighbourhood of Zittaw, occupied Görlitz (on the 12th), retook Friedland (on the 16th), drew Marshal Daun into Upper-Lusatia, and obliged him to abandon his plan of forming a junction with the Russians.

The prince had now attained the end he had in view. The communication had been re-established on the 12th of September. The marshal had withdrawn to Bauzen: the Russians, after having in vain expected him to strike a decisive blow, had marched towards Silesia through Guben, and appeared to have intentions to lay siege to Glogaw.

During all this time, Frederick had left the prince to act according to his own judgment. Satisfied with having saved the city of Berlin (which had been threatened by the Russians and the Swedes at the same instant), and with having detached some divisions into Saxony to check the army of the circles, he waited till Lower-Lusatia was clear, in order to traverse it; and having gained a march upon the Russians and arrived before them at Sagan, he at length joined his brother there.

Reinforced with a few battalions, with which the prince accommodated him, the king was able to cope with the Russians, as well as to prevent their undertaking anything against Silesia, and after driving them from the banks of the Oder, he forced them to take up their winter-quarters in the above province. Vanquished as he had been in the plains of Frankfort, he now caused his defeat to be doubted of, by thus chasing his conquerors in triumph before him.

While the king was approaching Sagan, Prince Henry was preparing a feint march in Silesia. He ordered the bridges and highways to be repaired, and sent forward his baggage. His real plan was to return to Saxony, and to draw the Austrians after him, while the king was ridding himself of the Russians.

The project was attended with success. Marshal Daun was a second time deceived. While a few baggage-waggons, for the sake of appearance, repassed the Neisse in order to rejoin the army by a circuitous way, the corps of Zieten received orders to march upon Görlitz, where the prince himself arrived in another direction. Thus united, the army moved on the 23rd in two columns towards Saxony, and marched upon Torgaw. Zieten commanded the van-guard. The marshal, apprehensive of the danger with which Dresden was threatened, followed the prince closely, and thus favoured the principal object of his motions. Silesia was thereby delivered of its troublesome neighbour, and the king was at liberty to direct his whole force against the Russians.

Notwithstanding the checks which the Prussian arms had still to undergo in Saxony, the prince was able to sustain himself both against the Austrians and the forces of the German circles; and the issue of the campaign, in which Zieten gave new proofs of his indefatigable activity, was, upon the whole, glorious,

On the march from Görlitz to Torgaw, Zieten had the satisfaction of seeing his regiment united, which during the whole campaign had been parcelled out into different divisions. In the month of February, five hundred of his hussars, under the command of Major de Zettmar, had been sent into Poland for the purpose of destroying the Russian magazines upon the Warthe. This corps (under the command of Major de Reizenstein, M. de Zettmar having been named *commandant* of the regiment), remained in Silesia, in the environs of Glogaw, till late in the spring. From thence having joined the army of Count de Dohna (commanded by General de Wedel), it covered its retreat after the unfortunate Battle of Kay.

At length, in the Battle of Frankfort or Kundersdorf, still more renowned and unfortunate, the detachment accompanied the king and sustained his right, when that prince, averse to give up the victory which he had so nearly gained, threw himself, at the head of a small party of infantry, into the thickest of the fray. His horse was killed under him, and his *aide-de-camp,* de Götz, immediately presented him with that on which he himself was mounted. At the same instant, Laudon's cavalry advanced upon him, and the king's peril was the more imminent as His Majesty was determined not to retreat.

In this critical moment, the hussars of Zieten rushed between the king and the enemy. They were at once stimulated by patriotism, honour, and vengeance; and falling with fury upon the Austrian troopers, they checked, and drove them from the regiment of Diericke, at the head of which the king had just put himself, and fought as they retreated with him. Lieutenant de Velten highly distinguished himself on this occasion, by repulsing a troop of horse grenadiers who had already surrounded the king and were on the point of taking him prisoner. Captain de Prittwitz had the address to lay hold of His Majesty, to bear him out of the fray, and conduct him through the defile of the mill as far as the bridge of Guritz, at which place the main body of the army had already rallied.

★★★★★★★★★★

> Captain de Prittwitz, since that time, general of cavalry and chief of the regiment of *gendarmes*. "The king would have been taken by the Austrians, had not M. de Prittwitz attacked them with a hundred hussars, and gave him time to pass the defile." *Seven Years' War.*

★★★★★★★★★★

These hussars have ever since been called the preservers of Frederick, the preservers of their country. The merit of this service extended to their general, who on his part was fond of cherishing the remembrance of this glorious event.

The campaign had not decided the fate of Prussia, nor did the winter procure the army the repose of which it stood in such urgent need. Obliged to draw his provisions from Saxony, and not being able to recover the Elbe, from the enemy after the unfortunate affairs of Maxen and Meissen, the king satisfied himself with confining the marshal to the narrow space that lies between Dresden and the valley of Plauen, by establishing his own cantonments from Dippoltzwalde within the Mulda, to Freiberg, Willsdorf, and the environs of Meissen. In this manner he protected the *marquisate* and the city of Berlin, while the corps of Fouqué, stationed in Upper-Lusatia, covered the lower *marquisate* and Silesia.

Zieten commanded the advanced-guard. He encamped round Kesselsdorf and the villages extending to the valley of Plauen, in the face of an entrenched enemy who had every advantage of ground in their favour. The king had ordered him to cover the cantonments of the rest of the army, and he had eight battalions, a division of *chasseurs*, and forty-eight squadrons of hussars under his orders for this service; his headquarters he fixed at Kesselsdorf. Here, surrounded by his troops who were encamped on the snow, he had to contend at the same time with the enemy and the inclemency of the season; with the various diseases incident to armies, and with a scarcity of provisions. Several battalions were obliged to be daily upon duty; and during the night, the dragoons and hussars kept their horses saddled, while numerous patrols were sent out in all directions to watch the motions of the enemy and secure the safety of the camp.

From the instructions given by Zieten to his principal officers, which are still extant, it appears, that on account of the magnitude and proximity of the danger, he considered it necessary to redouble his vigilance and severity. Yet, under the pressure of this new kind of service, the troops stood in need of occasional indulgencies, and their general thought fit to allow them to burn the paling, the stables the barns, and even the very houses, of the villages between Willsdorf and Kesselsdorf; and whilst the camp was laying the country waste in order to procure the means of subsistence, Zieten's sole consolation arose from the consideration of the efficacy of his measures, and the continual immobility of the enemy.

To the care of observing the enemy, was added another which Zieten partook in common with the king and the whole army; which was that of recruiting his regiment. The resources of Prussia seemed to be wholly drained, while those of the enemy were inexhaustible. On this circumstance the hopes of Austria were founded, and she remained obstinately averse to all pacific measures. She was not, however, sensible of the resources to be derived from the genius of Frederick; who, in effect, was soon after enabled to create an army of sixty thousand men.

Frederick, indeed, seemed conscious that every difficulty would give way to the efforts of his own will. He knew his generals; and the orders he gave them to complete their respective regiments, was the magic wand with which he created this new accession of force. Zieten received the following letter from him, dated Freiberg, February 8th, 1760.

> .... Exclusive of your hussars who are prisoners of war, you will put your regiment upon the complete footing of fifteen hundred horse. As to those prisoners, you are sensible they cannot be taken into the account. They are liable to death, to enter into the service of the enemy, or to make their escape; men thus circumstanced are never entirely changed.

Zieten was much embarrassed by the task of completing his corps. He, at length, succeeded: the very name the regiment bore, contributed considerably to his success, and in the spring it was not deficient in a single man.

The following letter from the king serves to manifest the obligations that prince lay under to him.

> My dear Lieutenant-General de Zieten.
> I hereby inform you, that instead of the stipulated allowance for winter-quarters, I have assigned you fifteen hundred dollars, which you will receive from the military chest. I sincerely wish that circumstances permitted me to express my satisfaction in a more efficacious manner. I acknowledge, as I ought, your many and indefatigable services. Be assured I shall never forget them, and that on every occasion I shall be happy to shew you, how much I am your affectionate king,
> Freiberg, April 17th, 1760.                              Frederick

We now come to the year 1760, the fifth campaign of this long and interminable war. After some short differences, Austria and Russia, being again united, conspired against Prussia, which they flattered themselves they should be able to crush by their joint-preponderance, and they now began to raise up storms against Frederick the Great. To quell these storms, he had marched early in the spring into Silesia;

from thence he had returned to Saxony, and laid siege to Dresden. He had likewise sent Prince Henry to the frontiers of Poland to oppose the progress of the Russians.

During the whole of this campaign, Zieten did not quit the king's army (whose, cavalry in the right wing he had under his command) except on marches, in which he was always stationed in the van or the rear, as circumstances requited. Such was the reputation he had gained, that the enemy were become fearful of attacking him; at least, with equal force. They could boast of success but twice;—the first time, owing to the fault of the king: the second, to their superiority of numbers.

On the 7th of July, the king headed a strong reconnoitring-party between Nieder-Gurke and Göda, neat Dresden, against the corps under the command of Lascy. Zieten commanded the detachment which acted as an escort. He had taken three hundred prisoners, and having fulfilled the object of the expedition, he solicited the king's leave to withdraw his troops. He had a conference with His Majesty at three leagues distant from the camp: the columns of Lascy began to advance and the danger, to which the Prussians were now exposed, was every moment increasing. Frederick was determined to wait for the grenadiers who were coming on at some distance behind: they arrived, but they came too late. The numerous cavalry of Lascy overthrew that of Zieten, which retreated as far as Welke upon the grenadiers. The enemy did not venture to pursue them any further; but two hundred brave men had already fallen in the encounter. The next day, the Prussians resumed their march in order to pass the Elbe, and lay siege to Dresden.

About the same time, a detachment of Zieten's hussars, being attacked and taken in their rear at Kalkowitz upon the Spree by those of Lascy, lost two officers, three petty officers and eighty-four private soldiers. They perished, but with the glory of having yielded to numbers only.

One evil now began to follow another in rapid succession, and the situation of the king grew extremely critical. Glatz had surrendered; Laudon was besieging Breslaw at the head of an army of thirty thousand men. The spirited resistance made by General de Tauenzien, who with three thousand invalids guarded nineteen thousand prisoners and defended the place, gave Prince Henry time to arrive, and to save Silesia for a second time.

Eighty thousand Russians were now in motion. They approached

Glogaw to assist the operations of the Austrians, and their junction seemed to be inevitable. The king had no other part to act but that of raising the fruitless siege of Dresden and hastening from the heart of Saxony to check them. For this purpose, he marched at the head of thirty thousand men. Ninety thousand Austrians pressed him closely. To the united army of Daun and Laudon, he opposed Zieten. The march from the banks of the Elbe to the town of Lignitz was one of the most painful and most perilous that had been undertaken during all the war; and the whole army bore testimony, that the skill and bravery which Zieten displayed in the van-guard, furthered the operations of the rest of the corps, and screened them from impending destruction.

The king, encamped at Lignitz, at a great distance from his magazines, confined to a small and inconvenient spot of ground, had chosen that position for the purpose of striking a decisive blow, which alone could save him. He was under the necessity of giving battle; and it was equally necessary to gain the victory. The battle was fought; and the whole army imputed the first success, that attended it, to Major de Hund of the regiment of Zieten, who had the good fortune to discover in time the enemy in full march.

On one side were the Austrians, on the other, the Russians. The intention of the former was to surprise, surround, and defeat the king. Of the latter, the plan was to obstruct the road to Glogaw, and cut off his retreat.

The king knew not that the Russians were in the neighbourhood, and when Lieutenant de Wolfrath, (since that time, lieutenant-general), of Zieten's regiment, informed His Majesty of this on his return from a patrol, he gave no credit to it. He nevertheless broke up his camp in the night of the 14th, passed the Schwarzbach in that of the 15th, and after ordering his troops to repose till morning, he prepared to gain the Oder.

While the army thus lay at rest, Major de Hund with Lieutenant de Wolfrath were reconnoitring the country, and their surprise was extreme, when, at daybreak, they discovered from the heights of Binowitz the columns of Laudon advancing to occupy that place, as well as a body of cavalry at Panten. Every moment was precious: they flew to apprise the king, and had the good fortune to find him, together with the Margrave Charles and Zieten, in a small wood, round a fire, and fallen asleep.

Without waiting for the king's orders, Zieten put himself at the head of the Prince of Prussia's regiment of *cuirassiers* which had not unsaddled. He repulsed the flankers, fell upon the infantry which followed them, and threw it into disorder. He learnt from some prisoners, that the latter was a corps of five hundred grenadier-volunteers of Laudon's regiment, which had been detached to make a bold stroke. The king availed himself of his corps of reserve in order to impede the attack, and at the same time made that admirable disposition which history has celebrated and success crowned. Attacked at once by Daun and Laudon, he threw himself between them, and separated them; his left wing beat Laudon, while his right, under the command of Zieten and Wedel, kept Daun and Lascy in awe, and prevented their advancement.

Had Zieten's orders been strictly observed, the batteries would not have played but on the near approach of the Austrians. They began their fire too soon, and the balls at first fell much short of the enemy.

The battle began before sunrise, and at five o'clock, victory declared in favour of the Prussians. Never was victory more decided than this; nor was ever conqueror more suddenly transported from the abyss of danger to the heights of glory. Deploring the calamities of war, ("When will my calamities have an end?" exclaimed the king on the field of battle), and the necessity he was under of prolonging them, he ordered discharges of ordinance and small shot to be made in honour of his gallant soldiers whose bodies bestrewed the ground, as well as to celebrate the successes of the day. Eighty-six officers, six thousand private soldiers, two pieces of cannon, and twenty-three colours and standards, were so many trophies of Prussian valour. The loss of Laudon amounted to ten thousand men; that of the Prussians, to six hundred killed, and double that number wounded,

Frederick and Zieten had passed the night together beside a watch-fire. Uncertain of the hazards they were going to incur, they had suddenly separated at the alarm given by Major de Hund. The one and the other had fought for glory and their country, and they met again on the field of battle, crowned with victory. Zieten congratulated the king; the king embraced Zieten, and advanced him to the rank of general of cavalry.

If the king owed this victory to the keenness of his military glance, and the extent of his genius which was ever able to avail itself of the moment, of the ground, and of the faults of the enemy; he was not the less indebted to the skilfulness of his officers and the bravery of his troops. Lieutenant-Colonel de Möllendorf, the same who had so splendidly contributed to the victory of Leuthen, supported by Major de Rhodich, (who died a lieutenant-general, and head of the war department), prevented a whole column from quitting the village of Panten, from whence it was even obliged to retreat. The regiments of Wedel, Forcade, Saldern, the guards, and especially that of Prince Ferdinand, acquired much glory. The latter regiment suffered prodigiously: when the battle was over, the king was pleased to decorate the few surviving officers with the order of military merit, and to assure them, that he should never forget their services.

Zieten had the greatest regard for this regiment; he distinguished it in the infantry, as he always distinguished the *cuirassiers* of the Prince of Prussia (now Schleinitz) in the cavalry—a corps which had proved of great use to him, in dispersing Laudon's volunteers at the beginning of the battle.

The victory of Lignitz had gained the king time, and weakened one of his enemies. It was now his business to rid himself of the other. General de Czernitscheff, who commanded the Russians, had advanced as far as Lissa: it was necessary to force him to repass the Oder. The army was in want of provisions, and they could only be procured from Glogaw. Prince Henry was at Breslaw, and Daun before Schweidnitz, it was necessary to join the one, and to turn the other. In all these fortunate operations, Zieten rendered the army the most important services. Ever opening or closing the march; always skirted, but never broke in upon, by Lascy; he was nevertheless able to take a considerable number of prisoners from Saint-Ignon and Nauendorf.

Frederick was enabled to drive the enemy out of Silesia, and to put Schweidnitz into a state of defence. This, however, was but one of the great tasks he had imposed upon himself: after so many painful marches and counter marches, he undertook that which had the re-establishment of his affairs in Brandenburg for its object. The Russians and Austrians had already taken possession of his capital; the circles were masters of the principal towns of Saxony, and, among the rest, of Torgaw, and his magazines. His Majesty detached a division to deliver Berlin, and conducted his army in person to Torgaw, which it was incumbent upon him not to leave in the power of the enemy.

Daun continually hung upon his rear: being in possession of Dresden, Torgaw, both the banks of the Elbe, and the whole of Saxony; he was enabled to cut off all his provisions and communications. The king's position was extremely precarious: he found himself, on the approach of winter, without magazines, without fortresses; having no other footing in Saxony than the narrow spot he occupied, and apprehensive of being insulated from Berlin. The Russians on the banks of the Oder, and the Warthe, threatened to establish their winter-quarters in the *marquisate* of Brandenburg. It was necessary to recover Torgaw at any rate, to regain the Elbe, to impede the junction of the Austrians with the Russians, and to deliver the *marquisate* from danger.

Marshal Daun was fully convinced of the importance of Torgaw. The king endeavoured by various marches and manoeuvres to draw him towards Dresden; he remained, however, immovable in his camp. The situation of the Prussians grew every day more critical and alarming. Encamped at Duben, (towards the end of October), and reduced to the sole magazine of that town, which could not afford a supply for more than four weeks, they were sensible of the necessity of either conquering or dying.

In this perplexity, the king reinforced himself with the corps with which Zieten was occupying Wittenberg, broke up his camp, and crossed the Elbe at Dessau, before the enemy, who were expecting this passage upon three other points, were able to take any measures to impede it. After being further reinforced by the corps of the Prince of Wirtemberg and General de Hulsen, who had just driven the Russians out of Berlin, and the army of the circles out of Saxony, he concentrated his forces; and impelled by all the courage of despair, he made ready for striking an important and decisive blow.

Frederick risked much, or, in fact, he had everything to risk. His great soul, for the first time, now gave way to melancholy presentiments. He hesitated, for the first time, on the part he had to act. Undetermined whether he should run this desperate risk, he held a conference with his generals in Zieten's presence. Depressed by apprehension rather than encouraged by hope, he imparted his doubts and surmises, and in this manner impressed them with the like sentiments. How, indeed, should they have ventured to recommend what his own courage had not already suggested, or take upon themselves a responsibility which he seemed inclined to charge them with in case of ill success. They kept profound silence; Zieten alone thought proper to break it.

"Everything is possible, sire;" said he. "It is our business to triumph over difficulties."

These few words decided the king, and the battle was instantly resolved upon.

His Majesty decamping on the 2nd of November, marched to

Schilde, established his headquarters at Lang-Reichenbach, and after being informed of the position of Marshal Daun upon the heights of Siptitz, he communicated to the generals of the left wing the disposition of the attack which was intended for the next day. With regard to the right wing, under the command of Zieten, the orders he gave that general were of a secret nature.

On the day of the battle (the 3rd of November) at half past six in the morning, the army began to march in four columns. Zieten's hussars preceded the first, which the king commanded in person. At ten o'clock, the corps of Zieten separated from the left wing at the moment in which Saldern's brigade had gained the causeway that leads from Leipsic to Torgaw.

The forces of Zieten consisted of four brigades, *viz*. Those of Saldern, Zeunert, Tettenborn, and Grumbkow.

His cavalry, commanded by the Duke of Wirtemberg, comprised three squadrons of lifeguards; five of *gendarmes*; three of life-*carbineers*; five of the *cuirassiers* of the Prince of Prussia; the regiment of Czettritz's dragoons; that of Normann's; and that of Krockow's.

Colonel de Kleist commanded the light troops, consisting of the regiment of Kleist's dragoons, that of Kleist's hussars, and one free battalion of Salemnon.

The king's intention was, that while Zieten should attack the enemy in front, he himself should fall upon their rear, and gain the centre of the heights of Siptitz at the moment of the arrival of his general there, and carry that position by storm. Zieten, in consequence of this, after having quitted the Leipsic causeway, was directed to advance along the road called the Butterstrasse, while the king should take the left direction, and file through the forest of Domitz in order to turn the enemy. Zieten had a march of two hours shorter than the king's to execute. To combine the two attacks, it was settled that he should remain concealed in the wood till the report of the cannon and small shot should summons him to advance, and begin the action.

Such was the plan of attack. That of the defence which Daun had determined upon, was not less formidable. His right wing was stationed among the vineyards behind the village of Siptitz, and was covered by the forest of Domitz and several extensive mounds. His left wing reached as far as Zinna. Opposite that wing and the centre, lay the Röhrgraben, a brook which takes it rise above Siptitz, traverses the village and several pools, and falls into the lake of Torgaw. The corps of Lascy was posted near Coswig; the reserve at Grosswig; two detachments at Weidenhayn and Vogelgang; and several flying-posts in the forest of Domitz and on the high-road to Leipsic.

The king and Zieten advanced with their respective corps. The progress of the latter was slow on account of several obstacles he met with on the road which was besides, much damaged by the late rains, and bordered by hedges and ditches which admitted but of few outlets. At the entrance of Klitsch wood, the columns of the infantry received orders to halt till Kleist with his van-guards had repulsed a body of light troops which infested that quarter. This operation took up an hour; after which, the cavalry continued to march along the causeway, and the infantry along the Butterstrasse for the purpose of gaining the heights of Siptitz.

The cavalry under the command of Zieten met a detachment of Lascy's corps which had taken post at the, (a ferry), Rothe-Führt on the Leipsic road, and which seemed determined to dispute the passage with two pieces of ordinance. A free battalion made ready to attack this detachment, when the enemy suddenly retreated, and left their cannon behind them. A mound which they had thrown up was now to be levelled, and the bridge of the Rothe-Führt to be repaired, which operations created further delay. Zieten, in the meanwhile, traversing the wood with his escort, in order to reconnoitre the enemy, discovered Lascy's division, whose left wing, composed of cavalry, had passed the Röhrgraben, and extended as far as the ponds above Torgaw. The right wing, consisting of infantry, touched Daun's left. These two wings formed together an obtuse angle which the Röhrgraben covered in its whole extent. At the right of Lascy's corps, was the take of Torgaw, a chain of small ponds, and a battery.

Scarcely had Zieten left the wood, when the first ball that came from the battery killed one of his suite: the youngest of his comrades, who had never before been in an action rode up to Zieten, and informed him of it.

"It is enough," said the general, with great composure; "there will be many more killed before the battle is over."

At the same time, a hussar arrived with dispatches from the king, which Zieten was observed to read over in apparent perturbation of mind. He then took out his watch, and exclaimed, "Is he out of his senses?" He thought he heard a distant cannonading, but the wind being contrary, he was not certain he was right.

The king, on his side, heard the report of every gun. He had imagined that the discharge he heard at the Rothe-Führt, was the beginning of the attack. He could not comprehend these precipitate proceedings, and he had now no other part to act than to adopt them; and the more so, as several peasants and fugitives informed him that Daun was about to pass the Elbe, that he had prepared his pontons, that his baggage had taken a retrograde direction, together with his artillery of reserve and his meal waggons. This was, however, a mere change of position, and which the king took for a retreat. He hastened therefore in order to begin the attack before the hostile troops could, as he imagined, recover their position. His first brigade, supported by Zieten's hussars only, without artillery or any of those appendages which serve to inflame the courage of the assailant, advanced against an entrenched enemy. The corps was destroyed rather than conquered, and it was thus with the lives of the choicest of his troops, that Frederick began to purchase the victory with which the day was destined to be finally crowned.

Had Zieten literally obeyed the king's orders, he would have marched directly to Grosswig, and from thence to the heights of Siptitz: instead of which, in order not to expose his flank to Lascy's division, which might easily have turned him, he took a circuitous way. He reinforced himself with his infantry, disposed it in two lines, with the cavalry on the right and a battery in front. In this order, of battle he attached Lascy, supporting his left by the mountain of Siptitz, and his right by the lake. A part of his cavalry having discovered a ford, took that of Lascy in flank and immediately repulsed it.

In the meanwhile, his troops were greatly annoyed from the redoubts of Zinna and the heights of Siptitz, against which he was now advancing. The general was riding slowly along the ranks of his cavalry, when a cannon ball took off the head of a *cuirassier* belonging to the Prince of Prussians regiment. His comrades were startled and alarmed at this accident: Zieten, however, revived their intrepidity by the example he shewed them of his own, and calmly said, "That worthy man, my friends, died an easy death."

The infantry, notwithstanding the terrible fire from the heights of Siptitz, still continued to march, on. Daun opposed his second line to it. Zieten drew out his, and stationed it on the left wing of the former. His view was to draw the whole attention of the enemy to this point in order to support the king's operations. He ordered the cavalry to remain behind on his left, to keep that of Lascy in awe, and yet to avoid coming to an engagement. The Duke of Wirtemburg, to whom he had imparted this order, caused it to be written down, word for word, by the *aide-de-camp*, who was the bearer of it, in order, as it seemed, to screen himself from all unnecessary responsibility.

Zieten was now full against the Siptitz, at the head of his battalions. He detached the regiment of Dierke from the line to carry a redoubt and a windmill which lay in his road to the village. The enemy withdrew, and occupied one of the neighbouring eminences, after having set fire to the outermost buildings, and obliged the regiment to retreat

In this attack Zieten narrowly escaped being killed through the imprudence of an artilleryman: at the moment in which the cannon went off, his horse fortunately reared, and sprang on one side. In the first emotions of anger, the general drew his sabre, and was on the point of falling on the gunner; but he soon recollected himself, and was satisfied with giving him a severe reprimand.

In the meanwhile, the Prussians endeavoured to gain the hill by another route. The brigade of Saldern traversed a small wood, and made an attack upon the vineyards, where a strong party of the enemy was posted. The regiments of Harrach, Sincere, Harsch, and Leopold Daun, received the assailants with a discharge of artillery and repulsed them with loss.

The day began to decline. The Prussians could distinctly hear, that in the quarter where the king was posted, the report of the cannon grew gradually less loud, and they concluded from thence that His Majesty was making his retreat. Thus persuaded, the troops were determined to make every possible effort to secure the success of the day. They had, however, few difficulties to encounter; the ground was slippery, full of swamps and springs, and unfit for the operations of the cavalry, and the transport of the artillery.

Zieten was not to be discouraged; and turning more to the left, he now braved the fire of the batteries. The silence of his march and the declining day formed a striking contrast with the discharge of the artillery. At length, victory crowned these repeated exertions of valour. Colonel de Möllendorf, the *commandant* of the guards, who had acquired so much glory in the battles of Leuthen and Lignitz, and who was well acquainted with the environs of Torgaw, discovered a dike between two ponds, which the enemy had neglected to occupy. At the head of Saldern's brigade, he was the first who advanced upon it.

**********

This dike was so narrow, that only three men abreast could advance along it. The company of Major de Lehman, forming a part of the regiment of the Margrave Charles was at the head of the column. At the moment in which they were about to advance, they perceived at the further end, two pieces of cannon which the enemy were pointing down the dike. The company halted in consequence of this obstacle, when a musketeer, of the name of Gulle, cried out, "It is of little consequence, whether I live or not, or in what manner I die;" and rushing upon the dike, he ran up to the artillery men, shot one of them dead, knocked down a second with the but-end of his piece, which having broken, he attacked the rest with the stump, and forced them to abandon their cannon. Three of his comrades joined, and supported him. The cannon were spiked and dismounted, and the column passed the dike, and proceeded to the attack of the redoubt. The hostile battalions opposed them in vain, and were soon obliged to yield. Gulle, to whom his officers promised signal recompense, dropt in the affray, and was feelingly lamented by his comrades. Fortunately, he was only wounded, and he soon rejoined them. He has been since forgotten, and now (1803), resides at Soldin, his native town, and receives the allowance of an invalid.

**********

The general and his whole brigade followed him, and began to attack a redoubt. Zieten being apprised of this, sent an immediate reinforcement, and the redoubt was carried. The Prussians occupied it, and maintained the post. Saldern receiving a dangerous wound, directed Colonel de Möllendorf, in the king's name and his own, to take the command of the brigade; Möllendorf made a second attack upon the enemy, which was crowned with success; but he was himself taken prisoner.

The Prussians had no other cannon than those which they had taken from the enemy. The hill was too steep and the ground too sandy for the transport of them. The horses would not advance, though every expedient was taken to impel them on. At length the brave infantry harnessed themselves to their field-pieces, and dragged them along. Zieten placed the heavy cannon on the right of the dike in order to secure the passage.

The want of artillery considerably retarded the victory; for, besides the first redoubt, others still remained to be carried. To shorten the operation, Zieten drew out his infantry on the other side of the Siptitz, and began an attack upon the principal battery. The enemy made a desperate defence; great carnage ensued, and success for a while seemed in a state of uncertainty: the battery and the field of battle had perhaps been possessed by the enemy, had not General de Lestwitz come forwards at this decisive moment, and sustaining the assault with his fresh troops, turned the balance in favour of Prussia.

The general had been stationed in the king's corps of reserve. He had just formed a battery, at the head of five battalions of grenadiers, for the purpose of protecting the retreat of His Majesty's cavalry at Neiden, and of repulsing that of the Austrians who endeavoured to harass it. Finding himself master of his post, he advanced to sustain Zieten, and having formed a junction with him, the last battery was soon carried, and the enemy obliged to retreat. The Prussians were scarcely sensible that they were conquerors, and waited for the return of day to be fully convinced of their good fortune.

The king, in the meanwhile, being driven with his cavalry as far as Neiden, passed a very anxious night in the church of that village. His anxiety increased every moment, and he impatiently waited for the break of day; when mounting, his horse, he left the place, and scarcely had he ridden a hundred paces, before the *chasseur* who attended him, informed him of the approach of an officer in a white cloak who came galloping in full speed. The *chasseur* advanced, and recognising Zieten, turned about, and announced him to the king. His Majesty not conceiving that the general himself could be the bearer of good tidings, received him with apparent disquietude; when in the usual attitude of an officer making his report,

Zieten stopped, and said, "Sire, the Austrians are beaten, and are now making their retreat," The king then alighted from his horse; Zieten sprang from his, and they mutually embraced each other. The king was in an ecstasy of joy; and his general, mute, and oppressed by his feelings, found relief in tears.

After having paid this first tribute to sensibility, Zieten recovered himself, and began to inform His Majesty of everything that had occurred the preceding evening; and, in his torn, he was apprized that the king's infantry, supported by the cavalry, had maintained their ground at the foot of the hills; that, consequently, the enemy's retreat had been general, and that there was no necessity of renewing the engagement. At the same time, he learnt, that the king had been exposed to great danger, that a ball had grazed his skin, and lodged in his *surtout*. After this interview, he returned to his corps, and arriving at the left wing of the infantry, he rode along the line, and exclaimed, "Comrades, the king has gained the battle, and the enemy are completely routed. Long live king Frederick!"

The whole corps replied. "Long live the king! Long live Fritz! and long live Zieten, our father, and the king of the hussars!" (Fritz was the war name which the soldiers usually gave the king, in abbreviation of that of Frederick. His Majesty seemed pleased at being called so.)

During the battle, the cavalry, under the command of the Duke of Wirtemburg, had kept the corps of Lascy in awe, and the cannon which had been taken from the enemy were pointed against the battalions which that general had sent to the succour of the heights of Siptitz.

We shall spare the reader such detail of this engagement as does not immediately relate to Zieten, and which, of course, is foreign to our subject. We shall beg to refer those who wish for fuller information, to the *Observations of an Austrian Veteran*, a work which does ample justice to Zieten, who contributed so essentially to the success of the day.

We shall close this subject with an anecdote. This battle, which was the last, in which either Frederick or Zieten engaged in personally was the first in which our general stained his sabre with the blood of the enemy. He had now made such violent use of it, that Fahrenholz, his *attendant*-hussar, from whom we have the anecdote, had a difficult task to clean and furbish it.

Zieten's hussars, who formed part of the king's army, acquitted themselves in too distinguished a manner, not to be entitled to some tributary mention, of their exploits. Before the battle began, they took General de Saint-Ignon prisoner, with the greater part of his dragoons; but they lost their gallant *commandant*, Major de Zettmar. When the king made the first attack with the grenadiers, he had no other support than Zieten's regiment, which stood him in the stead of cavalry of the line. The regiments of Bayreuth, of the Margrave Frederick, and of Spaen (commanded by Colonel de Dalwig, an officer of great merit), emulated the exploits of Zieten's corps on this day, and deserved the honour of being mentioned with equal praise.

The Battle of Torgaw secured the Prussians safe and commodious winter-quarters; and the Austrian Army being driven upon Dresden, took up theirs in that place. Some detached corps had succeeded in. dislodging the enemy from Silesia, the upper and lower *marquisates*, and Pomerania. The Russians returned into Poland; the Swedes repassed the Pene, and the siege of Cosel was not undertaken. All the advantage on the part of the Austrians was confined to the taking of Glatz. Both armies were considerably diminished in number; that of the Prussians suffered by the enemy's refusal to exchange prisoners; that of the Austrians was very ill paid. The finances of the empress queen were in great disorder, and the means and resources of Prussia now seemed to be inexhaustible.

The king marched deeper into Saxony, and fixed his headquarters at Leipsic, Zieten established his at Meissen, and his corps lay cantoned between that town and Nossen. This corps was very considerable; it was composed of eighteen battalions, and fifteen squadrons of dragoons. His advanced guard, consisting of two thousand light cavalry, and supported by a body of artillery, occupied the position of Siebeneichen, Wendischbohra, Robschutz, and Miltitz.

Previous to the dislocation of the army, the general had received the following letter from the king; a letter which does much honour to that prince's justice and humanity,

> My dear General de Zieten.
>
> You are now going into winter-quarters, and it is proper that the close of the campaign should revive a sense of due order in the army, and put an end to every kind of abuse which had gradually and insensibly introduced itself therein. The marches, the counter-marches, the various military movements and operations which have taken place during the campaign, have too often rendered violent and arbitrary measures expedient for the purpose of procuring provisions; and they have furnished such measures with an excuse. But, at the present moment, justice as well as the consideration of our own welfare loudly call upon us for the most exact discipline and regularity in the mode of procuring our subsistence, in establishing magazines, and in levying contributions in Saxony.
>
> I am therefore determined, that henceforth all violent expedients, all exactions, all arbitrary supplies, shall cease, I shall require the whole army to pay due respect to the laws of discipline, and shall cause every transgression of those laws to be severely punished, I particularly charge you, my dear Zieten, to inspect the execution of my orders, to inform the inhabitants of the country, wherever you command, or may afterwards command, that in case they are exact in furnishing the supplies, and the regular contributions laid upon them, they shall meet with no other annoyance; but, on the contrary, shall be protected and maintained in the possession of their property; and that no rigorous measures shall be put in execution against them, unless they themselves provoke such measures by their negligence in complying with what is reasonably required at their hands.

A proclamation, explanatory of every necessary particular, which I shall cause to be made, will be a sufficient guide to them in that respect. Furthermore, the orders contained in, this letter are not to be observed till after you have passed the Tribsche. From that moment, you will take upon yourself to maintain due order and discipline in the corps under your command. I am your affectionate king,
Leipsic, November 27th, 1760.                                    Frederick.

In the course of this winter, Zieten received several other letters from the king, which have been preserved among his papers. Their contents are not of a very interesting nature; they are chiefly answers to reports made by the general, instructions, information respecting the position of the enemy, and military discussions. We shall insert two of them, as they are characteristic of the king, and at one of them contains a postscript in his own hand.

My dear General de Zieten.
I have already informed you by General de Ramin of the success of Sybourg's detachment at Langensalza, and I shall now give you the particulars of that expedition. General de Sybourg has forced the pass of Instrut, and driven the French and Saxons, commanded by count de Stainville, beyond the town of Langensalza. The Saxons he has entirely defeated; Reinforced by General de Spörke, he chased the French as far as Eisenach, and afterwards took five pieces of cannon, five colours, sixty-two officers, and three thousand private soldiers. The enemy being pressed by General de Luckner, have since evacuated Eisenach and Gotha, and retreated to Vach; Duke Ferdinand of Brunswick informs me, that the hereditary prince has entered the Hessian territories and taken Fritzlar, and the immense magazines of the French there;
Moreover, I was informed by express the day before yesterday, that Prince Ferdinand has delivered Cassel, made the whole garrison prisoners, and taken possession of the magazines, together with a considerable number of waggons, I feel great pleasure in communicating this good news to you. On Sunday next, the usual military ceremonies will be observed in honour of these victories. The progress of Sybourg's corps furnishing me with continual occupation, owing to the occasional arrangements which the expedition requires, I shall probably stay here till the

beginning of March, provided everything remains quiet in your quarter. Should it happen otherwise, you will give me instant notice of it, and I shall be with you. Your very affectionate

Frederick.

2.

My dear General de Zieten.

I have received your letter of the 21st; and, convinced of the warm and sincere part you take in my service and concerns, I shall with great pleasure give you some further account of our successes in Thuringia. General de Sybourg being advanced on the 20th as far as Arnstadt, on the other side of Gotha, the army of the circles withdrew precipitately to Ilmenaw and Smalkalden. The whole country is cleared; for I have every reason to believe, that the rest of the troops of the empire in the circle of Neustadt will march into Franconia. As for General de Spörke, he has completely dispersed the troops of Stainville at Vach. Luckner has taken six pieces of cannon from them, and all their baggage. The account of Duke Ferdinand's expedition is confirmed. He has taken Cassel by storm, with six battalions, thirty cannon, and is likewise master of the magazines of Fritzlar.

All this will, I am persuaded force the disappointed French to leave the Hessian territories. I approve qf your intention to send the battalion of Quintus to Strehlen. With regard to the garrison and magazine of Lomatsch, the care of providing far them must be left to. Lieutenant-General de Forcade. His corps has not yet been weakened by detachments. You will impart your orders and dispositions to him, as if they came directly from me. I remain ever your affectionate king,

Leipsic, February 23rd, 1761.             Frederick.

*In His Majesty's own hand.*

Marshal de Broglio is arrived at Fulda with twenty thousand men, the remains of an army of sixty thousand. This may bring us peace,             Frederick.

The king's most ardent wishes were, indeed, for peace. The warrior, the conqueror, gave way to the feelings of the man, of the father of his people. Yet two years' hard trials were still in store for him; and it is well known, that the campaign of 1761 was the most perilous and desperate of any of the foregoing ones.

We leave it to the masters of the military art to decide, whether the junction of the grand Russian Army with that of the Austrians, was one of those operations which he had been able to impede, or whether this fatal circumstance was not the immediate result of the death of General de Golz. It is certain that Zieten, the general's successor in the command, arrived two days too late for such purpose. He had been previously charged with the care of putting the provisions and pontons in a place of security, as well as with covering the march of the king, immediately after, into Silesia.

Golz, who had gone forward with a view of falling upon the Russians who were still dispersed about Poland, and of attacking them separately, had fallen ill at Glogaw, and died before he had been able to execute his plan. The king sent Zieten to succeed him; but the Russian Army was now concentrated. Zieten, however, put himself at the head of Golz's troops, marched into Poland, and formed his camp at Kosten in face of the Russians, from whom he was separated by the Obra only. The king was at Schweidnitz, where he had Laudon to cope with; and uncertain as to the direction which the Russian Army might take, he sent orders to Zieten to reinforce the garrison of Brieg and Breslaw. These detachments having considerably weakened his corps, the general was obliged to confine himself solely ta defensive measures.

To this slight sketch, it may not be improper to add the particular journal of the operations of Zieten.

As soon as he had received His Majesty's orders to succeed General de Golz, he repaired to his destination. He arrived on the 29th of June, and on the next day he began his march to Kosten. In the meanwhile, the two first Russian divisions had broken up their camps, continued their march (on the 26th and 27th), and arriving at Moszina, had halted there on the 28th. The two other divisions (Fermor's and Czernitscheff's) had joined the above, on the 29th, and the united army proceeding on their march, had occupied the camp of Czempen, at a league distance from Kosten.

The corps of Golz, in the state in which Zieten had found it on taking the command, consisted of twenty-four battalions of infantry, and forty-seven squadrons of heavy and light cavalry. He had about twenty thousand men to oppose to sixty thousand Russians; yet, notwithstanding this great disproportion of forces, he advanced on the 30th, as far as Polnisch-Lissa and Borchen, and on the 1st of July, he arrived at Kosten. During his march, his advanced-guard, met a detachment of the enemy, under the command of Brigadier de Löpen, and having joined battle, took the brigadier prisoner, together with three other officers and forty Cossacks. But being too ardent in the prosecution of their success, the hussars of Zieten and Malachowsky advancing upon a large body of cavalry which General de Czernitscheff led, on in person, fourteen of them were killed and eighteen wounded.

Zieten, however, encamped in an excellent position at Kosten. His right wing extended to Czerkowa, and his left to Gukowa, while his front and right were covered by the town of Kosten, which he had garrisoned with a battalion of grenadiers. His front and two flanks were besides covered by a marsh four German miles in length, which was traversed by a single dike that led to Kotta. General de Tempelhof, who is a very competent judge of whatever relates to the military art, observes (*History of the Seven Years' War.* vol. 5), that this camp was one of the strongest that could be imagined, as two days' march was necessary for turning it and forcing the army which occupied it to take another position. An army so situated had, moreover, the advantage of retreating, at all events, through Schmiegel and Fraustadt upon Glogaw, without having anything to apprehend even from superior forces.

Zieten, however, did not long avail himself of the advantages which the camp of Kosten afforded him. Having been informed on the 3rd, that the enemy was proceeding to Dalskow, and apprehending the danger to which the fortresses of Silesia would be exposed, he marched to Storchnest, with which town he began the left wing of his camp, while his right extended to Kopkowna. He detached the Prince of Bernbourg with five battalions and fifteen squadrons for the purpose of securing the heights of Grätz, which covered his left wing. All his efforts to find out the position of the enemy were of no avail; M; de Anhalt at the head of four hundred horse, and M. de Dalwig with two battalions and twenty squadrons, were both equally unsuccessful in their attempts to pass the Obra; and the reports of these two officers gave him no better information, than that the camp and the main body of the Russians were at Dalskow,

Zieten had recourse to further attempts from day to day, and every new effort was thwarted by the numerous parties of light cavalry which were ever in motion around the hostile camp. Determined at length to remain no longer in this painful and dangerous state of suspense, he detached Dalwig, on the 8th, with two battalions and twenty squadrons, to Krzwin, to force the passage of the Obra in that quarter. This officer availing himself of a ford, led his troops across it; but scarcely was he arrived on the opposite bank, when he was received by so strong a body of cavalry that he was obliged by prudence to make a timely retreat. His loss was not considerable, but the expedition produced no new information.

On the 9th, Zieten was at last apprised that the Russians had left their position, and pitched their camp at Borcke. This intelligence was soon after confirmed. Czernitscheff had first occupied the place; the main army followed him on the 11th, and on the 12th encamped at Kobielin. This march clearly indicated that the Russians were proceeding on to Breslaw; and Zieten, in order to be beforehand with them, had marched on the 9th Bojanowa; on the 10th, to Trachenberg, and took his, camp at Brausnitz.

In this camp it was, that he received the king's orders to divide his corps into two equal parts, and to march directly to Breslaw. These two divisions, one of which was destined for Brieg, and the other far Breslaw, encamped separately in the environs of the latter city. In the meantime, the Russian Army approached the frontiers of Silesia; it passed them on the 15th, encamped at Henrichsdorf and Brzlavecz, near Militz, and advanced on the 17th, in two divisions, as far as Tscheschen. Of this march Zieten was informed by Colonel de Lossow, whom he had sent to Oels and Bernstadt, at the head of a reconnoitring-party, (consisting of Reusch's regiment of hussars,) and who, two days after, brought him four officers, fourteen petty officers, and a hundred and eight dragoons, whom he had taken from the Russians.

This movement on the part of the enemy obliged Zieten to camp near Breslaw, between Gubitz and Hufen, with the division that still remained with him, and which contained eleven battalions and twenty-two squadrons. He employed two thousand men in digging intrenchments to supply his want of troops.

Breslaw and Brieg were now secured from any sudden attack; Zieten defended the former, and General de Knoblauch the latter. If, however, Zieten, with the whole corps of Golz, had retained the position of Brausnitz, he had perhaps been able to have opposed the Russians, on their entrance into Silesia, with more effect; at least, he might have checked their progress for some time, and thwarted their junction with Laudon's army. Instead of which, being now masters of the dutchy beyond the Oder, they marched without any molestation to Militsch, Wartenberg and Namslaw, and having proceeded up the river, effected a junction with their allies.

From this moment the preservation of Silesia did not result from any decisive action; it was effected by the marches and countermarches, the manoeuvres, the positions, taken by the king, and, under his auspices, by the army, divided into several corps, commanded by his best generals, and disposed in such manner as to leave no unguarded spot to favour any incursion on the part of the enemy; At lengthy observing that the imperialists and the Russians began to concentrate their forces, His Majesty had no other resource than that of imitating their example: he therefore occupied a kind of fortress in the, open country near Bunzelwitz, and formed the celebrated camp which bears that name, in order to wait the crisis of affairs. This narrow space contained at once, the king, the army, and all the hopes of Prussia.

In this critical juncture, Frederick had reason to be well satisfied with the zeal and fidelity of his generals, as well as with their courage and activity. Zieten had just been recalled with his corps, and posted at Breslaw. He was one of the number of those who assisted the king with his counsels as well as with his sword; and, to the duties of his station, he added the most tender concern for whatever related personally to his royal master. He was not ignorant, that Frederick, in a moment of despondency, had declared that death was the last friend he had in store.

In their nocturnal conversations, when stretched upon a bed of straw, in a redoubt, exposed to the enemy's fire, the two heroes mutually communicated their pains and their secrets to each other—it was Zieten, who opposed the hopes that ever animated him to the melancholy bodements of the king;—it was Zieten who sustained the courage of his royal friend, by continually assuring him, that everything would turn out prosperously. He would pronounce these words with such seeming conviction, and had so often repeated them, and in so positive a manner, that one day, when the king was more than ordinarily depressed by the sense of his misfortunes, and weary of hearing a kind of consolation which did not at all coincide with his way of thinking, His Majesty asked him in a sarcastic tone—if a new ally had joined the Prussian Army.

"No, sire;" replied Zieten, "I know of no other than one who dwells above, and who will never forsake us."

"But," rejoined the king, "he no longer works miracles."

"Be it so;" said Zieten, "we stand in no need of any:—let him fight for us, and we shall not fall."

Soon after this, the king had an opportunity of observing the reasonableness of pious hope; that providence was not a vain name; and that the confidence of Zieten had been that of a Christian hero. The army came out unhurt from their camp, which had been transformed into a prison, and Frederick said to his general with affected indifference, and in the genuine tone of sensibility, "For this time you have been in the right, Zieten; and your ally has kept his word."

The warm attachment which he always had for the king, did not, however, render him the less jealous of his own rights, whenever it was necessary to maintain them. He possessed the art of uniting delicacy with firmness, and the present campaign will furnish us with a remarkable instance in support of the assertion.

It has already been said, that the king had sent him to Glogaw, upon the death of General de Golz, to succeed him in the command of the army, and to march against the Russians. Zieten's health, which had seldom been good, was at this time in a very alarming condition. The king was probably apprehensive of losing him as he had lost Golz, or at least was fearful, that his indisposition would render him incapable of pushing his operations with due vigour. Whatever might have been His Majesty's motive, he despatched M. de Anhalt, his first *aide-de-camp*, to join Zieten's corps, with secret instructions to take upon himself the management of the army as circumstances might require.

This officer, who was one of Frederick's chief favourites, arrived, announced himself to Zieten in a very respectful manner, and was extremely well received. Under pretence of taking orders from the general, he began to assume the task of giving orders himself; but Zieten, although he had from the first moment detected the views of the king and the object of the mission; and although this secret arrangement touched him to the quick; yet, without betraying his feelings, he remained immovable, continued to exercise alone the functions of commander in chief, and ridded himself of the importunity of his rival by making use of him as his *aide-de-camp*.

In such capacity he chiefly employed him; he sent him to carry and execute his orders, charged him with the most frivolous commissions, and soon deprived him of the consequence he had enjoyed in the king's army, and which he would fain have assumed here. Thus, foiled in his expectations, he solicited the king to allow him to return; "For," added he, in his letter to His Majesty, "there is nothing to be done with old Zieten, nor am I able to be of any service to him." The king immediately thought fit to recall him.

The close of this campaign was rendered remarkable by the surprise of Schweidnitz. This bold operation, which was conducted by

General de Laudon, was the only disaster which the united armies were able to bring upon the Prussians. The loss of this place, however, together with the prospect of the ensuing campaign, created many gloomy apprehensions in the mind of the king. The enemy had gained footing in Silesia. They had, as well as His Majesty, established their winter-quarters there. A body of Russians, under the command of General de Czernitscheff, (and which Marshal de Butturlin had given up to General de Laudon), had likewise taken their quarters in the county of Glaz. The main Russian Army returned into Poland, though not in time to hinder General de Platen from destroying the magazines of Posen, together with an escort of five thousand waggons. Marshal Daun and Prince Henry wintered, with their respective troops, in Saxony; Laudon at Schweidnitz, and the king at Breslaw.

The well-known attempt, made on the 30th of November, against the king's life at Strehlen, had filled the Prussian Army will indignation and alarm. While the troops had an open enemy to engage, they felt themselves supported by a proper sense of their own prowess; but they had now the machinations of treachery to cope with;—they had to combat against the dark arts of assassination, as well as the lawful operations of war.

If we make mention of this event and of some others relative to the king, in the course of these memoirs, it, is, because whatever concerned that prince and his country was no stranger to Zieten's heart. We now come with him to a period abounding in great revolutions.

Elizabeth, Empress of Russia, the personal enemy of Frederick, died on the 25th of December 1761. Her nephew and successor, Peter III, the avowed admirer of that prince, made peace with him, and endeavoured to engage the court of Vienna to adopt the same measure. On the refusal of that power, he sent orders to General de Czernitscheff to withdraw the twenty thousand men under his command from the army of Laudon, and to join that of the king with them. Sweden following the example of Russia, withdrew her troops from the coalition, and the king had reason to remember his invisible ally; to whom Zieten, however, did not fail to ascribe the glory of all these happy events.

Thus, under the most favourable auspices, opened the seventh and last campaign of this destructive war. The king began it in preparations for the siege of Schweidnitz, which he was determined to recover from the Austrians, Laudon, in the meanwhile, made ready for the most vigorous resistance. All the belligerent powers now considered themselves arrived at the last act of this bloody tragedy, and were determined to finish it with *éclat*.

Zieten had no particular corps under his orders. Continually stationed in the headquarters of the king, he was invested with the command in chief during the occasional absence of that monarch, and shared the command with him, whenever two operations took place at the same time. The object of the Prussians was to dislodge the Austrian Army which continued to impede the siege of Schweidnitz; but every attempt to effect this proved abortive. Intrenched upon their flanks and their centre, the enemy seemed to lie perfectly secure from every attack.

Marshal Daun had exhausted all his art in the choice of his camp. He had pitched it upon the heights of Burkersdorf; detached corps occupied the passes of the mountains, and forming a chain of communications with Schweidnitz, kept the whole country under subjection, and rendered the siege impracticable. The king, however, could not submit to leave this gem of Silesia in the hands of the enemy; and not being able to lay siege to it, he resolved upon taking the camp by storm.

His pupil, his rival in arms, Major-General de Möllendorf, whose success had equalled his valour in the battles of Torgaw, Lignitz, and Leuthen, put himself, on the 21st of July, at the head of his brigade, and in the face of the combined armies, and in the presence of the Prussians, scaled the camp, and completely carried it in the course of four hours. This master-piece of Prussian tactics was executed with as much precision as dispatch. The barriers were completely cleared; and the routed army could not refuse paying the tribute of admiration to the conqueror. With him, General de Lottom (afterwards *commandant* of Berlin: he died in the year 1774), shared the glory of the day; and the writer of these memoirs is proud to decorate his grave with a sprig of laurel, as well as to water it with her tears.

The success of this day proved of the utmost consequence to Frederick. He had just lost a powerful ally. On the ninth of July, a tragical revolution had taken place in Russia. Peter III. now dethroned, and no more, was succeeded by Catherine II. who adopted a new system of politics, and gave orders to General de Czernitscheff to march home with his troops. This intelligence, so afflicting to Prussia and so distressing to the king, had already transpired in the army. The Austrians could not long remain ignorant of it, and it was necessary to strike a blow before they might be enabled to render such step ineffectual.

Frederick had gained upon the heart of the Russian general, and not upon his avarice, as it has been falsely represented, and he had been able to persuade him to defer his departure for twenty-four hours, to support the attack of Burkersdorf. The general did more: he ranged his troops in order of battle, and thereby facilitated the success of the enterprise. His friend, Major de Berg, of whom mention has already been made in these pages, having asked him the next day, what he would have done, had the issue proved undecisive; "I would have advanced," said he, "and provoked my own destruction."

Zieten who had been informed of this great revolution by his *aide-de-camp*, Lieutenant de Kleist of the *gendarmes*, absolutely refused to give any credit to it. He considered it as a mere fiction, a political bubble. He was, however, desirous of further information, and having all the Russian officers, on that day, at table with him, he got up, and gave the emperor's health. The guests were much embarrassed: some of them rose and pledged him; the rest kept their seats. Zieten had now no longer any doubt of the truth of the report.

The separation of the two armies was equally painful on both sides. The Russian and Prussian officers were united in those bands of friendship which seem so naturally to bind the two nations together. What they were mutually apprehensive of, did not happen: they were no more to draw their swords against each other, and the Russians on their departure, implored heaven to crown the arms of Prussia with success.

After having dislodged the Austrians from Burkersdorf, the king, in the beginning of the month of August, undertook the siege of Schweidnitz. General de Tauenzien commanded the army engaged in this enterprise. That of the king was divided into two equal parts. The one, encamped at Lampersdorf, and alternately under the orders of that prince and Zieten, covered the siege. The other, under the command of the Duke of Bevern, who had just been restored to the service, of his country, was posted at Reichenbach. Marshal Daun, whose grand object was to force the Prussians to raise the siege, had taken a formidable posture upon the heights of Langenbeil.

The king continued to frequent the two camps successively, visited the intrenchments which had been opened on the 8th of August, and pressed the siege; was apprehensive of a battle, entrenched himself to avoid it on the defiles and even on the summits of the adjacent hills, and carefully kept up the communication between the two camps in order that they might be able to support each other in case of need.

The event justified all these measures. Marshal Daun had devised a plan of attack that seemed to be infallible. While General de Beck should fall on the left flank and the back of the Prussians, and Lascy attack them in front with ten choice battalions, General Odonell was to pass the Pailbach at the head of twenty-five squadrons, to gain the plains of Reichenbach, and cover the left of Lascy, by throwing himself between that corps and the succour which the king might afford the troops under the command of Bevern. Several detachments at the foot of the hills had the like destination.

A little before the engagement, the king and Zieten met upon their return from a reconnoitring party which each of them had separately been making. The king was attended by M. de Anhalt and M. de Schwerin; Zieten had his *aide-de-camp*, M. de Lestocq, with him. On the approach of his general, Frederick stopped, and not knowing on what measures to determine, he addressed these officers in the following manner: "What do the enemy's intentions appear to be? Do they mean to attack Lampersdorf or Reichenbach?" No one made any reply; they were fearful of hazarding their opinion. Zieten alone had an eye sufficiently correct, and presence of mind and courage enough to answer.

"Sire," said he, "whatever may happen, it will be necessary to station a wing of cavalry upon the heights of Reichenbach."

The advice was judged to be salutary; and the success of the 16th of August, on which day the battle was gained, was the consequence of it. Beck had already turned the corps of Bevern, and thrown it into some disorder. Odonell's cavalry was on the point of enveloping the duke: the danger was urgent, and it was necessary to apply for succour to the cavalry of the king. The Duke of Wirtemberg who commanded it, came up in time with his right wing, and re-established the line. Had he arrived later; had the advice of Zieten been forgotten or neglected, all would have been lost. Odonell had already passed the defile gained the plain, and formed his line;—when the horse artillery of Wirtemberg began a terrible fire upon his left wing, and General de Lentulus of Bevern's corps, fell upon his right.

The battle grew hot, the Prussian infantry advanced, the Austrian cavalry repassed the defile in disorder, the Duke of Wirtemberg pursued it, and took four standards and some hundreds of prisoners. The hostile corps retreated, victory declared in favour of the Prussians, and the siege of Schweidnitz was carried on with redoubled vigour.

During the battle, Zieten remained at his post. He commanded the camp of Lampersdorf, and his attention was engaged between the succour he had to afford the Duke of Bevern, and the resistance which it was necessary to make against the enemy.

After having detached the Duke of Wirtemberg with one half of his cavalry, he ordered the other half to sustain his left from Reichenbach, and his right from Roth-Vorwerk, in order to check the right-wing of the enemy which threatened his left. The *aide-de-camp* whom he had commissioned with this order, after having communicated it to the general who commanded that moiety, proceeded, on for the purpose of finding out the king, who had joined Severn, and to whom Zieten had to make his report.

General de Kiaw, either having ill-comprehended or ill-executed the order of his commanding officer, stationed his men upon the same line with the infantry, propping his left by Roth-Vorwerk and his right by the battery of Peterswald.

Zieten arrived, and perceiving the error, instantly rectified it, but fell into so violent a passion on the occasion, that the general in order to extricate himself, had recourse to falsehood, laid all the blame upon the *aide-de-camp*, and protested he had executed the orders that he had been given him. At this moment M. de Lestocq made his appearance: he had been the bearer of the order. Zieten caused him to repeat it, word for word, in the presence of the general. The falsehood was detected. Zieten could no longer contain himself: among other things which his passion prompted him to utter, he said to M. de Kiaw:

> You should be aware, sir, that it is not with such giddy heads as yours, that battles are won: and, pray observe, that such conduct will not be overlooked a second time.

Yet, when the first emotions of anger had subsided, Zieten refrained from making the king acquainted with the affair; and the general, more touched with the delicacy of his commanding officer, than hurt at the severity of his expressions, shewed him ever after the highest marks of attention and respect.

After so many unavailing attempts, the Austrians at length thought fit to abandon Schweidnitz to its fate, and withdrew themselves from before it. They did not, indeed, consider it as lost; for independent of its natural strength, they had a whole army garrisoned within its walls. The siege went on slowly, but it was attended with the less danger. Zieten enjoyed some occasional hours of leisure; and he employed them in conversing with his officers on the art of fortifying towns, and with the labourers on that of tilling their grounds. He frequently visited the trenches, exposed himself to the shells of the enemy, and saw them fall at his feet without any apparent concern.

This was the last time that Zieten was to behold the fire of the enemy directed against him. Four months after this period, the songs of peace and delight succeeded to the doleful cries of desolation and death. The country received her sons with open arms, and joyfully congratulated them on their triumphs.

Schweidnitz surrendered on the 9th of October, with its garrison of eleven thousand men. On the 29th, Prince Henry, whom history will ever call the Fabius and the Caesar of the Prussians, beat the army of the circles at Freyberg. Princes Ferdinand, Charles, and Frederick of Brunswick, gained new laurels on the banks of the Rhine, and Frederick the Great, the *Unique*, intwined those he had won with the olive of peace, on bestowing that blessing upon the world. (On the 16th of February 1763, at Hubertsbourg.)

The heroes of Prussia sheathed their swords, impressed with the pleasing and honourable conviction of not having drawn them but in the defence of their country. They had rendered their king immortal, as he, on his part, had rendered them invincible. Exalted to a higher degree of eminence than the greatest commanders that had preceded him had ever attained, he was nevertheless indebted in no small degree to his fellow-soldiers for his elevation and his glory. The army proudly cherished the remembrance of the seven years' war, and considered the happy issue of it as an ample recompense for their past toils; and history will consecrate some of her fairest pages to perpetuate their well-earned renown.

Since that period, a political and revolutionary fanaticism has thrown all Europe into disorder and dismay. A ferocious war has torn the vitals of the social system: whole nations, and not armies only, have risen in a mass, and joined in bloody conflict: and scarcely has land and sea afforded a theatre sufficiently vast for the operations of an uninterrupted warfare of ten years' duration. It will be the task of future ages to compare these two periods, to point out their leading peculiarities, to characterise them, and to pronounce with impartiality. Happy the universe, if in addition to these two wars, a third of a similar nature is never to be recorded.

We should add nothing to the glory of Zieten by the recapitulation of his exploits. The reader has accompanied him through his various campaigns; and this unadorned narrative of his achievements has become his eulogy. His own actions have spoken for him, and they have stood in no need of foreign ornament. We should, however, be wanting in our duty in an historical point of view, were we to pass over in silence the manner in which he uniformly acted with regard to the various corps under his command. Some detail on this head is due to our young military readers, whom his example is so highly calculated to instruct.

As a general, and a commander in chief, he was never known to neglect anything which had formerly been the object of his solicitude in the capacity of a subaltern officer. He extended to a whole regiment, to a whole army, the attentions he had at first began to bestow upon a single company. On the march, he was either at the head or the rear of the column, and always indefatigably employed in providing for every possible contingency. At one time, he would slacken the march, in order to allow the hindermost to regain the ground they had lost. At another, he would fill up the gaps, reconnoitre the bridges, the defiles, the face of the country; in a word, it might be said, that he never had a better quarter-master-general than himself.

When the army was encamped, Zieten was not satisfied till he had examined and adjusted everything, entered into the minutest details, supplied every omission, and obviated every inconveniency. Whenever the king, as he imagined, had neglected a point, he would look to it; he posted or displaced the guards of the camp, augmented or diminished their number. When the ground was uneven it was his care to remove all obstructions, facilitate communications, construct bridges and every other necessary accommodation; and his orders were ever attended to as much as the immediate orders of the king.

After having provided for the internal part of the camp, it was his custom to take a survey of its environs. By day and by night, while the rest of the army were taking their repose, he was on horseback, examining the face of the country in order to discover on what point the enemy might probably make an attack, and what spots were best adapted for making a defence. This was his invariable occupation, on the march, in camp, and in every position; whence the army had honoured him with the name of their guardian. When the infirmities of age began to grow upon him, and it sometimes happened that he fell asleep at the royal table, the king would never allow him to be disturbed. The first time that the company, upon such an occasion, were about to awaken him, His Majesty interrupted them, and said, "Let him sleep on; he has watched long enough for us."

Frederick esteemed him highly for the manly firmness of his character, which the greatest military disasters were never able to shake for a moment. Bred up in the midst of storms, he had learnt to face them without dismay. While others trembled, he remained calm, and placed his entire confidence in heaven. This placid intrepidity, this cool patience, this inexhaustible fund of resolution, had great influence upon the mind of his royal master, who had often, under the pressure of despair, sought the general's quarters, alone and during the night, in quest of consolation and advice. Often has the heart of the consoler been wrung with anguish, when instead of coinciding in his way of thinking, the desponding monarch has made him no other reply than, "It will not do; it cannot possibly succeed."

Zieten extended even to the private soldier, the happy talent he possessed of encouraging the disheartened. He was aware, that the inaction and languor of camps are apt to give birth to discouragement, and that in such situations the distresses of want and hunger are felt with double severity by the troops. To prevent or mitigate their murmurs, he would often visit the ranks on foot, as well as on horseback, and invite the soldiers to come out of their tents. "Well, comrades!" he would say, "What are; you doing there?"

As soon as his voice was heard, they would instantly appear, and cry out, "Long live our good father Zieten!"

"Well, and how do things go on with you?" he would add.

"Bad enough," should they say, he was nevertheless able to apply a word of comfort.

"Take courage, comrades," he would answer, "If things go ill today, they may grow better tomorrow."

He has been frequently seen to alight from his horse, and converse with his veteran grenadiers: he has dispelled the cloud that hung upon their brows, and often rendered them insensible to the torments of hunger by regaling them plentifully with hope. This great popularity, accompanied with a frank benevolence of disposition which extended itself indiscriminately to every individual in the camp, had gained him the respect and confidence of the whole army to such a degree that with one common accord, as we have just seen, the soldiers had no other name for him than that of their father.

In the various battles in which Zieten took an active or directive part, the youngest officers were well aware, that they should not escape the general's observation—that their exploits would be remarked, distinguished, and rewarded; In the Battle of Lignitz, at the attack of Laudon's grenadiers, previous to the general engagement, a young lieutenant of the Prince of Prussia's regiment, of the name of Calbo, had received a wound. After the victory, Zieten passed near an officer who was under the hands of the surgeon. The general recognised him, spoke in high terms of his courageous deportment, expressed his concern at his disaster, congratulated him that the wound was not of a dangerous nature, and took occasion to praise the services the regiment had done the army, and the bravery it had just displayed. Such procedure could not fail to gain every heart.

At the present day, M. de Calbo recollects this anecdote with singular satisfaction, and the impression it made upon him; an impression which upwards of forty years have not been able to efface. Thus, could a word of Zieten operate in the breast of the young soldier, and prove a powerful incentive to glory and duty.

Officers of merit, to whatever regiment they belonged, could confidently rely on his kind services and powerful interposition, in cases, when owing to the distance of their residence from the king, to some unforeseen accident, and not to any fault of their own, they had lost the good graces of that prince. Zieten would watch for and seize the favourable moment to combat his prejudices. Obliged often to repeat his applications, he would never cease making them till they were crowned with success. In the campaign of 1761, the king, with a view to hinder the junction of the two armies, had recourse to several extraordinary motions; and, one day, having ordered Zieten to make an expedition in his presence, in the neighbourhood of Klosten-Wahlstadt; the general detached to the left, for the purpose of reconnoitring a wood, two squadrons of the regiment of Finkenstein's dragoons—a corps which His Majesty had an aversion to.

The head of these squadrons met in a valley a body of Austrian cavalry, consisting (as it has since appeared) of forty-two squadrons. As they were confined to a narrow pass, it was possible to attack them with advantage, provided the charge was made in a bold manner, and with all the appearance of being properly supported. The commanding officers of the two squadrons (M. de Bergsdorf, and M. de Schatzel), determined upon making the attempt. Proud of repeating under the king's immediate inspection, the exploits which had rendered them illustrious at Crefedt and Minden, the troops were resolved to force from that monarch the approbation which he had hitherto so unjustly refused them. After having agreed among themselves not to waste any time in taking prisoners, and being properly assured that

Zieten would not fail to support them, they fell upon the enemy with loud shouts and inconceivable fury.

The king had scarcely taken notice of this movement, when he sent one of his *aide-de camps*, with all possible expedition, with these orders:

> Tell Zieten to prevent the two squadrons from attacking the hostile cavalry, as they are not sufficiently strong for the attempt.

The general sent back the *aide-de-camp*, with the following reply.:

> Inform the king that I request him to let them go on, and that he himself would have the goodness to be witness to their success; that I have always said they were brave troops; that it is now their business to shew themselves such; and that I shall take care to send the rest of the regiment to their succour.

The dragoons performed prodigies of valour, the promise of Zieten was realised, and the king, on their return, conferred upon every officer the order of military merit, and gave them leave to wear a particular kind of sabre in honour of the exploits of the day. From this time, Frederick continued to testify the highest esteem for the corps; and Zieten who had the happiness, or rather, the merit of bringing about this revolution in His Majesty's sentiments, never ceased to congratulate himself on having chosen the favourable moment, and turned it to so good an account.

Ever serious, often severe, with regard to the officers who were subordinate to him, and particularly when they were men of high rank, he required the same secrecy on their part, as he himself observed in his most trivial expeditions. He carried his scruples so far on this point, as never to give his troops any intimation of their destined march till the very last moment. On the day preceding any motion, nothing was allowed to transpire through the whole army, and the instructions or dispositions, which he had to give the generals, were dictated to them in private, after having caused their *aide-de-camps* to withdraw. One day, when General de Bandemer, whose hand shook on account of his great age, had requested that his *aide-de-camp* should be permitted to sign in his stead, Zieten granted him that indulgence with no small reluctance, and not till the general had made himself responsible for the discretion of that officer.

His new officers, his new *aide de camps*, and especially when they were recommended by powerful patronage, were destined to act at first but passive and secondary parts. He commonly employed them in the most unimportant commissions, and it was not till he had put them to the proof, and had become well acquainted with their several characters, that he gave them his confidence, and did proper justice to their deserts.

He made choice of his *aide-de-camp-majors* from among the best of his officers. To fill this post, great talents and great activity were always requisite. Severe to an extreme, with respect to them, and, at most, pardoning such errors as resulted from youth and want of experience, he inured them to a rough school of discipline. Two eminent general officers of the present day, (1803), were long engaged in this honourable post with him; the one, Lieutenant-General de Köhler, whom he always called his pupil, his friend; who was tenderly esteemed by him, and whom he particularly recommended to the king; the other, Major-General de Lestocq, who succeeded the former, and of whom we have already made honourable mention. They were both proud to acknowledge, upon every occasion, what they owed to their master, their father, their friend.

To the severity which Zieten exerted in everything that related to the military service, he knew how to add proper indulgence, whenever he perceived that the officer was still more jealous of his honour than prone to subordination. The case of M. de Romberg will furnish us with a proof of it. This officer, a man of eminent talents, and whom his country would have numbered among its best commanders, had not an untimely death interrupted his military career, was *aide-de-camp-major* to Zieten. One day being charged by him with a commission of small importance, and sensible that it was confined to the mere delivery of a message, he employed a *chasseur* to execute it, and despatched him for such purpose in the presence of the general; who struck with the lesson, turned coolly towards him, and said, "So, my good lieutenant, it seems you are become a great man."

On the same day, however, he declared at table, in the presence of several officers, that Romberg had done well not to have debased his rank; that, for his own part, he liked to see a man properly jealous of his rights; that a well-timed resistance indicated a good officer, and restrained the general within proper bounds by hindering him from degrading his subalterns, as he acknowledged he had himself done that morning.

Although during the latter years of the war, Zieten had seldom met his regiment, he was never neglectful of anything which he owed it in the capacity of its chief. The internal and particular arrangement of the corps was his own work, and its exploits his recompense. Through the whole army, and even among the enemy, one general opinion prevailed with regard to the good order and bravery of the troops. Governed by ambition, by emulation, and incited by glory, the hussars of Zieten, whether officers or private soldiers, were ever anxious to emulate their commander; and their commander carried the confidence he had in them to such a degree, as to imagine himself invincible at their head.

Whenever it happened, that he encamped in the midst of his regiment, he considered himself more secure than he could be in any other situation, and, in such case, he would generally take a sudorific draught, with which he took care to be always provided. It was then of little import to him, whether the enemy were near or at a distance: after having visited the quarters, he would retire to his tent and give himself up to rest. He was one day so slightly guarded, and lay so much exposed to a sudden attack, that an officer, belonging to another regiment, could not refrain from remarking the danger he was in. Zieten made him no other reply than, "Am I not in the midst of my hussars?"

The regiment caught the words; and what was nothing more than a well-deserved eulogium, proved a further encouragement to them, and strengthened the bands of affection and devotedness which attached them to their chief. After peace was made, his officers, petty officers, private soldiers, flocked to Zieten, as to their common father, to shew him the scars that graced their persons, and to remind him of the spots, and the honourable occasions, on which they had gained them.

His hussars had born a part in every principal battle. At Prague, they had snatched the palm of victory from the hostile cavalry, and prepared the success of the Prussians. At Collin, at Breslaw, they had no share in the defeat of the army. Before they assisted in gaining the Battle of Leuthen, they had already bound their brows with laurels at Neumark; and after the victory, they had driven the enemy out of Silesia. At Zorndorf, they added to their reputation; at Hochkirchen, they saved the army; at Kunersdorf, the king. At Lignitz, they were the first who discovered the enemy, and the last who remained on the field of battle.

Finally, at Torgaw they crowned their former exploits, in the resistance they made to a victorious enemy in pursuit of the king, by covering their vanquished countrymen; in repulsing a column of Austrian infantry; in routing a column of cavalry; in forming a junction with the Prussian Army, and in checking the career of the enemy in order to afford Zieten time to overcome them. And yet the regiment was not complete at this period: a part was occupied in guarding general Saint-Ignon with eighteen officers (among whom were one colonel, and two majors,) and four hundred dragoons, who had been made prisoners before the engagement began.

In general, there had been no battle in which this regiment had acted ill; no officer belonging to it, who had not, more or less, distinguished himself in pitched battles, encounters, or on particular occasions. To do justice to ally they should be all named; but their number would be great, and we must be satisfied with recording the names of Seelen, Möhring, Sommogy, Probst the elder, Troschke, Herrmann, Mahlen, Velten, Lenz, Zettmar, Hund, Prittwitz, Probst the younger, Köhler, Wolfrath, Berg, Lestocq, Kordshagen, Drössel, Schulz, Kalis, Köppen, Voigt, Schwarz, Reizenstein, Möllendorf, Puttlitz, Biela, Breetz, Bock, Löwenek, the two Quasts, the two Jurgas's.

Without presuming to decide whether the foregoing are the most celebrated, we may venture to assure the reader, that those we have omitted are highly entitled to honourable mention, and that none of them would disparage the list, whether those who have survived Zieten, or such, as having fallen in the field of battle, have preceded him to the grave. In general, from the camp of Pirna, down to the taking of Schweidnitz, there was scarcely an officer in the whole corps, who had not displayed talent, or courage, or presence of mind, or the union of these qualities together. Besides those who had been decorated with the order of military merit in the early campaigns of this famous war, there were several who owed that distinction to their exploits during the campaigns of 1760 and the three following years; and several to whom the king, since that period, granted patents of nobility.

The last battles in which Zieten's hussars had an opportunity of signalising their accustomed valour, were those of Langensalza, Rudolstadt, Saalfeld, Hoyerswerda, Ditmannsdorf, Tharon, Boraw, Pantenaw, Habersdorf, Plauen, and Gottsberg. In these various actions, they were commanded by Major de Prittwitz, except in that of Plauen (in 1761), whose unfortunate issue was owing to a point of honour which Major de Hund had carried to a romantic extreme.

The victory remained doubtful. In vain Major de Hund, who commanded the hussars, lifted up his hand, which had been just shattered by a musket-ball, in order to inflame his troops with courage and revenge; the enemy still remained invincible behind their entrenchments. At this moment, one of his brother officers was illiberal enough to observe to him with a sneer, that his hussars took care to stoop in order to avoid the enemy's fire; when M. de Hund, by way of answer to so unmerited a charge, rushed with M. de Schulz and his small troop into the thick of the battle; and, after fighting with the most desperate valour, they all perished to a man.

In 1762, Captain de Köhler displayed the talents, of a great general at Gottsberg, in conducting through a numerous body of the enemy, a square battalion of infantry, flanked by his hussars.

We should be fearful of fatiguing the reader by any further detail on this head, how so ever instructive it may prove to men of the profession, and although authenticated by the most respectable authorities.

What Zieten's feelings must have been, when at the head of his regiment, he entered the gates of Berlin; it is not easy to describe. Let the reader imagine what reflections must have engrossed his mind, during the whose march with regard to the issue of this long and perilous war, and the singular felicity of his having escaped without any accident, and returned with the perfect use of all his limbs. Thrice had he accompanied the king into Silesia; thrice had gathered laurels there, and acquired new glory. How sincere must his satisfaction have been, to have so religiously acquitted himself of his promise to fight and to conquer for his country! He might, indeed, have considered, as partly his own work, the future prosperity of a state, whose foundation had been laid by the war, whose after-progress would be the result of that glorious struggle; and such animating reflections must have afforded him no inconsiderable recompense for all his cares and toils.

These brilliant remembrances, the high rank to which his own merit had raised him, his intimate connections with the king, filled up the measure of his happiness, and left him nothing farther to desire. What he had formerly sown with pain, he now reaped with glory; and had it not been for the trials he had met with in the earlier stages of his life; the repeated victories he had gained over his passions; the progressive steps by which he arrived at so eminent a degree of perfection;—he would not have enjoyed, and preserved to the very close of his long career, that admirable serenity of mind which added new value to his existence and to all the advantages that attended it.

Each returning year produced him new sources of happiness and new honours. During the span of twenty-six years, his sovereign continued studiously attentive to distinguish him by fresh marks of his esteem, his friendship, it may almost be said, his veneration. The princes of the blood were eager to imitate the example of Frederick. Henry, Ferdinand, the presumptive heir to the crown, considered themselves honoured by the zeal they shewed to do justice to the merits of Zieten. The court, the strangers that visited Berlin, equally admired the attentions which were shewn to this hero by those whose birth and rank were so far above his own; and, it was a fine spectacle for the whole country to see the subject thus noticed and caressed by his masters and by the family of his kings.

These distinctions, for which Zieten was indebted to his merit only, were no longer imbittered by envy. His enemies had disappeared, and among the witnesses to his glory, he could only reckon applauders and friends. His countrymen in general, whether in civil or military capacities, whether inhabitants of towns or villages, esteemed him, cherished him, and looked upon him as a father, revered him as a hero, and considered themselves in some degree as partakers of his glory.

His renown was not confined to the limits of his own country: it reached the most remote nations, where his name was universally mentioned with that of Frederick the Great. Of all the Prussian generals, there was not one whose exploits excited the curiosity of strangers to such a degree, or their eagerness to know him. In visiting the monuments, the beauties, the extraordinary characters of Berlin, they could not refrain from paying particular attention to whatever related to Zieten. The Empress of Russia, the Queen of Sweden, were pleased to request his portrait; the latter presented him, in return, with her own. His illustrious chief, Prince Henry, likewise paid a similar attention to him.

It was not only in the field of grandeur that Zieten was loaded with, these flattering distinctions: a new kind pf glory attended him in the applauses of the lower classes of the people. His name was pronounced by them with enthusiasm; they paid him a kind of worship. There was scarcely a single person who was not accustomed to speak of him, who had not come striking particular to relate of him, who had not procured his portrait, whether well or ill engraved, and who did not take a pleasure in placing it beside that of the king. Zieten and his hussars were seen in the poorest houses, and their exploits and praises, in bad verses, were pasted against every cottage-wall. A tobacconist at Aken upon the Elbe, made choice of his picture to wrap up his wares, and the envelope soon rendered the manufactory celebrated, and its concerns extensive.

Those who were personally acquainted with Zieten, have generally acknowledged that it was not to his external appearance that he was indebted for the universal homage which was paid him: it was solely owing to the qualities of his mind.

Zieten was low of stature, meagre, but well built; his face was oval, his hair dark-brown, his forehead flat, his eyes large and blue. His mouth was somewhat wide, his lips thick, and the under one marked with a deep scar. (He was wounded in the mouth, when a lieutenant, upon a recruiting-party.) His features were strong, his countenance masculine and somewhat harsh, though not deficient in harmony. His looks were steady, his eye fall of expression and fire, and his face highly characteristic of seriousness and dignity.

His attitude was erect, his gait free and easy. He was brisk in his motions; could use his sword in either hand, a circumstance, that proved advantageous to him on several occasions. He danced with singular grace, rode boldly and with great ease; and to the very end of his life, he preferred the lightest and most mettlesome steed to any other. (He could not recollect to have danced more than eight times since he was a mere stripling.)

Whether on horseback or on foot, all his movements were alert: on all other occasions, they were sedate and slow; and he who saw him in his chamber engaged in his domestic affairs, could hardly suppose him to be endowed with that degree of activity, resolution, and boldness which always characterised him in public.

Averse to loquacity, he could say much in few words. His answers were just and precise; his replies not deficient in point and smartness. His voice was rough and manly: he gave the word of command with peculiar distinctness. His whole person announced serenity, experience, and firmness of character; commanded attention, obedience, and respect.

He was remarkably neat and clean in the article of dress. Such had been his practice from his earliest youth, and he never ceased to observe it to the latest period of his life. To that period, he was always found with his regimentals on, early every morning. He generally wore his hat in his room for the purpose of keeping his head warm. As soon as he was dressed, his valet was ordered to leave him: it was then his custom to say his prayers; a duty which he was never known to neglect, even during his severest indispositions.

His breakfast consisted of a bason of soup and some slices of bread and butter. He would never take either tea or coffee, except a kind of tea, made of lemon-peel, which he sometimes drank by way of diet drink, as prescribed by his physician.

He dined with good appetite, and commonly on three dishes. No other vegetable than carrots ever appeared on his table. He ate that root the whole year round for the sake of his health, and drank either water, or a diet-drink which he prepared himself from a receipt with which his favourite physician, M. Oehm, had formerly furnished him. (Hotz, the celebrated physician, brother to the Austrian general of that name, assures us, that the man who would eat carrots every day of his life would stand in no need of medicines.)

At supper, it was his custom to eat of two light dishes, almost always the same things, which he likewise partook of with good appetite, and without touching any other of the meats that were on the table. He had adopted this rule out of regard for his health, and every time he swerved from it, his intemperance was punished by indigestions; so that after many trials, he submitted to this regimen, which he continued ever after to observe very scrupulously, and at length it became a matter of no sacrifice to him.

The patriarchal simplicity in which he lived was practiced by him to the last moments of his life with such a degree of firmness, that at the age of eighty-four, his most intimate friends could not prevail on him to make use of an elbow-chair of a more commodious construction than that to which he had been generally accustomed.

His turn for hospitality increased with his years, and although he was so abstemious with regard to himself, he took great delight in having his table profusely spread with the best things each reason afforded. He was fond of seeing it frequented, as well as to share in the general hilarity of his guests. Without standing in need of any such amusements to fill up the vacuities of life, he indulged himself in them with the highest satisfaction: they by no means influenced his way of living, but rather tended to give it new charms; and the visits which he received at Wüstrau, and in the capital, became more and more agreeable to him. He received his friends with an engaging sort of kindness as bordered upon gratitude; and he was studiously careful to provide everything that could any way contribute to their enjoyments.

At Wüstrau, in particular, he would invite young people of both sexes to balls and social diversions. He was happy to be surrounded with officers of his own regiment, and that of Prince Ferdinand, which from the conclusion of the peace, he cherished almost equally with his own. Several witnesses to these agreeable rustic entertainments are still alive, in whose memories this brief description must awaken many a pleasing idea, and who must all allow that old Zieten, without derogating in the least from the native dignity of his character, was an adept in propagating delight, and in giving new zest to harmless frolics. To his more select associations he admitted officers of distinction and merit only. The conversation would then commonly turn upon military affairs, and in which he was always careful not to speak of his own exploits.

Every officer in the army who had distinguished himself by acts of valour or general probity of conduct, bore a high rank in his esteem. He would honour such as if their principal object had been to please himself only. He was ever looking after concealed desert; was fond of exposing it to view, and he has often been able, through his representations to the sovereign, to crown it with final, though tardy, recompense.

His gratitude to those who had rendered him services during the war, was boundless, and indiscriminately extended to all of them. Sometimes, indeed, he was apt to carry his attention, in this respect, too far. A spy who had been of use to him in the late campaigns, he afterwards made his *valet-de-chambre:* the man, however, not only abused the trust the general placed in him, but likewise his goodness and indulgence; and it was not before he found himself repeatedly and grossly deceived, that Zieten was induced to discharge him from his service.

In his youth, the general had been extremely fond of the chase: he afterwards neglected that diversion; and in the decline of life, he had seldom recourse to it but for the sake of the exercise it afforded him, and the pleasure it gave to his friends. He conquered, at the same time, another custom, which in his earlier years he had carried to excess. After having been the most inveterate smoker of the whole army; after having made his pipe his inseparable, and even table, companion, for forty years together, he suddenly refrained from the use of it to the great surprise of all his acquaintance. Matthisson the poet had procured a porcelain pipe ornamented with the portrait of Zieten: this pipe has since made part of the reigning Prince of Wittgenstein's collection of smoking apparatus, where it is now (1803), preserved as a relic. Zieten is represented as the patron of smokers, with the hussar-cap on his head, and, consequently, at a time of life, in which he had left off the use of the pipe.

With regard to his passions of a complexional nature, he had early learnt, by the assistance of reason, to gain the mastery over them; though he found it impossible to stifle them entirely.

To the thirst of glory and ambition, which during the period of youth had proved both his bane and good fortune, had succeeded a sentiment of honour of a more peaceable nature, though still founded upon a noble pride, which would never suffer him to give up the smallest of his rights, were it even to the first man in the kingdom. He had never varied his opinion with regard to these sentiments; they had actuated him from his earliest youth, and he considered them as peculiarly characteristic of the military profession; hence, one day, when a lieutenant, belonging to his regiment, was making complaint to him of some offensive language which had been given him by a senior officer, Zieten made him no other reply than this, "If you hesitate, Sir, on what part you have to act; I can have no advice to offer you on the subject."

Proneness to anger was the last enemy he had to subdue, and over which, it could not be said, he was ever able to gain a complete triumph. He was one day on the point of pushing downstairs an officer of another regiment, who had taken a hussar from him, and who had come to make his excuses in person. All his officers, without exception the moment they happened to depart from the line of their duty, were sure of incurring his anger, and of finding him inexorable. In all other cases, and where there was no question of military service, he acted in a very different manner, and those about him were scarce able to conceive him to be the same person.

It would be difficult to find a single instance of his having abandoned himself up to anger with any of his own servants or the peasantry of Wüstrau. He was satisfied with giving them a reprimand, and, at most, confined himself to threats of punishment, without ever having recourse to any acts of violence: and this distinction, which he knew how to make between the king's service and his own, shews the importance he affixed to the former, and the obligation under which he considered himself of not giving way to his feelings, but to have due respect for the invariable letter of the law.

It cannot be denied that, in his youth, Zieten was violently devoted to the passion of love, and that he was frequently entangled in its snares. His own experience, however, rendered him indulgent to the foibles of others, and his young officers had no occasion to complain of their general's severity on the subject of their amorous follies. He would often rally them at his own table, with great good nature and pleasantry, upon their good or ill fortunes: but whenever he discovered that innocence had been seduced, or abandoned by its betrayer to want and infamy; that the peace of a family had been ruined, and the sacred ties of the conjugal union violated, he was unable to set any bounds to his indignation and resentment. The tender passion may, indeed, have captivated, and led astray, his senses, but it was never able to subjugate his heart entirely: it never checked his activity, nor shackled his genius; nor ever palsied his arm. His country commanded his first homage; the fair sex had only a secondary claim to his attentions. He was ever alive to the power of beauty, to the charms of wit, and to the graces. Such sentiments, indeed, it was his pride to avow.

Self-interest was a passion to which he was, during his whole life, a total stranger. This passion is generally supposed to be the growing infirmity of age. He was invariably deaf to its suggestions: to his latest hour, he remained liberal, generous, sensible to the misfortunes of others, and totally indifferent to what related merely to his own welfare. The desire of amassing wealth could never find any place in his heart; that of bestowing took up too much room there, to allow of its admission. On the suppression of the right of commonage at Wüstrau, he resigned the most valuable portions to his peasants; upon every; occasion, he gave up his own privileges, augmented theirs, and was ever bettering their circumstances.

He planted colonies on his estate, built them houses and barns at his own expense, and extended his bounties to such of the neighbouring villages as solicited his patronage and protection. When he had at, length, by means of certain loans, acquired; the whole lordship of Wüstrau, and it was necessary to rebuild a part of the village, he employed, during the leisure of the winter season, all the idle hands in the neighbourhood, and generously rewarded their labour. So little regard had he for money, that one day he replied to a person, every way entitled to make representations on the subject of economy to him, "I hope you put no value upon that dirt of Eldorado."

The noblest point of view in which Zieten remains to be considered is that of a man, who invariably entertained the most hallowed regard for religion. Hence the pure source of all his virtues, and all his morality; hence that extreme indifference, that entire abnegation of himself, whenever his own interests came in competition with those of another; hence, from his earliest career of life, when he first began to push his fortune in the world, that uncommon delicacy of character which never allowed him to have recourse to any indirect or disingenuous expedients; and hence, when arrived to the summit of his glory, that noble serenity of mind, unembittered by reproach; that pure and unalterable felicity, which crowned the evening of his days, and repayed the toils of a useful and well-spent life.

The piety of Zieten was entirely distinct from all mechanical devotion or superstitious servility. His sentiments of religion were pure and simple. He considered it as an homage due to the supreme being; and as long as his health permitted him, he was a constant frequenter of public worship.

At no time, indeed, was he ever neglectful of the duty of prayer; nor did a day pass over his head, without his having acquitted himself of it in the silence of his closet, excluded from the observation of the whole world. His prayers were not limited to any fixed periods; he consecrated to that duty his occasional moments of solitude, his watchings, his sleepless hours; and his couch was often found to have been watered with his tears.

The alarms of war were now over, and Frederick and his fellow soldiers were at length to taste the sweets of repose. The wounds of their country began to close up, and the reign of order to succeed to that of tumult and destruction. It was Zieten's particular object to re-establish that order in his own regiment, The discipline of camps too frequently grows relaxed; the duty of a hussar, during the campaign, is attended with innumerable deviations which are inseparable from the nature of war, and to which hostilities of seven year's duration seemed to have given a sanction.

When returned to their garrisons, the soldiers had to lay aside the habits of a vagabond life, and to submit to the yoke of a new system of things. Zieten thought fit to begin this reformation with his officers. On their march from the theatre of war, he found it necessary to treat them with a severity which they little expected after their exploits and the indulgence he had usually shewn them during the late campaigns;—and ere they came within sight of the walls of Berlin, they had already acquired a competent idea of the spirit of order which was to reign there.

The regiment approached the capital, and formed in a line before one of the gates. Zieten despatched an officer to Prince Henry, to announce his return to him in the king's absence, as his senior general; During the time in which the prince was expected to arrive, in order to put himself at the head of the regiment and conduct it in triumph into the city, the general reviewed the equipments of his officers, into which several alterations and abuses had lately found their way, and he declared to them his resolution of restoring things to their former state. In the meanwhile, the officer despatched to Prince Henry, announced, by mistake, the arrival of the troops to the Prince of Prussia, afterward Frederick William II.

The heir to the throne appeared: he was Zieten's junior general. The latter taking him for Prince Henry, gave the signal of salutation, drew his sabre, and ordered his hussars to do the same: but perceiving his error, he loudly blamed the officer who had been the cause of it, and peremptorily commanded the troops to sheath their swords; nor did he pay the prince his particular homage before he had executed what the laws of subordination and military etiquette required at his hands.

Happy the subject, happy the inhabitants of a country, where the laws are paramount to every other consideration; where the general may venture to withhold military honours from a prince of the blood and heir to the crown, should his rank in the army be beneath his own, Happy the country, in which that prince was the first to applaud the conduct of Zieten, who had thus acted the part of a general in preference to that of a courtier.

After having made every necessary arrangement in the garrison and provided for the accommodation of his regiment, Zieten visited his favourite villa at Wüstrau, from whence he had been so long absent. The pleasure he felt on this occasion was heightened by a circumstance that had taken place there since he had last left it, and which did great honour to the Swedish troops. In one of their campaigns, they had penetrated as far as this village; when hearing it was the property of the celebrated Zieten who was waging war against them and their allies, they not only refrained from touching anything that belonged to him, but manifested the high respect they bore him by placing sentinels before his house, examining his portrait with admiration, and by many other traits, equally flattering and agreeable.

From Wüstrau, Zieten went to Carlsbad with a view of recovering his health, and he had every reason to be satisfied with his excursion. He gained much with regard to health, and was highly flattered with the attentions paid him there, as well as upon the road. At Zwickaw, where he had often appeared as an enemy, a guard of honour was given him; and although he staid there but a few hours, the officers of the garrison, with the magistrates, waited upon him in a body to pay him their respects.

The inhabitants assembled before the post-house to see the man, who, during the late war, had so essentially mitigated its horrors, who had encouraged them to support the hardships it laid them under, with patience and resignation, who at one time, had joined them in their public devotions, at another, partaken of their balls and entertainments, with a view of affording his officers an example of order and decency, and the town, a mark of his benevolence. At Görlitz, at Schneeberg, and, in general, along the whole road, the inhabitants were eager to give him the most honourable reception, and in a manner that shewed he had treated Saxony and Lusatia more like a benefactor than an enemy.

When he arrived at Carlsbad, he met with several Austrian generals, among whom were Counts Wartensleben, Harrach, and Buquoi; M. de Nugent, M. de Stampach, and General de Laudon. It was a fine spectacle to behold Laudon and Zieten, after having exerted their military talents with so much ardour against each other, now united together in the bands of friendship and become inseparable companions.

On this journey, Zieten made the acquaintance of Gellert the poet, who during the late war had been honoured with that of the king. In one of the letters of this celebrated writer, the general's portrait is drawn in a masterly manner, except in one particular point, in which the poet has not done him justice. Gellert represents him deep in the decline of life, and even bordering Upon a state of decrepitude. This was not at all the case-with our general. In his sixty-fifth year, far from giving up the enjoyments of life, he was paying his addresses to a lady to supply the place of the excellent woman he had lost before the beginning of the war.

He had not, indeed, waited for peace ere he formed this project: he had made an excursion from his winter quarters at Meissen as far as Wüstrau, and seen the lady, to whom he secretly destined his hand, at that place, where she then was upon a visit to his family. He made her an offer it on the conclusion of peace, and the offer was accepted. This lady was Mlle. de Platen of the house of Mesendorf in the province of Prignitz: she had no fortune, but had received an excellent education, and was a woman of sense and of an amiable disposition.

Zieten gave the king a very agreeable surprise by requesting his consent to this marriage; and this may be perceived from the gay turn of His Majesty's answer.

My dear General de Zieten.
By your letter of the 4th instant, you ask my consent to your marriage with Mlle, de Platen. I grant it with great pleasure, and wish you all possible happiness on the occasion. If I knew where the nuptials are to be celebrated, I should not fail to be with you, on purpose to dance with the bride. I remain your affectionate king,
Potsdam, April 7th, 1764, Frederick.

The ceremony was performed at the bride's sister and brother-in-law's. (M. and Mad. de Blumenthal of Krampfer in the province of Prignitz.) The next day, a ball was given, and notwithstanding his thirteen lustres, Zieten who had arranged the whole entertainment, astonished the company by the grace and agility with which he went down the dance. The king, though absent, signalised this *fête* by a present of a valuable diamond ring which he sent to the bride.

The following year. Mad. de Zieten brought him a son; and the king, who had promised to be sponsor to the child, came to Berlin from Potsdam on purpose, to be present at the ceremony of baptism. His Majesty was pleased to advance the new-born infant to the rank and pay of a cornet in its father's own regiment, and made Mad. de Zieten a present of four magnificent silver *girandoles*.

To the satisfaction he felt on the birth of his child, was added that which resulted from the warm part the king took in his happiness, and the flattering and distinguished manner in which His Majesty was pleased to shew it. It was not every day that Frederick appointed officers in their cradles, or waited on his subjects to hold their children at the baptismal font.

Sensible of this favour, Zieten was far from making an improper use of it. He brought up his son in those principles which were one day to make him worthy of these anticipated advantages. At the age of twelve, he placed him in the academy of nobles, without allowing him to advance at all in his regiment; and when his friends would urge the king's intentions and the sanction of custom, in opposition to his measure, he would reply with warmth, and observe, that his son was but a mere child.

At length, when the boy was incorporated in the regiment, the general consented to his being named second lieutenant in the place of M. de Malzahn; and in this manner it was, that the delicacy and scruples of his father prevented him from attaining to the rank of lieutenant earlier than the year 1782; seventeen years after he had been appointed cornet. The regiment, the army, the public, admired this disinterested procedure, and acknowledged the, greatness of the sacrifice. The paternal heart of Zieten had long resisted its own impulses, together with, the repeated remonstrances of his friends. It was in vain, that M. de Krockow, at that time *commandant* of the regiment, with the whole corps of officers, solicited him to avail himself of the royal bounty in behalf of his son; the more they urged it, the more obstinately he persisted in his refusal.

At length, M. de Krockow perceiving, that no impression could be made upon the determined firmness of his mind, he was induced to make direct application to the king, without the general's knowledge, and to propose his son as lieutenant in the place of an officer, who had just died. Frederick approved of the colonel's zeal, while he honoured the scruples of the general, and replied with regard to the young man, that he waited till his worthy father should himself make the application.

Zieten was kept a perfect stranger to this business, which might have exposed the colonel to some friendly reproaches on his part. Soon after this, he afforded the generals of the army an example of another kind, in the readiness of his submission to the orders of the king. A new military arrangement, which had lately taken place, was at this time, the subject of much discontent. The king had destined his regiments to undergo a very severe scrutiny, and given such extensive powers to the different inspectors, as to enable them, in a great degree, to represent himself. The multiplicity of his labours, and the manifold branches of administration, justified such step, as well as rendered it necessary; yet it was calculated to affect in a very sensible manner, a great number of officers, who were thereby made subordinate, not only to their equals, but to their juniors.

The time drew near, when the several inspectors were to review the regiments which belonged to their division. That of Zieten, which was submitted to the inspection of General de Lölhöfel, attended on the Wilhelms-Platz. (A fine square in Berlin.) The eyes of the whole garrison were fixed upon this regiment, and upon its chief. The latter had hitherto concealed his sentiments with regard to this novel arrangement, and he was now about to manifest them. The generals were impatient to see how he would act on this occasion: he soon exhibited a line example, and it was cheerfully followed by all of them. Though the inspector was by far his junior, he waited for him with the same attention which the lowest soldier could have been expected to pay him.

He was on foot, with his drawn sabre in his hand; and in such respectful attitude, he remained standing at the head of his regiment. General de Lölhöfel could scarcely believe the evidence of his own eyes: the moment he recognised him, he alighted from his horse, and accosting him, begged that he might no longer be put out of countenance by such a singular act of condescension; when Zieten, without changing his posture, and with a view of instructing him in the nature of his duty, replied, "General, you represent the king, and it is to him, and not to you, that my homage is addressed."

At the grand reviews, he was always charged with the command of the cavalry. The inspector received his orders, and caused them to be executed in the line. Lieutenant-General de Krusemark, who was inspector in the year 1773, having died a little before the review, and the post still remaining vacant, Zieten undertook to command the line in person. He was now seventy-six years old, and it was imagined that the task would prove too hard for him. General de Wiersbitzky sent to beg leave to attend him for the purpose of executing his orders. Zieten informed him by his *aide-de-camp*, Lieutenant de Jurgas, that it was needless to give himself any trouble, and that he was requested to remain at the head of his own regiment: but, having observed the general had said something to that officer, before he could prevail upon himself to yield to the injunction, Zieten made inquiry into the nature of it.

Wiersbitzky, it seems, was fearful that the general's voice would not be heard along the whole line, and had desired the *aide-de-camp* to make a signal with his cap the moment Zieten should have given the word to halt after the charge. The latter, piqued at this precaution, commanded his *aide-de-camp* not to take any notice of it. "We want no signal;" said he, "nor can I allow of any, as it is not our custom; they will see when I lower my sabre and turn my horse."

At this moment, the king came up. His Majesty knew Zieten, and of course was aware that he was still able to perform his duty. The charge was sounded; it was begun without the least confusion, was carried on and concluded, to the astonishment of all the spectators, and to the entire satisfaction of His Majesty. On the second day, everything proceeded well, and on the third, notwithstanding his infirmities and the impaired state of his memory, Zieten was able to retain the king's disposition, and to communicate it in a correct manner to the several generals under his command. Furthermore, two extra manoeuvres, which he executed off-hand, and which made no part of the general plan of the day, were honoured with the warmest applauses of the sovereign.

This was the last time that he undertook the command at a review; and if he was afterwards present on such occasions, it was only as chief of his own regiment; and whenever he failed to attend, it was on account of indisposition.

In the year 1790, he was for the first time detained at home by illness. When the review was over, the king, much alarmed at the general's situation, rode directly from the field to his house to see him; and after conversing for some time with him, he said, "I am not the only one of your old friends that pay you a visit; there is another of them waiting in the anti-chamber; can you guess his name?" It was the reigning Duke of Brunswick, the father to the present, (1803), one.

Every reader of feeling will certainly participate in the satisfaction and triumph of Zieten; who, if he owed in part this distinction to his military exploits, was likewise indebted for it to his singular probity of character.

In the course of this year, the king made him a present of ten thousand dollars, on account of a considerable loss he had suffered at Wüstrau from a epidemical disorder that raged among his cattle. He had lately made an acquisition of two thirds of that manor, together with all the livestock, and, as it has been already observed, had raised money to make good his purchase. (The proprietors of land, in this country, as well as in many other parts of Germany, furnish their several farms with cattle and with various utensils of husbandry.) The disaster was severely felt by him; yet it was foreign to his disposition, and inconsistent with his principles, to complain; nor would the king have heard of this accident, and the embarrassment in which it involved the general, had not Colonel de Prittwitz, the *commandant* of his regiment, thought fit to let him into the secret.

The king partook of Prittwitz' kind solicitude, and determined to administer relief. The affair was negotiated with the greatest delicacy and concealment; Zieten had not the least suspicion that his colonel had done him this piece of service; nor did the circumstance transpire till a long while after, through the confession of third person, who was privy to the transaction.

From the cessation of hostilities till the death of Zieten, several court-martials had been held at his house; and the following letter from the king is the only document of this nature, that has been found among the general's papers.

My dear General de Zieten.

In answer to your report of the 10th, relative to the court-martial for the purpose of inquiring into the conduct of Generals de Finck, de Gersdorf, and de Rebentisch, I hereby inform you, that I have named de Wedel to attend it in the capacity of lieutenant-general. I have likewise named de Czettritz and de Wylich in the same capacity. I have been unable to make any further nominations, on account of the distance of the parties. As to major-generals, colonels, lieutenant-colonels, and majors; there are many of them at hand, and you may make your own election. Furthermore, I shall myself inform the three lieutenant-generals of the choice I have made of them; and I remain your affectionate king,

Berlin, May 19th, 1763.                                      Frederick.

*In his own hand.*

Forcade may be admitted into the court-martial.

In one of these court-martials, he had an affair with General de Ramin, the Governor of Berlin, which made too much noise at the time, not to deserve some mention here.

A court-martial was appointed to be held upon General de Reizenstein. The king had named Zieten president, and Generals de Ramin, Wedel, Krusemark, Koschenbahr, Braun, Steinkeller, together with the colonels, and left to him the task of giving the usual notice to the lieutenant-colonels and majors. Zieten made ready to obey the king's orders, and despatched his *aide-de-camp* to invite the generals and colonels to the session, and to dine with him. He gave him particular directions to request General de Ramin to convoke the necessary lieutenant-colonels and majors.

The general, in a moment of ill humour, refused the commission, and alleged, that he could see no reason why the president had not done that himself. Zieten, much astonished at this answer, inquired if the general was indisposed, and was informed, that he was in perfect health, and just going out upon a shooting-party. The president grew angry, and sent back his *aide-de-camp* to the governor, not to request, but to order, him to execute the above commission. The second message proved as unavailing as the first. The governor replied, that Zieten might address himself to the place-major, and make his arrangements with him. (A place-major is an officer who is charged with the detail of the garrison.) The *aide-de-camp* began to remonstrate, but he was soon interrupted, and sent back with instructions to repeat what he had just heard. Zieten, more astonished than ever, replied:

> I cannot conceive how General de Ramin can thus neglect my orders. Return immediately to him, and tell him, that if he persists in not giving notice to the officers, I shall put him under arrest, and make report of it to the king. Take one of my horses for the sake of expedition.

The task was an unpleasant one; but Zieten was not to be trifled with; the *aide-de-camp* mounted the horse, and arrived at M. de Ramin's: it was late, and the governor was already gone to bed. It was with great difficulty that he could get himself announced: he was at length admitted, and received the following answer:

> Well, Sir, I shall take care to summons the officers in question, because, it seems, I am compelled to it; but I shall not stay to dinner.

In the seventy-ninth year of his age, Zieten experienced one of the most painful trials he had ever met with in the course of his whole life. It was in 1778: the Bavarian war had just broke out; the troops received orders to march; his equipments were ready, and he himself was likewise prepared. A new ardour circulated through his veins, and restored the vigour of his better days; but he was soon informed that the king was going to make the campaign without him, and that his name was not inscribed in the war establishment. He immediately wrote His Majesty a very pressing letter, and received the following answer.

> My dear General de Zieten.
> The apprehension I am under, that the state of your health will not allow you to undertake the present campaign, is the sole reason for my not having appointed you to accompany me. I am extremely mortified to be forced to leave you behind me; yet you cannot but be aware, that at your time of life, and after the fatigues you have already undergone, you would be unable to support the toils of a new war; and you must likewise feel that you stand in need of repose. I remain your affectionate king,
> Potsdam, March 25th, 1778.                                    Frederick.

Zieten was not to be repulsed at the first blow. He returned to the charge, redoubled his solicitations; but the answer he obtained was similar to that he had just before received.

My dear General de Zieten.
In reply to your letter of the 27th, I hasten to inform you how mortified I am to leave you in garrison on account of your health, which, as I have already said, will not allow you to go through the labours of the campaign. I am convinced of your good will; but no man is required to exert himself beyond his powers, and all you have now to do, is to rest from your past fatigues. I remain your very affectionate king,
Potsdam, March 26th, 1778,                                    Frederick.

We shall not attempt to describe what Zieten felt, when he saw the departure of the king and the army. The day on which his regiment left Berlin, was a day of mourning to him. Before sunrise, he was in the circus, near the Halle-gate, to take leave of his pupils, his children; and he exhorted them, in a short and pathetic speech, to be mindful of what they owed to their country, to their profession, and to their reputation. The good old man could not refrain from shedding tears, nor was the regiment less affected on the occasion. The tears of the brave are graceful, and the hardiest soldier needs not blush to give way to them. On his return to his house, and for a long time after, the conflict of his mind was visible on his countenance.

His grief was, indeed, mute but it was the more pungent: it broke out in complaints but once, and that happened on the day of the departure. In the midst of his family, and surrounded by the group of females who chiefly composed it, he suddenly exclaimed, after a very long silence, and with a deep sigh; "Alas! I have now nothing to do but to raise a regiment of women!"

At length he could no longer bear to reside in Berlin: he went to Wüstrau, but unaccompanied with the ardour and activity which had hitherto attended him there. He caused several tables to be placed together in his dining-room, covered them with the best maps he could procure of theatre: of the war, and passed whole hours in poring over them. In a short time, he began to recover his former tranquillity of mind, became more gay and communicative; and, at this time it was, that the grateful woman, whom he honoured with his friendship and his confidence, and, who has since ventured to compile these *Memoirs*; attentive to these recitals, snatched from oblivion such particulars as discretion permitted him to impart to her, and has incorporated them in the monument she has raised to her hero.

In the recitals and various details into which he entered, he refrained from touching upon one point only—his own panegyric. Lavish in the praise of others, he often withheld that justice from himself which was his acknowledged due; and instead of enlarging upon his proper exploits, he dwelt only on the trials and vicissitudes of his life. When he came to the story of his duel in Prussia, to the brewer's lever which he wielded for want of a sword, the old man seemed to forget his age, and starting from his seat with all the fire of youth, put his recital into action. It was thus, that instead of requiring from the companions of his retreat and sorrows, the consolations they were ill-able to afford him, he took pleasure in contributing to their amusement and instruction.

But scarcely had he heard that the king, with the Prussian Army, had returned in peace, than he hastened to meet his regiment; and great was his satisfaction to find it considerably improved by the exercise the campaign had afforded it. He had next the pleasure to welcome his royal master's return, and to find that his friendship for him had not been at all diminished by absence. This moment effaced the remembrance of that of the departure; he forgot the refusal which had given him so much pain;—and which was the last vexation that embittered his life.

Happy in the repose his country now enjoyed; happy in the return of his beloved regiment, in the reiterated marks of the favour and esteem of his sovereign, and in the peculiar felicity of his own family, he had now nothing more, on this side the grave, to wish for. At Wüstrau, (where it had been his custom since 1766, to pass some months in the year,) his peasantry and all his neighbours ever rejoiced sincerely at his return. On his arrival, his first care was to examine the progress of various improvements which had been carried on during his absence; on his leaving the place, he planned new ones, and began to anticipate the future satisfaction they were to afford him. The last satisfaction of this nature was the improvement of a waste and sandy spot of ground, which he had rendered arable and fertile, and which had produced him a remarkable fine crop of barley.

He never calculated the advantages or expense of such undertakings; he was satisfied with the idea of clearing, building, embellishing, finding useful occupation for a multitude of hands—of employing his own time in a useful manner, and, in a word, of promoting honest industry throughout the whole neighbourhood. When he had already passed his eightieth year, he undertook a considerable edifice, which he had long had in contemplation, and which he still hoped, to see completed, though a work of some years. This was the steeple of the parish church of Wüstrau, which now (1803), serves as a principal ornament of the village. He applied a great portion of his pay and rents to the gratification of his passion for building; and the able economy of his lady, to whom he committed the entire management of his family concerns, rendered these extra-expenses less prejudicial to his fortune than they were generally supposed to be.

We would wish to be able to describe his domestic happiness;— but to have an adequate idea of it, the reader, should have seen, experienced, and partaken of it with him. His lady, his children, all who were about him, or served him, were indebted to him for the happiest moments of their lives. He was the beloved master of his family, the boast of all who belonged to him. His domestics were proud to be in his service, and to wear his livery. Of his three children, the eldest, a daughter by his former lady, was married during her father's lifetime, to M. de Jurgas, of the house of Ganzer. His other daughter, after his death, married Major de Zieten, of the *carbineers*, a gentleman of the family of Wildberg. His son, the godson of Frederick the Great, quitted the army on account of his health, soon after his father's decease: the states of the county of Ruppin have lately named him their provincial counsellor.

It was, indeed, an engaging spectacle to see the old general, with his white head of hair, in the midst of his rising family, taking part in their pastimes, superintending their education, declaring himself to be the happiest of fathers, and returning thanks to heaven for having given him so excellent a wife. With regard to the delicate attentions he always shewed her, the most tender and complaisant of lovers could not easily surpass them. He anticipated, rather than gratified, her wishes; and in endeavouring to make her happy, he considered himself as merely paying a debt. One day he expressed in one word, his high opinion of her merit, when, with a tear starting from his eye, he exclaimed to her; "God reserves such women as you for those he loves."

It has been already remarked that Zieten, as he advanced in years, became more gentle, communicative, sociable, and indulgent; and that he took more delight than usual in opening his heart to some of his most intimate friends. While other old men obstinately refuse to advance with the world in their career, and form a contrast with the century in which they live, Zieten, in most respects, kept pace with his, by his ready approbation of such modifications as time and custom had introduced therein. Among other particulars, he ceased to insist upon a point, in which he had ever been extremely rigid—the cut and fashion of the military dress. He allowed his officers to comply with the modem mode, under certain limitations which he thought fit to prescribe and to insist upon with severity. With regard to the females who composed his family, he wished to see them dressed with neatness and taste; in all other respects, he referred them to the tribunal of fashion.

Ever satisfied with the present, he would not, like most other old men, complain that the world, of whose enjoyments he could not, as formerly, partake, was no longer the same, but that it was every day growing worse. On the contrary, Zieten could sincerely welcome the verdure of spring, could bask in the sunshine of summer, relish the fruits of autumn, and live upon hope during the rigours of winter. The various vicissitudes of nature, the war of the elements, an agreeable prospect, were all capable of affording him delight; and those who have accompanied him to Wüstrau, have often witnessed and shared his transports on such occasions.

His free and unprejudiced observation enabled him duly to appreciate the moral as well as the physical world. The experience of his younger days had taught him, that close to the man of worth are often found the wicked, the impostor, the intriguer, and the base, engaged in the same pursuit in the road to fortune: and having, during his whole life, entertained a proper distrust of those who had owed their advancement to indirect practices, he rendered double homage to such as were obligated for their success to their talents and virtues only.

In general, while his bodily frame was sinking into decay, his mind seemed to lose nothing of its accustomed vigour. He never yielded, but to himself: no one was ever known to have triumphed over his inclinations; he had never either said or done, but what he himself had purposed. In the latter days of his life, one of his most intimate friends, who knew him thoroughly, who saw him every day, and by whom he was highly esteemed, having pressed him to relate the story of his duels, Zieten shewed him the crooked finger of his right hand, and observed, that he did not come into the world with that blemish. More, he could not be prevailed upon to say.

With regard to what related to executive justice, he was never known to err. Indulgent to all around him, particularly to such as were weak and unprotected, he would allow no one to give him offence, or do him any wrong. As soon as the business admitted of any doubt, it was his custom to appeal to the decision of the laws. Without having ever liked litigations, he never avoided them when he considered such proceedings as necessary to the maintenance of truth and justice.

He never spoke of death as an event near at hand. That mixture of devotion and discontent, so common among old people, was entirely foreign to his disposition. On the contrary, he delighted in consoling such as trembled at their dissolution, and he would encourage them with hopes of long life by every argument that reason, good humour, and his own example, could suggest. He had, however, long betaken himself to prepare in silence for his own exit; and, as if he looked upon it as near at hand, had recourse to a precaution which manifested his fidelity both to the king and the state, and the tranquillity with which he considered that awful period.

He committed to the flames the principal documents of his correspondence with his sovereign during the three wars. This task was performed at Wüstrau, and in the following manner. After having employed his son-in-law and another confidential person, to carry into his bedchamber and place before the fire, a large box filled with letters, many of which were written in ciphers, he requested to be left alone. When his friends returned to him, they found the box empty. Zieten thought it a duty incumbent on him, to destroy papers, the communication of which might have proved dangerous, and their abuse, pernicious.

During his residence at Wüstrau, he never failed to visit Berlin once a month, for the purpose of seeing his regiment, of which, as has been already observed, he was extremely fond. The further he advanced in years, the more he grew attached to his corps of officers. He delighted in having the senior ones at his table, to see the young ones on horseback, or in groups on the parade. He admired the gracefulness of their carriage, and their expertness in military exercises; nor was he a little proud of his nursery of heroes; and though short of stature himself, he liked tall men, and had made choice of such, in preference, for his officers.

With regard to his veteran companions in war, they impressed him with sentiments of a different and more serious cast. As soon as he recognised one of them (for he began to grow near-sighted), he was sure to receive him with a friendly and affectionate exclamation. One day, Colonel de Lentz accosted him; "What! is it you, my old comrade?"

he cried, "Come, we have had many a hard day together." At another time (it was new-years' day, on which it was customary for the whole corps of officers to pay him their respects), he perceived Lieutenant de Kalis in the throng; and having called him, presented his cheek to him, and cried; "Embrace me, my good friend; you were of great service to me at Domstädtel."

One of his old officers having lamented to him, that he had not yet received the military cross, of which, he took occasion to remark, he considered himself as deserving as the rest of his comrades; and, at the same time, accusing one of the generals of having forgotten him; Zieten replied:

> Be satisfied with the consciousness of having merited the distinction you have not received. Honour does not consist in decorations; and the reputation of a brave officer is worth all the ribbons and all the crosses in the world.

During his whole life, he strenuously endeavoured to estimate the true value of things; not to rate the advantages of fortune and glory at more than they were worth; to enjoy them with moderation and dignity. We have seen his king, his country unweariedly lavishing the choicest honours upon him. When turned of fourscore, he was still treated with the like enthusiastic attentions; the pleasure of seeing him seemed to have lost nothing of the charm of novelty. Whenever he appeared in the streets of Berlin, the passengers stopped to look at him, saluted him with respect, shewed him to one another, and kept looking at him till they could see him no longer.

In the capital, every time the king gave out the parole at the palace, and Zieten was among the generals who attended to receive it, His Majesty would embrace him in the kindest manner, and inquire into the state of his health. One day, at Sans-Souci, after the grand manoeuvres, he had taken leave of the princes and dismissed the generals, without having discovered that Zieten was hid in the throng; when recollecting himself, he looked about for him, ran after him, embraced him several times over, and seemed quite loath to leave him. During the winter, on his return from the exercise-saloon, he frequently went to Zieten's house to visit him, often entered his chamber by surprise, and would never allow himself to be conducted to the door by him at parting.

It was an agreeable spectacle to see Frederick the Great, at seventy years of age, in his carriage covered with snow, paying a visit to his general who was turned of eighty, forgetting the grandeur of his condition, or rather asserting it, at the gate of his subject. The princes of the blood were happy to imitate the monarch's example. The Prince of Prussia, since that time, Frederick William II. never failed to visit the general on his birthday; and Prince Henry has often come on purpose from Rheinsberg, to spend a whole day with him.

The Prussian generals stood in no need of such examples of an homage which they paid unanimously, not to his birth, nor his rank, nor the favours he enjoyed; but solely to his person. Those expressions of respect which custom has consecrated for the use of children, and which the imprescriptible rights of man seem to refuse to every other relation in life—the highest military characters did not hesitate to bestow on Zieten: nor could they, at the same time, refrain from pressing to their lips his hand, or the regimentals which he wore, which also became an object of veneration! In this act of humility, the spectator considered only the sentiments which dictated it, the generous minds of those who gave way to it, and the superiority of the man who was the object of it.

Such like attentions one day produced a scene at Zieten's own table that much affected the guests. He had invited a large company of friends, among whom were several ministers of state and general officers. They all drank to his health; and, contrary to his usual way, he ordered his glass to be filled for the purpose of drinking that of the company; when General de Krusemark, who sat next him, an infirm old man and already on the brink of the grave, sensible that neither he nor Zieten could bear the liquor, chose to sacrifice his own health to preserve that of his friend; and snatching the glass from him, cheerfully drank it off.

Nothing could be more painful to him than to be prevented by the ill state of his health from assisting at the annual manoeuvres and reviews. He would sometimes attend without having duly considered his strength, and he was one day carried back from the field, halfdead with the fatigue he had undergone. From the year 1780, he had obtained the king's permission to appear on the first day without the incumbrance of the tiger-skin upon his shoulders and the eagle's wings on his cap, which it was usual on such occasions to wear. The king had likewise written him a very gracious letter on this subject.

My dear General de Zieten.

I shall always see with the same pleasure, a general of your age and distinguished services appear at my reviews, and I approve of your laying aside the tiger-skin, as well as the ornament of your cap. Yet, should the weather prove cold, I must conjure you to consult your health and stay at home. Whoever has like you, served so long and so gloriously, has an undoubted right to avail himself of the privilege which the Romans allowed their veterans. Pay some attention to this advice, if you wish to oblige your very affectionate king,

Potsdam, May 17th, 1780.                                         Frederick.

Zieten was upwards of eighty years old, when early one morning he rode out of the gates of the city, at the head of his regiment to attend a special review. The remembrance of this day is still fresh in the minds of those who were present, and particularly his own regiment. Scarcely had His Majesty perceived the general, than he galloped up to him, alighted from his horse, and expressed both his pleasure and his concern to see him. Zieten who had just gone through his task of duty, who had presented himself and his regiment to the king, and witnessed the condescension of that prince, appeared on his return, a regenerated man. Mounted upon a fine charger, he preceded his corps as if he had still been in the vigour of life; and his officers, his hussars, and himself, seemed equally proud of belonging to one another.

We should ill perform task of an historian, if we pretended to deny, that notwithstanding the regard which the king had for Zieten, and the gratitude which he owed to, and always paid, his services, he did not consider him a perfect adept in the art of war. Yet, impressed as he was with this opinion, he was always careful, not to give him the least occasion to feel the consequences of it. The following anecdote will suffice in support of this.

Frederick, it was well-known, was fond of conversing with his generals at table, on the subject of his campaigns. He was one day speaking of Torgaw. Zieten, who according to his late custom, was dosing, awoke at the mention of that name. The king supposing him to be still asleep, enlarged in a loud voice and without the least restraint, upon what he was pleased to call the delays and errors of our general, and concluded in these terms; "Zieten was, indeed, on the point of doing a very foolish thing."

**********

Frederick ever persisted in the same opinion. "M. de Zieten, instead, of making an attack, amused himself for a long while with a body of *pandours*, which he found in his way in the forest of Torgaw; he then cannonaded a considerable time the corps of Lascy, which was posted, as we have already said, behind the ponds. In a word, the disposition was not executed; the king made his attack alone, unassisted by M. de Zieten, and totally unsupported by his cavalry. At length, M. de Zieten being arrived at the place of his destination, began the attack, etc." *Seven Years' War.*

★★★★★★★★★★

As he pronounced the words, he cast his eyes upon the sleeper, who, in return, looked him full in the face: he had listened with great attention to what had been said, but had not ventured to interrupt a discourse, which admitted of much to be urged in contradiction of it. The king, confused and quite out of countenance, added not a single word, but laid down his napkin, and rose from the table.

We now come to the last period of the life of Zieten. For several years past, his infirmities had increased upon him. His nights grew restless, and, he became subject to a feverish complaint which proved extremely troublesome to him, and sometimes threw him into a delirium. His character, however, was still the same, even under the most violent pressure of the disorder. One night, when he was severely attacked by his fever, he imagined there was a fire under the floor, and that he felt his bed burning beneath him. He called his valet, who endeavoured to calm, and undeceive him. His efforts were vain: the sick man persisted in his opinion, and the valet was obliged to call M. de Jurgas to his assistance. Zieten fell into a passion at the sight of his son-in-law: "Do not conceive," said he, "that I am at all afraid of the fire that is under the bed."

In the daytime he appeared weak only: yet it was easy to perceive his general decay, and particularly that of his sight and hearing; but his intellectual faculties still remained sounds and he grew more than ever fond of the company of his nearest relatives. He felt himself revived by their converse; he acknowledged it, and repeatedly thanked them for their assiduities. In general, he redoubled his kindness to all around him.

Besides the best of wives, he had the good fortune to have about him, for the last six years of his life, a person who rendered him the most essential services, and who was considered by him as the support of his old age. Such merit is of too uncommon a nature among the class of mercenaries, not to induce us to distinguish from the crowd, the man who possessed it. This was M. Wagner, his *valet-de-chambre*, at present (1803), steward of the royal kitchen. The worthy man was thoroughly acquainted with the humour and way of life of his master; by day, he would amuse him, at one time, with books of devotion, at another, with subjects of rural economy, at another, with treatises on politics.

At night, he usually sat up with him, attended him with unremitting care; he, indeed, scarcely quitted him for an instant, at any time, and cheerfully sacrificed all kind of recreation out of doors for his sake. He possessed the entire confidence of the general, acted not only as his valet, his reader, but likewise as his secretary. As long as his master lived, he refused various establishments that were offered him; and at length, he was appointed, on the recommendation of the late M. de Werder, minister of state, to the confidential post which he has continued to fill in an honourable manner to the present day (1803).

The last letter from the king to Zieten is in answer to one which the general had written him on the return of the new year.

> My dear General de Zieten.
> I feel the value of your good wishes, and am truly grateful for them. I wish, in return, that your strength may be renewed and firmly established, and that your health may equal your contentment. The accomplishment of these wishes would afford me the highest degree of satisfaction, and I remain your very affectionate king,
> Berlin, January 1st, 1785.                              Frederick.

Several circumstances have given rise to a belief that the king had a presentiment of the approaching dissolution of his general, A man indeed, on the verge of eighty-six, must naturally have been expected to die soon; and that the public, ever fond of the marvellous, should choose to make a miracle of His Majesty's apprehensions, is likewise far from having anything extraordinary in it.

A peculiar incident soon enabled the great Frederick to give his general a last proof of the high esteem he bore him, and of the manner in which he was pleased to recompense true merit.

It happened in the course of the winter of 1785. The king, had returned to Berlin in a bad state of health. On the 22nd of December, Zieten, in spite of the burden of eighty-six years, went to the palace, at the end of the parade, to pay his sovereign this last tribute of respect, and to have the pleasure of seeing him after six month's absence. The parole was given out, the orders imparted to the generals, and the king had turned towards the princes of the blood, when he perceived

Zieten on the other side of the hall, between his son and his two *aide-de-camps*. Surprised in a very agreeable manner at this unexpected sight, he broke out into an exclamation of joy, and directly making up to him; "What, my good old Zieten! are you there?" said His Majesty, "How sorry am I, that you have had the trouble of walking up the staircase. I should have called upon you myself. How have you been of late?"

"Sire," answered Zieten, "my health is not amiss, my appetite is good; but my strength! my strength!"

"This account," replied the king, "makes me happy by halves only; but you must be tired;—I shall have a chair for you."

A chair was quickly brought. Zieten, however, declared that he was not at all fatigued: the king maintained that he was. "Sit down, good father;" continued His Majesty, "I will have it so; otherwise I must instantly leave the room; for I cannot allow you to be incommoded under my own roof."

The old general obeyed, and Frederick the Great remained standing before him, in the midst of a brilliant circle that had thronged around them. After asking him many questions respecting his hearing, his memory, and the general state of his health, he at length took leave of him in these words;

> *Adieu*, my dear Zieten! (it was his last *adieu!*) take care not to catch cold: nurse yourself well, and live as long as you can, that I may often have the pleasure of seeing you.

After having said this, the king, instead of speaking to the other generals and walking through the saloons as usual, retired abruptly, and shut himself up in his closet.

This interesting scene, equally worthy of Frederick and of Zieten, brought tears into the eyes of the hardiest of the spectators. Zieten was himself too much affected to be able to shed any; nor can language describe what he felt on the occasion. The graver of Chodowiecki has preserved this interview in a plate, which, among its other excellencies, is remarkable for the likenesses of the group, and which is well known throughout all Europe.

The sun of Zieten hastened apace to its decline, and the edifice of his bodily frame fell fast into decay. He had now scarcely any desires to animate him: he had drunk out the cup of life, and had fully tasted of its glory and its enjoyments. His favourite wish of living to an advanced age had been granted him: he had run his long career with a conscience void of reproach, and he began to feel the want of repose; he cherished the hope of immortality, and prepared for death, as an event he neither desired nor feared.

He was now in his eighty-sixth year; and on the 25th of January, after having taken a ride in his carriage with Madame de Zieten, he felt himself in such spirits, that he planned an excursion to Wüstrau with her, and from thence, to his brother-in-law, who had invited him to stand godfather to his child. He spent the evening at home, and was remarkably good-humoured, conversed gayly with his children, and observed to his youngest daughter, that he hoped soon to see her dressed in a new gown he had just bought her. They all sat down to supper, when, on a sudden, and for the first time in his life, Zieten complained of being unwell. The consternation was general: every possible assistance was administered to him; and, in a little time, he grew better. He then went to bed, and the family had no apprehensions of a relapse.

The night, which was the last of his life, afforded him but little rest. He was heard to pray aloud, and at several different times. At four in the morning, he called his valet, who on entering the room, saw the image of death upon his master's countenance. He immediately rung for assistance. The dying man had not, however, lost his senses; he coughed, and spat; asked if it was blood, and before any assistance came, or his valet could answer his question, Zieten was no more.

The death of Zieten, though inevitable in the natural order of things, filled the whole city with alarm and sorrow. Throngs of people hastened to see his corpse as it lay in state; and among the soldiers of all orders and descriptions, who paid this last tribute of respect to him, there was one, who rushing through the crowd, approached the body, and from the abundance of his heart, addressed it in a speech that was worthy of being preserved, as well as the name of the man who delivered it. This was an old grenadier, who had often fought under the general's banner, and whose enthusiastic affection inspired him with a flow of language, little to be expected from an unlettered common soldier. (This anecdote renews the remembrance of another. A French soldier at Strasbourg visited the monument of Marshal Saxe. He drew his sword, laid it upon the tomb, sheathed it again, and withdrew in silence.)

The corpse, attended by young Zieten and Captain de Velten, was carried without pomp to Wüstrau, and laid in the family vault in the churchyard of that village. A plain stone, bearing a trophy and a bundle of fasces, which allude to his double capacity of officer and commander in chief, covers his remains. His name, his dignities, the day of his birth, that of his decease, and his seventy-three years of service, are engraved thereupon, within a wreath of laurels.

His family have erected a splendid monument to him, in the church, which bears the following inscription.

> HE LIVED WITH FREDERICK
> IN THE ANNALS OF HISTORY,
> ADMIRED AS A HERO,
> BELOVED AS A MAN, AND A CHRISTIAN.
> HE WAS BESIDES, THE HAPPINESS
> OF HIS DISCONSOLATE WIFE AND HIS CHILDREN,
> WHO HAVE CONSECRATED
> THIS MONUMENT TO HIS MEMORY.

Frederick the Great has likewise honoured the memory of Zieten by the following letter to his widow.

My sentiments, Madam, with regard to your late husband, are too well known to you, to render it necessary that I should tell you how severely I feel his loss, although his advanced age should have prepared me for the shock. To doubt it would imply an incapacity of appreciating merit like his. Of that merit I was truly sensible, and I now bewail it. I take this opportunity of condoling with you and your family on the melancholy event, and hoping that my affliction may tend to alleviate yours, I conclude with assuring you, that on every occasion, I shall continue to be both your and their affectionate king,

Potsdam, January 28th, 1786.                                Frederick.

The king survived his general but a few months only. Instead of the usual pension, His Majesty had made a present of ten thousand dollars to Madame do Zieten and her children. The finances of the deceased, which had been considerably disarranged by his liberalities, stood in need of this reparation.

To the regrets of the great Frederick, we must join the remembrances of his august brother. In the year 1790, Prince Henry of Prussia erected in the park of Rheinsberg, a pyramid to the memory of his favourite brother, Augustus William, grandfather to the present king. On the four sides of the pyramid were inscribed the names of twenty-six warriors who had been particularly esteemed by him, with a short description of their several merits and exploits. The inauguration of this monument took place in the year 1791; and to render it the more solemn, the prince had collected from the neighbouring garrisons all the troops, from the general down to the common soldier, who had served in the seven years' war.

A signal being made, the monument was uncovered; a fine harangue, of the princess own composition, was pronounced; the heroes paid the tribute, of a tear to the memory of the illustrious dead, and celebrated together the anniversary of this famous war. The front of the pyramid is crowned with a medallion of Augustus William. In the middle are the names of Keith, Schwerin, Prince Leopold, Prince Ferdinand, Seidlitz, the Duke of Bevern, Platen, and that of Zieten with the following eulogy, composed by the prince.

GENERAL DE ZIETEN
ATTAINED
TO A HAPPY AND GLORIOUS OLD AGE;
EVERY TIME HE COMBATTED,
HE TRIUMPHED.
HIS MILITARY GLANCE, JOINED
TO HIS HEROIC VALOUR,
DECIDED THE FATE OF BATTLES;
BUT WHAT DISTINGUISHED HIM
STILL MORE,
WAS HIS INTEGRITY, HIS DISINTERESTEDNESS,
AND HIS CONTEMPT FOR ALL SUCH
AS ENRICHED, THEMSELVES AT THE EXPENSE OF
OPPRESSED NATIONS.

Finally, to crown the glory of Zieten, the successor of the great Frederick placed him in the military Pantheon by raising a statue to his memory. In perpetuation of the signal services, which during the two preceding reigns, the general had rendered his country, Frederick William II. caused it to be erected in the Wilhelms-Platz, at the end of the Mohren-Strasse. This fine piece of sculpture is worthy of the taste of the king who ordered it, of the hero whom it represents, and of the artist who executed it. (M. Schadow of Berlin, whose chisel would have acquired him a name, even in the age of Praxiteles.)

The statue, which is the subject of the frontispiece to this volume of memoirs, is the fifth which ornaments the square. The other four, which were erected during the reign of Frederick the Great, represent Schwerin, Winterfeld, Seidlitz, and Keith. They are all wrought in the finest Carrara marble. That of Zieten, including the pedestal, is fifteen feet and a half in height. The pedestal which is eight feet high, is composed of grey Silesian marble. It is inlaid with four blocks of white marble, which surround it, and are raised in *bass-relief.* The first represents the tiger-skin which is worn by the officers of the regiment at the grand reviews: the middle of the skin contains the inscription, which is a follows:

> JOHN JOACHIM DE ZIETEN,
> GENERAL OF CAVALRY,
> SERVED FROM MDCCXIV TILL MDCCLXXXVI,
> UNDER
> FREDERICK WILLIAM I. AND FREDERICK II.
> THIS MONUMENT WAS ERECTED TO HIM
> BY FREDERICK WILLIAM II.

The three other sides compose the frontispiece of this volume. They are descriptive of three memorable events in the military life of Zieten, taken from the different wars in which Frederick engaged for the purpose of conquering Silesia, and of securing that splendid and important acquisition. On the *bass-relief* on the left, is represented the Battle of Rothschloss.

The artist has made choice of the moment in which Zieten, at that time lieutenant-colonel, having driven the enemy against a watermill, discovered their general, and was on the point of taking him prisoner. Baronay springs from his horse, and by the assistance of a grenadier, crosses the stream upon a plank. At the sight of the precipice which borders it, Zieten checks his steed, and threatens the fugitive with his drawn sabre. The mill on the left, Baronay's charger without its rider, the trumpeter in the middle, who sounds the alarm behind Zieten, and a hussar on the foreground, who turns at the noise, fill up the rest of the space. Over the *bass-relief* is read the following inscription.

> ZIETEN AND HIS FORMER MASTER, BARONAY.
> Rothschloss, July 22nd, 1741

The second, which is on the back of the monument, represents the surprise of the Saxons at Hennersdorf.

Zieten appears in this group as a general: he is giving his orders, and a trumpeter attends near him for the purpose of receiving them. One of his hussars fires at the kettle-drummer of Obyern's regiment.

The horse is fallen, and the bridle cut. In the background the Prussian hussars are charging the hostile cavalry. The cottages indicate the village. The inscription runs as follows:

### ZIETEN TAKES FOUR SAXON REGIMENTS.
Catholic-Hennersdorf, November 23rd, 1745.

The last *bass-relief* represents the Battle of Torgaw.

Zieten on horseback, is looking towards the heights of Siptitz, which rise on his left. Everything announces the commander in chief. Behind him, is an *aide-de-camp* belonging to the regiment of Kuhnheim, one of the first at the attack. Before him, appears a sergeant of the *gendarmes*, holding his hat in his hand, and in the act of making his report. An *aide-de-camp* sets off at full speed with the general's orders to the heights, where the Prussians are seen mounting to the assault. At the same instant arrives a Prussian grenadier, bearing an Austrian flag, in token of victory. All is effort and activity; but it appears to be exerted late. Zieten's horse seems worn out with fatigue, and that which carries the officer with the general's orders; gallops with apparent difficulty. The inscription is as follows.

### ZIETEN CARRIES THE HEIGHTS OF SIPTITZ.
Torgaw, November 3rd, 1760.

Though several years have elapsed since its erection, this fine monument still continues to excite the curiosity of the inhabitants of the capital, as well as the strangers who visit that place; and this short account of it, it is hoped, will not prove unacceptable to our readers.

## ALSO FROM LEONAUR
### AVAILABLE IN SOFTCOVER OR HARDCOVER WITH DUST JACKET

**THE FALL OF THE MOGHUL EMPIRE OF HINDUSTAN** by H. G. Keene—By the beginning of the nineteenth century, as British and Indian armies under Lake and Wellesley dominated the scene, a little over half a century of conflict brought the Moghul Empire to its knees.

**LADY SALE'S AFGHANISTAN** by Florentia Sale—An Indomitable Victorian Lady's Account of the Retreat from Kabul During the First Afghan War.

**THE CAMPAIGN OF MAGENTA AND SOLFERINO 1859** by Harold Carmichael Wylly—The Decisive Conflict for the Unification of Italy.

**FRENCH'S CAVALRY CAMPAIGN** by J. G. Maydon—A Special Correspondent's View of British Army Mounted Troops During the Boer War.

**CAVALRY AT WATERLOO** by Sir Evelyn Wood—British Mounted Troops During the Campaign of 1815.

**THE SUBALTERN** by George Robert Gleig—The Experiences of an Officer of the 85th Light Infantry During the Peninsular War.

**NAPOLEON AT BAY, 1814** by F. Loraine Petre—The Campaigns to the Fall of the First Empire.

**NAPOLEON AND THE CAMPAIGN OF 1806** by Colonel Vachée—The Napoleonic Method of Organisation and Command to the Battles of Jena & Auerstädt.

**THE COMPLETE ADVENTURES IN THE CONNAUGHT RANGERS** by William Grattan—The 88th Regiment during the Napoleonic Wars by a Serving Officer.

**BUGLER AND OFFICER OF THE RIFLES** by William Green & Harry Smith—With the 95th (Rifles) during the Peninsular & Waterloo Campaigns of the Napoleonic Wars.

**NAPOLEONIC WAR STORIES** by Sir Arthur Quiller-Couch—Tales of soldiers, spies, battles & sieges from the Peninsular & Waterloo campaingns.

**CAPTAIN OF THE 95TH (RIFLES)** by Jonathan Leach—An officer of Wellington's sharpshooters during the Peninsular, South of France and Waterloo campaigns of the Napoleonic wars.

**RIFLEMAN COSTELLO** by Edward Costello—The adventures of a soldier of the 95th (Rifles) in the Peninsular & Waterloo Campaigns of the Napoleonic wars.

AVAILABLE ONLINE AT **www.leonaur.com**
AND FROM ALL GOOD BOOK STORES

# ALSO FROM LEONAUR
### AVAILABLE IN SOFTCOVER OR HARDCOVER WITH DUST JACKET

**THE 9TH—THE KING'S (LIVERPOOL REGIMENT) IN THE GREAT WAR 1914 - 1918** by *Enos H. G. Roberts*—Mersey to mud—war and Liverpool men.

**THE GAMBARDIER** by *Mark Severn*—The experiences of a battery of Heavy artillery on the Western Front during the First World War.

**FROM MESSINES TO THIRD YPRES** by *Thomas Floyd*—A personal account of the First World War on the Western front by a 2/5th Lancashire Fusilier.

**THE IRISH GUARDS IN THE GREAT WAR - VOLUME 1** by *Rudyard Kipling*—Edited and Compiled from Their Diaries and Papers—The First Battalion.

**THE IRISH GUARDS IN THE GREAT WAR - VOLUME 1** by *Rudyard Kipling*—Edited and Compiled from Their Diaries and Papers—The Second Battalion.

**ARMOURED CARS IN EDEN** by *K. Roosevelt*—An American President's son serving in Rolls Royce armoured cars with the British in Mesopatamia & with the American Artillery in France during the First World War.

**CHASSEUR OF 1914** by *Marcel Dupont*—Experiences of the twilight of the French Light Cavalry by a young officer during the early battles of the great war in Europe.

**TROOP HORSE & TRENCH** by *R.A. Lloyd*—The experiences of a British Lifeguardsman of the household cavalry fighting on the western front during the First World War 1914-18.

**THE EAST AFRICAN MOUNTED RIFLES** by *C.J. Wilson*—Experiences of the campaign in the East African bush during the First World War.

**THE LONG PATROL** by *George Berrie*—A Novel of Light Horsemen from Gallipoli to the Palestine campaign of the First World War.

**THE FIGHTING CAMELIERS** by *Frank Reid*—The exploits of the Imperial Camel Corps in the desert and Palestine campaigns of the First World War.

**STEEL CHARIOTS IN THE DESERT** by *S. C. Rolls*—The first world war experiences of a Rolls Royce armoured car driver with the Duke of Westminster in Libya and in Arabia with T.E. Lawrence.

**WITH THE IMPERIAL CAMEL CORPS IN THE GREAT WAR** by *Geoffrey Inchbald*—The story of a serving officer with the British 2nd battalion against the Senussi and during the Palestine campaign.

AVAILABLE ONLINE AT **www.leonaur.com**
AND FROM ALL GOOD BOOK STORES

www.ingramcontent.com/pod-product-compliance
Lightning Source LLC
Chambersburg PA
CBHW031622160426
43196CB00006B/235